DON'T TRY THIS ALONE

DON'T TRY THIS ALONE

The Silent Epidemic of Attachment Disorder

How I accidentally regressed myself back to infancy and healed it all

Kathy Brous

For information please contact Kathy Brous at AttachmentDisorderHealing.com.

Cover design by Danny Dayton, Dayton GraphX, Anaheim, CA <DaytonGraphX@PacBell.net>
Printed in the United States of America

ISBN-13: 9781976120121
ISBN-10: 1976120128

Library of Congress Control Number: 2017914201
CreateSpace Independent Publishing Platform
North Charleston, South Carolina

Publication Data:
Brous, Kathy
Don't Try This Alone: The Silent Epidemic of Attachment Disorder.
How I accidentally regressed myself back to infancy and healed it all.
Summary: Attachment disorder is a little-known condition facing up to 50% of Americans. It can be emotionally excruciating, or we may be unaware of it because we've repressed it. It stems from disruption to an infant's bond with the mother. Damage can start at conception. I functioned at a high level for three decades with no hint of illness, then suddenly had five life disasters at once. It came to where my father died and I couldn't cry. Then I couldn't get out of bed. Therapy failed me so I quit, "did it myself," and fell into a layer of emotional pain so severe I became suicidal. I learned the hard way: *Don't try this alone.*

1. Psychology 2. Developmental Psychology 3. Developmental Trauma 4. Attachment Disorder

Dedication

to

Randy and Steve
and
Sherry and Cynthia
and
John and Henry
and
John and Russell

Thank you for saving my life.
Repeatedly.

Many thanks to Danny Dayton at Dayton GraphX for the cover design.
Much gratitude to Steve McWhan for his extensive graphics support.
Blessings to Donna Bunce for her insight regarding the title.

All names have been changed beyond recognition except that of Joe the electrician
from Freeport, Long Island—in hopes that Joe might read Chapter 9
and know how much he meant to me.

Contents

Preface: Parts of My Brain Were Dark

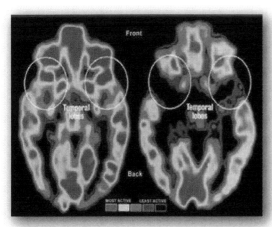

i. PET brain scans. Left: Attached child. Right: Attachment disorder. (First 5) (1)

Are parts of your brain dark? Silly, you say. Well, did you ever have a broken heart? I functioned so well I had no idea, but parts of my brain were dark and my heart was 'way far broken.

So goes attachment disorder, and I believe some 50% of Americans have a degree of it. No wonder we've got a 50% divorce rate and a government that can't function, not to mention the ratty odds in Internet dating.

Science has only recently shown that unless kids (and other mammals) receive deep emotional connection from birth from adults, infant neurology just doesn't develop well.

A baby's brain requires stimulation by an adult's eyes and facial expressions to "attach" to people. Loving interactions with the mother cause an infant's neurons to fire in neural circuits for affection, stimulating growth there and in the brain generally. The positron emission tomography (PET) brain scan on the left side of Figure i shows an attached child raised by its parents. Neurons are firing in most brain regions.

When an infant instead experiences excess stress or lack of response from adults, its instincts read that as a survival threat. This floods the baby with fight-flight stress chemicals like cortisol. If an adult doesn't help it, stress chemicals overwhelm the baby's brain and within 45 minutes it goes into shock. (2) The scan on the right side shows a child raised in an orphanage; many brain regions are barely firing. The interaction to fire up these pathways in a healthy way never came. Excess cortisol also destroys brain tissue. That's attachment disorder.

What began as emotional stress ends in physiological damage. I literally felt this as a "hole in me." It causes intense pain to be transmitted to neurons around the heart and other viscera, producing, literally, a broken heart. Yet, it is definitely not "all in our heads." *Attachment disorder is a medical condition at the interface between the emotions and the body.*

This means a lot more of us need help than we realize. Babies have no thinking memory, so we can't cognitively recall infancy, and the trauma goes unrecognized for millions.

The American Psychiatric Association (APA) reserves the word "disorder" for the visibly, radically ill with Reactive Attachment Disorder (RAD), a tiny percent of the population. That avoids the cost of treating larger numbers of people. (3)

My attachment damage wasn't visible, but it nearly killed me. I'm calling that a disorder.

In fact, psychological studies using the Adult Attachment Interview (AAI) show that 45-54% of Americans can't attach well enough to sustain deep relationships. A major medical study, the Adverse Childhood Experiences (ACE) Study, also shows that 42-66% of us have significant childhood trauma, which means attachment damage, too.

Neuroscientists call it a "Hidden Epidemic." *It can also take 20 years off your life.* (4) Yet it gets little press because, absurdly, there's no agreement on how to handle numbers this big. See the Appendix for the science.

Now to my story.

I performed for three decades as an economist, technical writer and classical singer, with no hint of illness. Suddenly in 2006, I was in divorce from a 27-year marriage to my college sweetheart that left me bankrupt. I ran

3,000 miles from the East Coast to California. Then both my parents died and I had two bad rebound affairs—five life disasters in two years.

It felt like being hit by two cars, two trucks, and a jet airplane. It came to where my father died and I couldn't cry. Then it came to where I couldn't get out of bed.

I saw one therapist who listened helplessly and a second who said, "grow up." Next I read enough studies on the incompetence of psychotherapy to quit and try to "do it myself." (5)

I got a book on grief and wrote Grief Letters about the pain I felt for my ex, Mom, and Dad. I mourned my feelings for my ex for 18 months, even held a funeral for my lost marriage. (6)

"This is going to flatten me for a few days," I thought, "but then I'll be ready to re-marry."

But we can't just order out grief to go. After a week's relief, intense "breakthrough" grief about my Dad popped up. Taking a deep breath, I had at it again, but the more grief I addressed, the more and deeper layers of pain surfaced.

The feelings coming up, I gradually saw, were those of a younger and younger me. Writing letters to my ex, I felt back to my twenties. Writing letters to my Dad, I felt back to grade school; the voice of a little girl literally spoke up in my chest. (I'd sung Verdi's *Joan of Arc* in 1996, but this was a stretch.)

Then writing letters to my Mom, back, and back, and back I went—*but where was the bottom, with a mom?*

I "did it myself" for three years. I didn't know it, but I was drilling down into my past.

There were so many layers, it felt like falling through miles of rock as deep as the endless striated walls of the Grand Canyon—to a level earlier than thought.

I began to feel pain, including physical chest and gut pain, resembling a 24x7 bone marrow transplant without anesthesia which went on for about three years. It often felt like crawling across Mordor naked with orcs gnawing on me.

ii. A Grand Canyon worth of pain layers.
(Steve McWhan)

It was an accident. I didn't mean to do it, a point I never tired of making later to astonished doctors and in prayer. (God took it in stride.)

But once I began falling through the layers there was no way to stop, short of alcohol or the like, which disgusted me, or suicide, which often seemed attractive. Imagine my annoyance when I had to rule out even suicide after observing the effect on a friend whose spouse took that route.

I had No Exit and it stank—so down and down I went, through layers of memories and hurt, until one morning at 2 a.m. I found myself on the bedroom floor in a fetal position. I was clutching a large stuffed dog and eyeing a soggy toothbrush with which I had not been able to brush my teeth before crumpling.

The phrase "*She's not old enough to be dropped off at school*" repeated in my head. I crawled to the sink but had to hang on to the toy dog to stand and brush.

I found out the hard way that night: do-it-yourself psychology can be life-threatening.

Don't try this alone.

Somewhere in a textbook I had read about regression, the devolution of the mind back through childhood developmental stages. With my extensive notes of the last few years, I staggered into yet another therapist's office, presented the goods, and asked, "Do you think I've just accidentally regressed myself back to infancy?"

Upon examination, he leaned forward, eyes wide, and nodded solemnly, "Yes. Aren't you scared?"

You said it, brother, but not nearly as scared as I was gonna be. Since the sperm hit the egg, I'd had attachment disorder, and bad.

When I accidentally began to unfreeze these buried feelings, it felt like frostbite thawing: agony. But as with frostbite, we've got to feel the pain of unfreezing, to discharge the stored-up fight-flight energy inside us. Otherwise it sits and eats at us.

So the bad news is: *this is really gonna hurt.* Attachment disorder comes with trauma to the brain stem; when we first wake up to it, the emotional pain is unbelievable. When I say chest pain, I'm talking knife-stabbing levels.

I'll walk you through my story as it happened. See and feel the experience through my eyes and heart. If you have attachment disorder, my tale will resonate if you let it.

Hopefully it will draw you to reflection, quality therapy, and healing.

Because the good news is: as I healed, I felt so much better than I'd ever felt in my life, that you'll never believe this, either, until you experience it. You will never trade how you lived before, for how alive you'll feel now, in the fullness of feeling everything wonderful that you haven't been able to feel all your life.

Specialists compare recovery from this trauma to a metaphysical awakening or an experience of God, the relief can feel that profound. (7) Weeping for joy can become an odd habit. The sheer gratitude has put me on a first-name basis with God, and He's a really nice guy.

These days my doctor looks at my blood work and asks, "Do you plan to live forever?"

Meanwhile, friends smile when I repeat, wherever we go:

"I can't believe how much better I feel than the last time I was here!"

Notes

Check the Notes after each chapter alphabetically in the References section at the back, to get the full citation. Often, Internet links are included in the reference. Copying each reference into an online search box will give further detail and more references.

1. First 5 (8-2-13); Felitti (2003; 2011 p.16); Felitti in Grant (6-14-16); Redford (2015).
2. Verrier (2003, p.8).
3. APA (2013).
4. Brous (10-2-13, 4-12-17); Felitti & Anda (1998); Lanius (2010).
5. Lewis et. al. (2000, p.189ff).
6. James & Friedman (1998).
7. Levine (2005, p.4, p.79-81).

Prologue: The Silent Epidemic

iii. QR code for my website. (Kathy Brous)

I first heard the 50% range estimate for the prevalence of attachment damage in 2010, on an old CD by a local therapist. While many folks are able to relate, he said, almost as many are not, because they experienced painful relationships as kids. Worse, when that happens, we often pick spouses and friends who can't relate, so we keep getting hurt.

Asked about the odds, he replied that 55% are considered "securely attached," but 45% are "insecurely attached." That means almost half of us have trouble maintaining deep relationships. (1)

This wasn't academic to me. I'd barely survived 30 years of my life being destroyed by a bad marriage. I needed to know why, and how to avoid more such relationships. I worried about our 50% divorce rate.

Then I did a lot of dating and wound up with one man after another who couldn't relate. I had the same problem finding new girl friends after moving to California. It felt as if the entire population were more like 75% unable to relate. So I quit dating and set about healing myself.

Years after events in this book, I finally researched the 45-55% issue. The scientific proof of this "Hidden Epidemic" is in the Appendix.

My website, AttachmentDisorderHealing.com (QR code above), has dozens of blogs on the brain science of attachment. It also features the healing tools that helped me, led by neurofeedback. (2)

More important, the proof's inside so many of us. Why would we want to live our lives with blinders on, with a 50% chance of walking off a cliff?

Cases like mine, in which people somehow touch into their past and realize they have attachment damage, occur often enough that "we hear it every day," UCLA attachment specialist Allan Schore told me in 2013. (3)

Many are high-performers, as I was. Many are corporate or government leaders.

Attachment trauma doesn't respect zip codes.

"Nice families" frequently suffer attachment disorder due to moms working long hours or living under stress. Mothers who as kids had little air time with their own mom are often tone deaf as to how to attune to a baby's emotional states, and pass on the damage to their infants.

"As long as you were performing and trying to be perfect... the misery was silently gnawing away," the local therapist said back in 2001, just like Schore: "*We hear it every day*, from very successful people who've got it all and just want to know:

"'Why do I still feel so bad?' " (4)

Notes

1. Cloud (2001).
2. AttachmentDisorderHealing.com/blogs
3. Brous (5-16-14).
4. Cloud (2001).

Death and Taxes

1.1 I'll just find a good man. (Steve McWhan)

This book was originally titled *Death and Taxes*, a spoof on dating in America's post-divorce shark pool. When my divorce hit, I was a consultant for Washington DC defense contractors and my friend Denise was an IRS official.

I was "death" and she was "taxes." We thought it was funny because we were such soft-hearted women. Still, given all our adventures, it had the potential for quite a movie script.

We crossed paths the week both our marriages collapsed in 2006, raw, uninformed and in extremis, at a women's divorce seminar in DC's Virginia suburbs.

"This is not California where each gets half the assets," the female lawyer said. "In Virginia, ladies, you are up a tree. If you go to court, the fees could eat your settlement, or the judge could make you pay alimony for years. If you don't go to court, you might not get anything, either."

Denise and I looked at each other and said, "Anyone want to network?" Nothing, in short, was certain, except death and taxes. We started meeting in restaurants and calling each other at night for moral support.

The first thing we noticed, after her 20-year marriage and my 27-year marriage to my college beau, was that neither of us had children. This detail had hitherto escaped our attention. Had I explored it, I might have had a clue that something was amiss, not just with my ex, but with my own ability to attach.

Instead we blamed our spouses; they didn't want children. Only much later did we realize: these men couldn't attach. Gals at the seminar would ask each other, "how did you get divorced?" and the cause was always the same: someone couldn't attach.

Denise benefited financially from her marriage. She would wow visitors with her stately home and swimming pool.

Then on the second floor she would escort us to a certain room. All four walls were filled with rank upon rank of bookshelves. On the shelves were arrayed: Teddy bears. Rows of pink Teddy bears. Rows of blue Teddy bears. Calico Teddy bears. Teddy bears in cowboy suits. Teddy bears dressed as firemen. Purple People Eater Teddy bears. Teddy bears in tuxedos and top hats and sequined gowns and tiaras. Naked normal Teddy bears.

Denise developed a dramatic flair for it. She would usher someone inside, let it register, pause, then sweep her arm in the grand manner and proclaim: "And this, is Donald's teddy bear collection." Donald was her ex.

Clearly Donald had better uses for his time than attaching to Denise. One day he left her for his masseuse. She never saw it coming and wept for months. Not until years later did we realize: he never presented her with the need to attach. She stayed and stayed despite his distancing behavior, until *he* left. Staying didn't require her to attach.

I stayed longer, 30 years counting courtship. We were New Yorkers, and my ex was sweet during our early Manhattan years, but once he moved us to Virginia he lost interest. Larry drove off one morning and never returned until past midnight—for about 15 years.

Larry had business start-ups, political ambitions, and expensive hobbies, so I had to support him. I flew around the world doing economic consulting while he stayed home. In my ten years of travel he never made one trip.

I'd return from weeks in Asia to find that the litter box for our two good-sized indoor cats had not been touched by human hands since I left. The cats, at least, had the presence of mind to feel abandoned.

With all his Washington Beltway talk and protestations of love I didn't see it, but Larry lived by the law of the jungle. He had less than zero regard for my actual welfare. One day I got a lucrative consulting gig and he quit working, leaving me with the mortgage.

Soon I was working two jobs, 14-hour days, six days a week. This went on another ten years. The money was gambled away in Larry's business and political schemes. He'd hand me his credit card bills in the $20,000 range and say, "pay this."

Finally I googled "domestic abuse" and was shocked to read that it didn't require beating or rape. Verbal, emotional and financial mistreatment are also abuse, said a major university website.

I had been clueless. "Whu Nu? He was the first Prime Minister of Burma," I moaned.

Late one night Larry moved to take most of the equity out of our house, demanding that I sign a $280,000 refinance. When I refused and tried to leave, he did get physically violent. "You've got to protect my credit rating!" he bellowed.

I ran for the bathroom and locked myself in, but never thought of calling 911 on the man I loved. At dawn I crawled out, signed the papers, then looked at myself in the bathroom mirror and said, "You just signed your home away because you're afraid to be alone at this age." I was at that divorce seminar in days.

I left in July 2006, but not until years later did I see: Larry never presented me with the need to attach, so I stayed until he slapped me into leaving.

Why try to change death or taxes? Apparently both Denise and I had long considered poor treatment just as inevitable. We'd been in a sick system so long, we were numb to it.

Especially me. What was wrong with me?

This book shows how I found out the hard way. See through my eyes what I saw, walk through events as I did. You've got a ringside seat as I enter a maelstrom ferocious enough to make Edgar Allan Poe pass out.

Unless I walk you through it, you'll never believe what happened—or that this might also be you.

I Thought I was Dead

For 30 years I coped by singing classical music, lots of it, in several languages. It substituted for the communication missing in my marriage. "Most of my friends are dead," I often joked about Mozart and Beethoven.

But by 2006, so was I.

"I've been left home alone for so long that when I finally left home, I thought I was dead," I journaled then. For 15 years I'd had no "How was your day?" or breaking bread together, and no physical contact. I used to joke that my furry tomcat Tom (who slept on my shoulder) was my real husband, but Tom died in 2004 and it wasn't funny anymore.

Why did I tolerate a marriage with no children and a husband who was never there, to hang out with men who died 250 years ago? Neither the husband nor the dead guys required me to attach.

Yes, classical is great music. Yes, it requires concentration span to write, perform, and hear. Mozart extended the length of a song from three minutes to 23 minutes, the length of an opera from one hour to four. Asked why a CD is so long, the Tokyo engineer who invented it replied that it had to hold Beethoven's *Ninth Symphony*.

Yet what I didn't know was that my peculiar musical fervor stemmed from my illness. "Sie feuhlt was sie singt (She feels what she sings)!" said a German tourist after one of my concerts. "It was always going to be different when you sang," my best friend Cynthia added.

At least I could feel Wolfgang and Ludwig blasting out their megawatt feelings. But all this was actually a sign that my real emotions were almost 100% numb, aka repressed.

Then I lost even my music. Commuting on the Beltway one day I popped in a CD to sing along with Bach, but instead had to pull over, collapsing on the wheel in tears. Suddenly I couldn't bear classical; it dredged up all those years of marriage, now lost. Here was my first taste of "breakthrough grief," the blinding emotional pain that hits from nowhere which would become a regular event.

Back on the road, I scanned the radio in a daze. Mostly there was country music, a genre so foreign it coulda been in Transylvanian. But it was a riot, with lines like "I met a man in Hollywood, a credit to his gender/He really worked me over good, just like a Waring blender." (1)

I needed a laugh, and somehow had the urge to dance. I began soaking it up like a sponge.

When I turned 50, a friend asked if I ever thought I'd live that long. "No, I guess not," I admitted, "Is it so obvious I'm burning the candle at both ends?" I'd been lost in East Berlin on the wrong side of the Wall. I'd been deep under the Korean DMZ in a miner's bucket. I'd been on so many adventures that another gal asked, "Is there anything you *haven't* done?"

Well, there were still a few things, and now I was going to do 'em all.

As I was boxing up my life in Virginia, I got a call from a friend in California who was ill. When her hair fell out, her husband divorced her; attachment was not his thing, either. She needed help so out I flew. On my first trip to California, all I saw were courtrooms and hospitals.

On my second trip I stepped onto Newport Beach and the beauty of the area hit me hard.

"Why not me?" I thought, looking at the ocean, the sailboats, the rows of green palms and red tile roofs sweeping into the bright blue distance. Why should I shovel snow to commute the rest of my life, when I could live here?

Larry was so mean for so long that by the time I left, I felt nothing but the sheer relief that I'd stopped banging my head against the wall. Just to breathe felt like a party. On my third California trip in late July 2006, just to see the sun on the ocean and the palm trees made me want to dance, and so I did.

I danced a lot of two-step and wailed to hard rock. I sang a lot of country. I raced sailboats, ocean kayaked, and hiked mountains.

I also dated up a semi-tropical storm. I had no intention of not doing the right thing. Fun appeared to be the only intensely rational thing to do.

In reality, however, I was in so much emotional pain when I hit Newport Beach that I couldn't stand to feel it. So I proceeded to serial-medicate myself with partying. Whu Nu? I had so much pain that I didn't even know I had pain.

It's simple, I thought. "I married a bad man; he was mean to me. Now I'll just find a good man."

The Singing Nun

Trouble is, divorce doesn't come with a Surgeon General's warning, "Caution: Rebound Affairs Can be Hazardous to Your Health." The women's center experts didn't tell us that 70% of divorced folks have a second divorce.

That's because divorce hurts; it hurts a lot. So people medicate the pain. Medicating includes alcohol, drugs, food, workaholism, Internet fixations—anything to avoid feeling the loss of an entire life.

At the top of the list is the feel-good of new romance, but rebound affairs right after divorce can't work. We've had no time to heal the losses of marriage. We're all hurt and no judgment, so mismatches are legion.

"Whu Nu?" I sure didn't. I didn't get the memo because there was no memo—another reason for this book.

One day back in Virginia, boxing up to move out West, I fell into a vat of the ultimate pain medication.

Every summer Sunday for 20 years I'd gone to a local pool. The first Sunday in August 2006, by then living in Cynthia's basement, I went to my pool only to find it bulldozed for the construction of a warehouse. Onward I drove to another pool in Maryland 20 minutes away. It was an innocent family spot where I'd never set foot before and from which I'd soon be 3,000 miles gone.

I was minding my own business, secure in the glum knowledge that Larry found me unattractive and no man would ever look at me again. It was 90 degrees in the shade and I was half asleep in the pool, holding onto a ladder, when he hailed me:

"Hey, ladder lady."

I thought he wanted the ladder, so I swam away.

Minutes later he appeared at my lounge chair, a wiry fellow with burning blue eyes, hitting on me like a ton of bricks. My jaw must have dropped a foot, but he wasn't looking at my jaw.

He chatted and handed me his business card, which showed that he managed billion-dollar equipment at Washington National Airport. "Come to my house for dinner," he urged. "I'm moving to California; I've got a car trunk full of boxes to prove it," I said. "It's pointless."

I hadn't dated since college. I knew the financial markets, but when it came to romance I was like the Singing Nun out of a cloister, or a dead ringer for Wilma Flintstone from some pre-historic time capsule with a bone in her hair. To say I knew nothing about men was an understatement. I had no tools to handle anything remotely approaching this.

Dan Heller, for his part, had quite a toolbox and was not to be deterred. Three Sundays at the pool he came at me; he had beautiful eyes and knew how to use them. Finally he realized that I was fascinated by air travel and offered me a "back stage tour" of the airport.

That Wednesday I met him outside his office. We climbed into his Jeep and roamed the airfields, examining the great machines which move people and equipment all over the world from angles a passenger never sees. We toured construction sites, fuel tank farms, hangars with aircraft of every kind, and I learned the difference between a taxiway and a runway.

The coup de grace was a ride to the top of the new Air Traffic Control Tower, not yet in service, with a breathtaking 360-degree panoramic view. We were alone at sunset, Dan was in his element, and I folded.

Entering Dan's Maryland farmhouse for dinner, there was a great room with cathedral ceiling, a bay window with a lake view, and a promising grand staircase. "Ah built this house with mah own two hands," he drawled.

Killer southern accent? He was from southern New Jersey, I was from southern Long Island—and I was toast. I had no idea what goes on in the world. I thought he was looking for love.

But no.

He had a closet full of hunting rifles and camo, and he was looking for a deer to take. Once he had the carcass, he was going to lose interest in that deer fast. I, however, was Ms. No Eye Deer.

Enter the Dragon

Before I knew it, my years of marital pain were being medicated into oblivion.

For weeks Dan pumped a flood of dopamine, oxytocin and other bonding chemicals through my bloodstream with enough intensity to knock a gal senseless. I was like a Stradivarius manhandled by a ham-fisted drummer, then tossed into storage, then found by a master violinist.

In college Dan was seduced by a diplomat's wife who taught him more about female anatomy than Henry Gray ever dreamed possible. Some intelligence agency should have had him teaching grad courses in persuasion.

Dan was systematic at ensuring my chemical addiction, but he wasn't just shining shoes. He took the delight of a kid in an ice cream store in his craft, so I thought he considered me a keeper. "If you enjoy something, why wouldn't you make it last as long as possible?" he'd say, going into hour three at 1 a.m.

1.2 Systematic addiction. (Warner Brothers)

Remember Bruce Lee's film *Enter the Dragon*, in which Han the drug lord builds a factory for the prostitution slave trade under his chateau? Stealing in to investigate, Lee discovers rows of red cages, each holding a kidnapped girl. Nurses in crisp white uniforms systematically inject them with heroin to addict them so that they never attempt escape. (Figure 1.2)

All those organic chemicals Dan pumped into me had me rowing in the same slave galley. Far-fetched? Nope. Helen Fisher, the anthropologist upon whose work Match.com and Chemistry.com are based, wrote a book about it. (2)

It was a trip from nothing to a whole lot of something.

Ms. New York City found herself on another planet, playing farm wife complete with apron. "A woman should be chained to the bed with a chain long enough to reach the kitchen," Dan would drawl. I posed on his tractor, but no matter how I tried to "go country" I still resembled nothing so much as Martha Stewart. Suddenly I had a taker for all that country music I learned.

We'd ride around in his four-wheel drive singing "I Ain't as Good as I Once Was" by Toby Keith at the top of our lungs.

Imagine my surprise when after a few months, Dan announced that he needed space. "Why can't women be like my guy friends? If Ah don't see them for two weeks, they don't care," he said. "Doin' them same gymnastics with the guys?" I wondered silently.

"Women are obsessed with relationships," he said. "Guys don't care about that stuff. Relationships are for marriage, marriage is for children, and Ah'm done with that. Women who can't have sex without getting attached should grow up."

I was a No Eye Deer at the time, but it was a classic case of "Come Here—Go Away." Dan did everything to make me attach like crazy glue, then flipped and dismissed me.

I didn't know it then, but our brain has distinct lobes, which behave very differently. First we develop a "reptilian" brain stem for survival functions like breathing. Later we develop a "mammalian" brain for emotions like attachment. (3)

Reptiles don't attach and don't carry their young; they eat them. That's because reptiles have no emotions, since they have no mammalian brain. Mammals developed this higher brain to carry and care for their young, and found emotions like attachment quite useful.

Dan militantly opposed mammalian attachment, and of reptiles he was rather fond. I once envied an iguana he played with for hours in Mexico, it got so much TLC. Years later I learned how to detect human reptiles, but back then, Whu Nu? (4)

To be fair, Dan had suffered serial cheating and a nasty divorce decades before. He went ballistic and vowed never to attach again. "Ah ripped out my heart with an ax and Ah like it that way," he would repeat. "She did me a favor: she made me bulletproof."

Dan had also learned that telling his sorry tale with his fluffy blue eyes full of hurt was a surefire way to lower a woman's defenses. It brought out the mom in her and all her bonding hormones. With a gal in the grip of this mindless emoting, he could get away with psychological murder. It *was* crazy-making. Didn't his physical actions speak louder than words? Nope.

Not only had Dan declared war on attachment; he sold war bonds to me.

I knew the foreign exchange markets but I was clueless in this ball park. Was he right? Maybe maturity means we rule ourselves by the mind and don't let emotions sway us? I wondered if all men were like this, for what did I know of men? My ex made even less of an effort to relate. It's possible Dan spent more time touching me in those months than my ex had in 30 years.

Either way, why argue? If I just kept showering Dan with love and compassion, his heart would eventually melt, right?

Finally I did move to California in late November 2006, but Dan wasn't done. He kept calling; he knew I had Washington clients with lucrative gigs to bring me to his door every few months. I couldn't say no to the money or to Dan.

The rest of 2006, all of 2007, and more than half of 2008 was a blur of transcontinental red-eyes, 70-hour defense work weeks, and flights to meet Dan on the farm or in Mexico. The guy had a distance thing, all right. A 3,000-mile distance thing. The only reason he kept calling was that I'd moved to the opposite coast.

During those two years I was often reduced to writing doggerel in an attempt to figure out how Dan's mind worked (there's an oxymoron), or trying to make him "get it." Still, considering my cross-eyed state back then, the insight in the lines below about "to feel or not" is oddly on the money.

All's Fair - April 7, 2007

We had some good times baby, that's a fact,
Ran down the river 'til the trains came back,
Laughed ourselves silly, danced our brains out flat,
But now I'm outta there. It ain't love,
It's war—and all's fair.

You've been a hunter baby, all your life,
A seasoned expert, arrow, gun, or knife,
In charge and on your game, each bullet is just right;

You sort your own underwear. It ain't love,
It's war—and all's fair.

I've got the wanderlust born in my veins,
The woman on the ships and planes and trains,
A gypsy spirit watches over me,
I like the wind in my hair; and I'm free,
To go anywhere—and all's fair.

You're a lyrical miracle, you're so good at sex,
All the women who know you want to shoot your ex.
She hurt you so deep, and she hurt you so hard,
You built a medieval fortress in your back yard;
Now you're stacking the turrets and manning the guns,
And Lord help the girl who has too much fun!

So look inside yourself a little more,
Know what you had last time I stood in your door,
You can rise above the past, I can stand there once more—
(I like to mess up your hair…)
If it's love, or it's war, all's fair.

But whether I go, or whether I stay,
Will never be the real issue anyway.
The issue is emotion versus Novocaine,
And whether you'll allow yourself to feel again.

So take a deep breath, breathe in the fresh air,
And we can make it up as we go from there.
If it's love, or it's war:
All's fair.

"You wrote a country song!" exclaimed a friend, reading it. Yep.

When I left home, to repeat, I thought that I was dead. I wrote to friends many times in the months to follow that Dan had brought a dead woman back to life.

"I was dead, now I want to be alive," my journals repeat. "You gave me life, I owe you life/Call upon it if you can," ends another poem.

I didn't learn for years that this feeling of being dead has a technical name: *dissociation.*

Toward the end of 2007, after one visit to DC contractors and Dan, I flew back to LAX in the worst fire season of the decade. From the air, flames and black smoke rose from the desert to the city as far as the eye could see. It was a descent into Hell, literally and emotionally.

My California dream had become a nightmare. Dan the anti-Christ of anti-bonding was eating an ever-wider hole in my soul. I spent the first quarter of 2008 writing a billion-dollar proposal for radar systems near LAX by day, and scribbling poems in an attempt to work Dan out of my system with a crow bar by night.

No matter how I tried to improve my present life, it never hit me that all this emotional pain might be caused by something in the past. Yet who in their right mind would put up with Dan's treatment for two months, let alone two years?

Something definitely not mental health was up.

Notes

1. Ronstadt (1996).
2. Fisher (2004).
3. Lewis et. al. (2000).
4. Baer (2-7-13).

2

No Tears for Dad

2.1 Never walk alone? (Fred Ward/EPA)

Reality hit when my father died and I couldn't cry.

I saw an ad for a concert in Huntington Beach of my all-time favorite, Mozart's *Requiem,* and moved to take back my music. On May 15, 2008, I performed it with full chorus and orchestra. Finally, a new California life!

Next morning my brother-in-law phoned from New York to say that my Dad in Florida had had a heart attack, so catch the next plane to Miami. Goodbye, new life.

Back across the country I flew, Mozart's fearsome call of Judgment Day ringing in my ears. Back to my "family of origin," to my parents and my sister (Miami Beach, 2.1).

Back, back, back in time.

My father lay in the hospital dying. He had an oxygen mask over his face and could do little more than groan and wave penciled lists of things to do in the general direction of my mother.

Dad was wonderful man who worked long hours into the night and Saturdays, yet there was something strange about it. He was "controlled access only." He'd come home late, Mom would allow us a quick hug, say "Daddy's tired," seat Dad in a back room with dinner and the TV, and close the door.

"They never knew his name was Ralph," she used to joke. "They thought his name was 'Daddy's Tired.' "

Dad grew up in a Long Island mansion with showcases of silver, plastic slipcovers and tennis courts. His father commuted to Manhattan by train. Grandpa lost everything in the 1929 crash, but went to the station every day for weeks and sat there to keep up appearances. One day Dad had to bring Grandpa home. Hearing this story, I realized that appearances had always been really important in our family.

Watching Dad now waving lists, I saw he was still trying to keep up appearances, trying to control events in a situation where that is notoriously impossible. I recalled this later when my younger sister Linda and I found Dad's huge cartons of nail clippers, pencils, pads, and bills from decades past, an empire of things he spent years trying to control.

Days later as we sat in the hospital, my phone rang with a call for a $35,000 contract in Washington DC that I couldn't refuse. Back on the plane I went. I was in so much pain from seeing my family that I couldn't even feel it. Instead, I proceeded again to medicate.

Straight to Dan's farm I flew, where his cocktail of organic chemicals numbed me up right fine. I was caught in a giant nation-wide merry-go-round jetting from LAX to Miami to DC then back to Miami.

On June 23, 2008, Dad passed away. Back to Florida I flew.

Mom had written funeral scripts for everyone but me.

When my sister asked me to start the service, something in me balked. "No," I said, "I'm the eldest, I'll go last." Linda's sons read their scripts, then extemporized as teens do. Linda's husband spoke, then Linda spoke about the greatest Dad on earth. Mom didn't speak.

No one had any idea what I would do, least of all me, until the last moment. "Everyone's already said what a wonderful father Dad was. I'd like to do something for my family," I said.

And suddenly, I sang. It was "You'll Never Walk Alone" from *Carousel*, a family favorite. The hundred-person audience in the upscale Miami retirement home cried, then almost applauded the long high note at the end.

Everyone cried, except me. I sang that whole slow sustained song a cappella and my voice was entirely clear. "I never thought you'd make that high note," whispered sis, "but you nailed it." I was shocked, too. The emotional soprano could not find tears for her Dad. Actually I had tried to cry for days.

I was worried, but somehow I felt nothing.

My Dad had died, but I couldn't cry.

Accept the Loss

Off I flew to a new Washington gig and Dan. Imagine my surprise when five days after my father's death, Dan sat down to the nice dinner I'd prepared for him and asked me to leave.

"It's just not happening for me," he announced. "Ah want mah house back. Ah'm just not comfortable with you."

After two years and endless hours of intensity, I was completely blindsided.

Later that night (much later, after the inevitable rematch) I asked Dan what I'd done wrong, so I could at least learn something. All he could do was repeat, "I was comfortable with my wife. I'm just not comfortable with you."

I left and rented a room near Washington National Airport to finish my project. My Dad was dead, I couldn't cry for him, but now I was crying buckets over Dan, a stranger I'd known barely two years.

Over the July 4, 2008 weekend, I dutifully googled "grief" on the National Institute of Mental Health (NIMH) website. "How will I know when I'm done grieving?" it said. "Every person who experiences a death or other loss must complete a four-step grieving process:

1. Accept the loss.
2. Work through and feel the physical and emotional pain of grief.
3. Adjust to living in a world without the person or item lost.
4. Move on with life.

"The grieving process is over only when the person completes these four steps," it concluded bluntly. (1)

I've kept that text in my wallet all these years. It proved to be deadly accurate. I posted "Accept the Loss" in large letters on my laptop and taped it everywhere, but couldn't understand it. I was sure that the shattering loss I felt was heartbreak over Dan.

I was working 14-hour days on a Homeland Security contract and leading a double life, interviewing top executives by day, crying into my phone to California friends by night. I'd been on a psychological drunk with Dan, I told them, to cover up the loss of my long marriage, my overseas projects, my music and my life.

I couldn't "Accept the Loss" of my entire life; I couldn't accept anything.

"I just ran," I said. "First to Dan, then to California, dancing, singing, sailing, then back to Dan. Now I've lost Dan, my last umbilical cord to the East Coast. What do you do when the champagne factory shuts down?"

Me? I churned out doggerel into the dying hours. I didn't feel angry while I was crying so hard that summer of 2008; I didn't feel angry for another year.

But I'd kept an empty bean can on a high shelf in my rental. It had a half dozen jagged wounds from the May afternoon when Dan posted it as a target in a mountain field and tried to teach me to shoot. Something inside me resonated oddly to think that I had actually pumped this piece of metal full of lead. I was not aware of any anger, but one poem told another story.

Tin Can Shot Full of Holes – July 13, 2008

It's sitting on the wall ledge above my closet door,
It sits and stares right at me; I know what it's staring for:
To think a serious woman like me would be concerned,
For such a pile of tin and rust, and might even get burned;
The more I think about it, the less I can control
A visceral reaction to that tin can shot full of holes.

I met a man in Mexico, he had an eagle eye,
He warned me not to feel too much; he warned me not to fly;
He warned me there was nothing alive behind his smile;
He smiled so warm right through me, it almost seemed worthwhile.

I thought his smile might save him, as bright as burning coals,
But nothing could bring comfort to a tin can shot full of holes.

We went up on the mountain with little more to say,
I did my level best to focus on things far away.
We used tin cans as targets to practice pistol shots,
But never could be certain to hit any given spot.
Like Dorothy I've traveled over Oz from pole to pole,
But all I've come away with is a tin can shot full of holes.

I hate it when these poems just overflow my mind;
I'd rather more be sleeping and my work is far behind.
I see him in the shadows, I see him in the sun,
I see him in the grasslands, I see him on the run,
He'll have to run forever, for he's running from his soul;
My heart goes out in pity to the tin man shot full of holes.

Summer 2008 surely, I thought, was the end of my world. Surely it could get no worse than this.

Financial Holocaust

Returning to LAX on July 18, 2008, however, it went downhill from there.

The Great 2008 Financial Meltdown was on, banks were crashing across America, and California jobs were doing a Japanese duck pop. That's a term I heard from a Korean War vet in the '80s. Imagine a duck flying along fast, then sticking his head up his rear… until pop! He simply disappears.

I'd met a lot of people in Newport by volunteering at Opera Pacific, but after 22 years, the opera went bankrupt in 2008 and closed its doors. Then an opera friend invited me to a Newport dinner party.

The lady on my right asked what I did. "A writer? Fabulous," she said. "I run a fund for clients investing $5 million and up. I need a ghost author for my book on investments. Come to my office on Monday." Soon I was typing up her book as she rattled it off. We talked global finance and she spoke of hiring me to help her with clients.

Here was a new California Dream.

Then one day I arrived to find that the Wall Street investment bank where she kept her clients' money had folded, bringing world markets down with it. Her three cell phones were ringing off the hook, computers were going haywire, irate clients were pulling up in limos, and her husband and son ran in and out with slips of paper.

It was like trying to write a book on nuclear war in the middle of a nuclear war. There went another California Dream.

Next, consulting near LAX imploded. Suddenly defense companies were closing their LA offices and shipping the gigs back to Washington from whence I'd just escaped. My career was done unless I moved back to DC, world capital of Pentagon suppliers, rain, sleet, and Dan Heller. I physically couldn't do it.

I was stuck in my California one-room, little more than a shack with no kitchen in a young couples' back yard. I had $30,000 of my ex's debt on my credit cards, my business wardrobe, my stellar resume—and I was curled up in a heap on my bed like a spider checking out for good.

Earlier, dating in California to replace Dan, I'd met Pete the management consultant. He read *The New Yorker*, took me to Zagat-rated restaurants and toured me in his Lexus to fine museums. Surely he was a gentleman.

Pete was also the first person in this adventure to say that I ought to have my head examined. Now, as my world collapsed, we talked about my Dad's death, and Pete said that I definitely needed help.

He should know.

Initially Pete drank St. Pauli Girl NA. That means "non-alcoholic," but Whu Nu? Months later he began to have a glass of wine with dinner; then it was a bottle of wine with dinner.

Later it was a bottle of vodka, after which Pete passed out. The last time he asked me to dinner, I pulled up to the restaurant to find Pete outside with a canned Manhattan. "Please put that away; it's me or the booze," I said. He popped the lid, I drove off, and never saw him again.

Five months later, his boss informed me that Pete, 55, had died alone with his three cats in his home steps from the sand in Huntington Beach. At the funeral before I sang "Ave Maria," Pete's ex revealed that Pete had been in alcoholic rehab clinics since age 15. He died when his gut rotted through.

Despite Pete's elaborate front it was remarkable: I'd again found someone who couldn't attach.

I had no way to know that Pete drank when we met. Yet anyone who drank that hard for 40 years had his head so far up a bottle that he couldn't possibly relate—and I chose him.

I didn't get that back then. All I heard was the "T" word: therapy.

I Oughtta Have My Head...

If you'd told me in 2005 that I'd move to California, land of fruit and nuts, I'd have rolled my eyes.

If you'd told me that I'd move to California and get a therapist, I'd have laughed my level New York head off.

But by July 2008, I was ready to believe it: I definitely needed to have my head examined.

Out of the dating shark pool I stumbled, into the therapy jungle, despite the social condemnation, time, and terrifying expense.

How did I find a therapist? Checking singles events in the newspaper. Amongst the dances, jazz concerts and "Chocolate Lovers of America" events, I saw a therapy group: "Support for dealing with divorce."

At the first meeting, Dr. Matt went around the room of ten women, asking what brought us in. "I've moved seven times in two years," said one. "I left my husband, moved in with my daughter, then with my boyfriend, then I left him. I'm miserable everywhere I go. No wonder I can't find someone to love me; I don't even love me."

"I lost a 27-year marriage, my Dad died, then I was dumped by the rebound guy and he's all I can think about," I said. "I feel like I'm crazy because I can't cry for my Dad." The other women had husbands deep in substance abuse who were wrecking their finances or cheated on them or beat them.

We were all repeating painful relationships from childhood, announced Dr. Matt.

"When a child has emotionally unavailable parents and is ignored, criticized, or under tension at home, the child believes that 'I *am* bad,' " he said.

I resonated on all cylinders. A part of me had felt that ever since I could remember. My parents never drank, smoked or did anything but work, but they did argue and get angry.

Suddenly I was cowering in the back seat of the car in grade school while my parents laced into each other up front. "Please don't fight, please don't be angry!" I scrawled madly. "What did I do wrong? Why won't you love me?"

Out of nowhere, I'm in grade school. Oh my. Asking my parents, "Why won't you love me?" Huh?

"When family stress occurs, a child learns wrongly 'I caused it, I've got to fix it,' " Dr. Matt went on. "We develop 'repetition compulsion.' As adults, we re-stage our childhood drama, trying to go back and fix it."

"Why are you telling me I broke it and demanding that I fix it?" I scribbled to my parents.

Dr. M. even diagnosed my marriage. "In the absence of the father, some mothers lean too much on their sons, so the son has a deep compulsion to escape. Later this man is allergic to relationships; he always has one foot out the door."

"Larry always had one foot out the door!" I scribbled. Larry's Dad traveled on business and his mom turned her first-born son into a prince. Plus yikes, Dan always had one foot out the door.

What Inner Child?

The Rx which came next hit me like a hammer. "You have a hurting child inside," said Dr. M. "Introduce your adult part to your hurting child part, and let them sit together for awhile—alone."

It sounded like gibberish. I had a sinking feeling. I went home, tried to do it, but felt much, much worse. After a week I was in such panic that I was nauseous.

I just couldn't find a "child" inside. No such thing!

My Dad died, but I can't cry, remember? That's why I'm in therapy. I came for help but now I felt worse.

"My husband didn't love me for 30 years," I said next time, "the rebound guy didn't love me, and looks like my parents didn't do emotions. You say 'Go love yourself'? At least with the rebound guy I didn't feel alone.

"I can't find any child inside, and the more I try, the more panicked I feel. It feels like being told to go have a homosexual relationship with myself. There's something pornographic about it."

"If you feel it's pornographic, you have severe trauma," he said. It didn't sound like "Wow, let's get you help right away." It sounded like, "You're bad. Try harder or you won't fit in."

Think of me as a frog on a lab table. It felt as if my belly were being slit open and no one could understand that simple fact when I told them. Instead they treated me like a broken widget refusing to behave.

The emotional pain was bewildering.

On August 1, I got a second opinion from Pam, a local church divorce counselor. "Your hurts go too deep for group therapy," she said. "Stop the Superwoman act and take better care of yourself. Go get individual therapy."

It was deep in the Crash of 2008, I was out of work and horrified, but Pam convinced me by sheer compassion. She even gave me a referral to a local charity. To this day I love her. I was in a second therapist's office for individual treatment on August 5, the pain was that intense.

Dr. Rita was full of textbook wisdom, but she didn't want to deal with my Dad grief, either. "If your father never came home, it's like the death of a stranger," she dismissed it. "Naturally you can't cry for him."

Now what?

"Make an emotional connection with yourself," said Dr. Rita. "Make a connection with your inner child."

Not again!

"Inner Child Theory," she expanded, "has a documented history of success. A part of you is a hurting child inside. You've got to learn to comfort that child yourself." I wrote it all down but I couldn't feel any of it.

I understood even less what "comfort" meant. Chicken soup? A hot tub? "Take two chickens and call me in the morning?" I'm alone in the world and horribly ill. What's the difference between your theory and "go stuff it"?

For weeks I tried to explain the disconnect to Rita.

"Stop taking all those notes and let yourself *feel* it!" she'd command.

"Feel what?" I'd say.

"Your inner child of course," she'd reply. "Why don't you stop emotionally blocking and comfort the child? You can't do it because you're not willing to give up being the victim!

"You've got to go deep within and feel the inner child's *guilt*, her *shame*, her *anger*," she'd say.

"I don't have that; I don't even know what you mean by shame," I'd protest. "I go right to panic!" That always drew a blank.

"Get down on your knees and comfort the child!" Rita finally exclaimed. "There are books on the Inner Child; there are exercises to do. Your emotional block is the problem! You have to take it on faith and try."

If that makes no sense to you, fine; it made no sense to me. I was in no position to do it myself; that's why I went for help!

No wonder top psychiatrists are writing critiques of their profession.(2) But I didn't know that then.

I Flunked Bonding

So in September 2008, I slunk down in shame to Barnes & Noble to buy the *Inner Child Workbook* and do my homework like a good little, er, child. It put me through 36 pages of exercises. (3)

First I had to interview relatives to ask how my parents were with me.

"I could never understand why your Mom was so mean to you," my older cousin Bonnie said, just like that. "I noticed it when you were about four. 'Why are you so mean to that little girl?' I used to ask her. She was mean to you in public; the aunts saw it; everyone saw it. But then she was mean to your father, too. I guess she just wasn't a very nice person."

Well, er, but Mom was a fact of life. Then I heard similar stories from other relatives.

Finally on page 37 the *Workbook* reports that "infants need attachment," something neither of my therapists ever mentioned. "From birth to 18 months, the developmental tasks you needed to master were bonding with mother, nurturing and trust," it said.

"If you were left for long periods to cry… if the arms that held you were rejecting and rigid, you would not have felt safe. If you did not feel safe, you would not have been able to bond enough to develop trust," it adds. (4)

Terror struck. I had no information on my first 18 months (no one can remember it), but something deep in my chest knew in that moment: my problem was a lack of bonding. Yes, I could still feel those rigid and rejecting arms. No, I never felt safe with Mom; she was always so critical. "Trust" and "bonding" were not words I could associate with her—or with anyone. I didn't even know that we're supposed to feel trusting or bonded.

Wham, it hit me: I had failed to accomplish the task of infant-mother bonding.

I couldn't feel the "inner child" thing, but this I could really feel.

I had flunked bonding. It felt like a death sentence. I had only myself to blame for my gross infant incompetence, and only myself to fall back on. But I was the broken one; how could I fix it?

Could I bond with myself? Could I get bonding from a book? Do they sell bonding at Walmart? Or for a price, Nordstrom's?

On and on the *Workbook* went with the damaging ramifications of an infant's failure to bond. If we flunked bonding as kids, now as adults we're empty inside and too needy for attention. "I'm screwed," I wrote in the margins over and over, "I'm just screwed."

Hadn't my ex and Dan both said I was too needy? Don't the latest books and films like *He's Just Not That Into You* say that women who want relationships are too needy, just as Dan said?

The *Workbook's* Rx was the same issued by my two therapists: hole up alone and heal your inner child.

It instructs us to lock ourselves in a room alone and do exercises. First, lie down on a sheet on the floor and get in touch with the child by sucking on a baby bottle or eating applesauce by hand as if unable to wield a spoon, smearing yourself with it. "Find out what it feels like to be a helpless infant," it advises.

I underlined chapter after chapter, scrawled reams in the margins, and forced myself through the exercises.

Every time I picked up that book I felt like committing suicide. After a month I hid the *Inner Child Workbook* under a stack of other books where I physically couldn't see it.

Over a long education and global travel I have read hundreds of books spanning three thousand years of world literature including Dante's *Inferno* in Italian, a very scary place. But this is the only book I have ever hidden.

Looking at it even now sends a shiver down my spine. Some days a book burning didn't seem out of line.

Isolation Row

I was too terrified to describe this to Dr. Rita. She had her own agenda.

"Close your eyes," she said, "and imagine you're going down, down, down below the ground. You emerge onto a path to a secret garden. You see a little girl about five. Imagine you take the child's hand." Nuts. I still couldn't find a child.

"Let's ask the child some questions," Rita went on. "Respond without thinking, from the gut. What's your first memory of Father?"

"A pair of slacks going behind a closed door," I mumbled.

"What's your first memory of Mother?"

"I swallowed a penny at four and was rushed to X-ray. Mom was so furious that I thought she would kill me."

"Your parents rejected you," Rita announced. "Now you're compelled to find men who reject you, to recreate the problem so you can go back and fix it. But you didn't break it—you don't have to fix it." I wrote that on a large 5 x7 file card and it's still on my desk.

But why didn't she tell me about adult attachment disorder? *Why didn't she tell me it wasn't my fault?*

Instead Rita lowered the isolation boom again. "You have to feel the little girl in your heart and comfort her," she intoned. "You have to do it alone: that's the whole point."

"You don't need Dan," she scoffed. "You don't need *anyone* else. What you need is to stop trying to heal the child who's sick, with some guy's d–k. Just heal yourself."

I may have New York potty mouth, but that did *not* come from me.

That, verbatim, was the instruction from my therapist, at my financial and emotional expense. I wrote that quote from this refined lady in the middle of her technical shrink-speak in my 2008 notebook, and I doubt she coined the rhyme. It must be trade jargon in some PhD circles.

Note the irrational assertion that only total isolation can work. Going to others, anyone at all, is linked to the mortification of "some guy's d–k."

Was there no middle ground between isolation and that? A women's group, a divorce seminar, a girl friend, a pastor?

Or maybe–gasp–go to your *therapist* for emotional support?

It did turn out that neither sex nor romance can heal childhood emotional pain.

But can it be done by lying alone on a sheet covered in applesauce?

Death Sentence

"But this feels like a death sentence," I kept telling Rita, "This isn't working."

"Something feels terribly wrong! It makes me queasy to say I have to do it myself, I'm not good enough that someone else would love me enough to help. It's a sinking feeling."

By demanding I find a phantom inner child which I could not find, both therapists were saying: "You're the problem."

All I could feel was a bottomless well of emotional pain and terror like something out of the real Inquisition. I felt terror at something horrifying deep inside. I had nightmares about dead fish with hideous eyes. No inner child, just horror.

Is that horror, me? Am I a freak with an inner dead fish?

All I could do was to sit in my room hugging a pillow and moan about how badly I wanted to be held. Then I'd think of how Dan held me for hours on end for the first time in my life.

"You just take all the tension out of my body," I used to tell him. I'd walk into his room after work, take off my watch, throw it against the far wall, and we'd both dissolve laughing.

Now that was gone, and I was the living opposite of relaxed.

How was I to avoid men, when romance was the only thing left on the planet which offered holding? I felt sure this must be bonding. All I could think of was: could I please get some bonding before I die?

I'd written something in a notebook, then blanked it out and put it away:

"Dan loved me more than anyone in my entire life has ever loved me."

An astonishing thing to say, given Dan's predatory behavior. Now I stared at it for a long time, then had to admit it was true.

Not that I'd dare tell anyone, least of all my, er, therapist.

I hadn't gotten anything near the love Dan gave me, however meager, from my husband, father, mother, or anyone else. Ever. Sad, but the truth is the truth.

Compared to both my therapists, Dan also loved me a lot more. What did they give me? No wonder I kept trying to crawl back into Dan's arms in subsequent romances; at least from Dan I got something.

Hadn't Dr. Rita read about attachment? Where were the diagnostic tools, or any diagnostic method? (5)

Once again I thought, surely Fall 2008 was the end of my world. Surely it could get no worse than this.

Notes

1. SAMHSA (undated, p.2).
2. Lewis et. al (2000). Norwood (1997): "You cannot apply Self-Help to a problem from which the Self that's trying to provide the Help suffers."
3. Taylor CL (1991, p.37).
4. There's a distinction between attachment and bonding, but many therapists use them interchangeably.
5. Brous (4-12-17).

Thanksgiving in Cambodia

3.1 Mozart's "Requiem."
(Rosie Barana)

B ut 2008 did get a lot worse. The gods of Pain had barely started on my file.

By September I couldn't take any more isolation row, and the bills were mounting, so I worked out my anxiety in a whirl of new business projects.

I wrote a three-page memo to a company in San Diego, offering to market their power plants in Asia. I e-mailed it to the vice president, left a voicemail and nearly passed out when he called back next day. He said the memo was "brilliant" and two days later I was in his office.

Negotiations with his staff, however, dragged on for months as they awaited the November 2008 election. They worried that the new Administration wouldn't support nuclear energy (it didn't). They worried that the crash meant no financier appetite for new ventures (there wasn't any). They worried gas prices wouldn't stay high enough to make the new reactor competitive (they didn't).

Meanwhile my friends at the South Korean central bank were calling in a tizzy (wouldn't you), worried that the US market crash would take them with it. They had a consulate official take me to dinner in Los Angeles.

He asked me to write a white paper for South Korea to take to a world financial summit, on how to stop the meltdown of global foreign exchange. No pressure, just in my spare time. This project didn't resolve quickly, either.

Then on the East Coast began a series of events which pushed me, my crisis, and my needs for emotional help well and truly off the agenda. It more like buried me under a very large landslide.

Mom.

Mom had been "home alone" in Florida since Dad passed in June, and my sister Linda in New York thought we should check on Mom regularly. In mid-September, in the middle of furious negotiations in San Diego over the fate of the Pacific Rim's electricity grid, it was my turn.

Landing in Miami, I phoned Mom from the cab to say, "Surprise! I'm on the way." Her reaction shocked me, even at that late date. "You can't do this to me," she yelled, "I don't want to see you; leave me alone!" By the time she hung up, Mom was in hysterics.

I phoned sis in New York. "I'm afraid to give Mom heart failure, plus I feel really awful," I said, "maybe this wasn't a good idea?" But Linda had spent so much time in the last six months in Florida tending to our parents that she was concerned about her job. Someone had to visit Mom and I was elected.

"*Couldn't you just be sweet?*" Linda asked.

The problem was that if I couldn't make it work, *I was* the problem.

No one in our family would dispute a cousin's recent statement that "when your Mom wasn't happy, no one was happy." But we all thought it was our job to make Mom happy, and now it must be my fault if she weren't. I didn't realize until years later that no one (including me) ever considered the collateral damage to me.

I ignored the terrified looks from the cab driver and dissolved in sobs in the back seat. We arrived and Mom asked if I'd come to institutionalize her. When I said no, she calmed down a bit. The visit proceeded, then I returned to my negotiations in San Diego.

On October 5, 2008, I again performed Mozart's *Requiem*, this time as soprano soloist, in Anaheim, California. After the events of 2008 you can see my glazed stare in the concert photo above.

Three days later, as my last dream to reestablish my international business was in play, my phone rang again from back East, just as it had after I sang the *Requiem* in May.

It was Linda calling to say that Mom had been hospitalized in Miami with hemorrhaging. Yes, this actually happened a second time. Whenever I sing Mozart's *Requiem*, a parent begins to die.

Again I left my meetings and got back on the plane to Florida. I'd be afraid to ever sing Mozart's *Requiem* again if I had any more parents. All my life it was my favorite piece, and I don't have any more parents, but I haven't sung it again.

Forget me. Now it was all about Mom for real.

I'd long worried that Mom lacked perspective; one rarely heard her speak of the eternal nature of love or immortality. I'd been concerned that she might not be at peace when the time came. Indeed. Peace, to paraphrase Henry Kissinger, was the light at the end of the tunnel that was the headlamp of an oncoming train. October and November 2008 with Mom in Florida were my psychological Cambodia. It didn't feel like one person's story; it felt like a crisis of civilization.

First came the homicidal doctors with the insurance hounds at their heels. Their sole concern was to remove Mom from whichever ward she was on, before the Medicare police found her and cut their funding. They moved Mom from ward to ward, forcing her into vigorous physical therapy which given her condition was brutality.

Finally Mom collapsed and the doctors booted her out of the main hospital and into the hospice wing, saying she'd have to leave soon, one way or the other. Ouch. "Welcome to the US healthcare system," said Linda.

Where's My Daughter?

Then there was Mom. She began to snarl when I arrived at the hospital and continued to do so for six weeks. It wasn't that she was in pain; the nurses saw to her meds.

Mom, simply put, did not want to see me, as she had said for decades. About seven minutes into each of my weekly Sunday phone calls to her, for about 30 years, Mom had a habit of hanging up on me.

She always put on a happy face and was entertaining at her retirement complex or with shoe store clerks, but now it was remarkable to watch the change. Now Mom was hanging up on friends and relatives, too. She folded the phone even on her bridge partners. She flat out didn't care anymore what anyone thought.

Mom never had time for questions such as "why and for what do we live?" She dismissed them as nonsense from fools who haven't worked hard for a dollar. She was pragmatic to the point of scorning ideas. Now when the time came for faith and belief, they were in short supply.

"Oh God, it is fearful thing, to see the human soul take wing," as Byron says, when it has no wing to wing it.

Mom seemed to get no comfort from God nor even be aware of the subject. She seemed to get no comfort from my sister's loving smile or even the appearance of Linda's two handsome sons from New York. She seemed to take no joy in bringing her family and Linda's family into being; having a long and until now healthy and prosperous life, nice clothes, fine homes, international vacations. Everything she always said was so important brought no solace in the end.

I had to spend hours watching this and felt driven to make sense of it. Mom appeared to be terrified of something, but I couldn't dismiss it as fear of death, since people do die in peace. It would have been gut-wrenching to watch just as an observer.

But then, I was not an observer. I was the designated pincushion. Mom had made no bones for decades that she didn't want me anywhere, least of all in that hospice.

I'd arrive in her room mornings and Mom would roll over and turn her face away. When the nurses dressed her or when she wanted something, she'd raise her voice and say, "Where's my daughter?" whether I were standing there, or down the hall on a business call. I'd say, "I'm here, Mom," and she'd growl, "Not you. Where's Linda?"

Scholars note that Buddha, Moses and Jesus all had trouble with their families when they went home. That's because those to whom we're closest are those to whom we're most vulnerable, so that's where we can be hurt most. We may develop a "need-fear dilemma;" we need closeness, but we fear it. That was me, all right. (1)

It was so intense, what if it were just my paranoia? Maybe Mom was fine and I was projecting my own neurosis onto her?

I sure didn't want to demonize my own mother.

Mommy Doesn't Like Me

Most of my life I just took it for granted that Mom didn't like me much, and so what? Lots of people simply don't get along. Mom was like the weather: a fact of life. You don't like the weather, you move. So I got moving.

I graduated both high school and college early, went to Japan at twenty and then medical school in the Philippines. It felt natural that I was alone on the other side of the world among strangers, killing myself pulling all-nighters.

Later I flew home to New York at 25 to visit and Mom was suddenly very proud. She feted "my daughter the doctor" like a returning astronaut at a string of family dinners.

Yet arriving home it hit me: I was doing something I didn't want to do. Mom wanted me to be a doctor and I saw that's why I was doing it.

3.2 Third-grade blues.
(Ralph Brous)

"I just realized that I'm not in med school for myself," I told my parents.

"I can't do something this serious the rest of my life for someone else." I said that I couldn't return to Manila and wanted to stay with my college boyfriend Larry in New York.

"You're throwing your life away!" said Mom in a rage. She despised Larry's politics and that became grounds for a sudden explosion: Larry "killed my daughter," she said, by ruining my medical career. In 20-20 hindsight, he did have lousy politics. No mom would want to see her daughter mixed up in that.

But it could have been discussed in the bosom of the family. I could have left U Manila and gone to work in New York while I figured out what I wanted to do or where to attend grad school.

Instead I was booted out of the house so fast it made my guts spin. It was not just "no more parties." It felt like one minute I was John Glenn and the next I was Lee Harvey Oswald. It was "Go and Never Darken My Door Again."

I couldn't think; I just wanted to die. Where was Jack Ruby when I needed him?

I had been excommunicated.

There's that odd feeling again; why does something always remind me of the Inquisition?

Not until decades later did I notice the real shocker: everyone accepted Mom's ruling as a *fait accompli*. I can't recall any debate from anyone, not from my father nor anyone else. It never entered my head to debate it, either.

Everyone including me seemed to agree that I was wrong and Mom was right. It was as if I'd broken all Ten Commandments. I condemned myself guilty as charged and slunk away.

What crime had I committed to merit this? I didn't steal from my dad or sleep with my sister's boyfriend. I just said, "I can't go to medical school and I'm seeing a guy whose politics you don't like." Yet suddenly it was "Off with her head!" Not until decades later did I realize it was nuts.

No one ever said, "*He's a bad man, he'll be bad for you. We love you, stay with us!*"

I would have stayed with my family in a New York minute. I was just trying to come home from the other side of the planet to find a little love for my mixed-up heart. But then I jumped out of a certain controlled script.

No one said, "But we want to see her!"

It was as if everyone was muttering, "Whew, glad it's not me."

Now here I was in 2008 in Mom's Miami hospice while she demanded, "Where's my daughter?"

How could Mom and I have run so far off the rails? I had plenty of time in that hospice to agonize over it and it didn't start after college. Mom hadn't wanted me all my life. When I left med school she finally found a reason to get rid of me.

That's me in the photo at eight in third grade. (Figure 3.2) What kind of a face is that on a kid?

Mom had been hostile ever since I could remember. I had memories of it predating my sister's birth. That puts the first time at age four, when I swallowed a penny and was rushed to X-ray late one night. I was terrified by the huge cold black machine, by being held down, and by Mom's rage at me for causing all that trouble.

When I was four, Mom also took me aside and said of my playmate Michelle, "I don't love her, but I like her. You're my daughter so I have to love you, but I don't like you." It stung so I never forgot it. I can still see the family dinner table where it happened.

I recalled cowering in the kindergarten bathroom at five, trying to erase a B grade and pencil in an A, afraid to come home with less than perfect, and then Mom's fury at the lie.

As a kid I could never fathom this pain or talk to anyone about it. We didn't discuss such things; there was too much to get done at home, work and school. I was too mortified to tell anyone at school. It was a serious Ugly Duckling routine which never got to the swan part.

Another puzzle piece appeared in January 2006 when I flew from Washington DC to my parents' 50th anniversary dinner in a swank Miami bistro. With my sister and her family in their finest, amid the champagne toasts, Mom suddenly announced that she'd never enjoyed my existence.

Fixing an eye on me across the table decked with flowers and candles, she said out of the blue:

"I nearly died having you; you almost killed me. You gave me an infection that put me on my back for weeks. I was so sick that Grandma begged Dad not to have any more children." As if I'd done it deliberately.

Stunned silence. I looked into Mom's eyes in panic, but there was no way to make a connection with what looked back. It looked like either a very cold fish or something much more dangerous.

I made a beeline for the ladies room and collapsed in a stall in a blur of chiffon, stilettos and tears. Eventually my sister pulled me out. Everyone acted as if nothing had happened. Again. My sister blanked it out and denies to this day that any such event occurred.

Later I recalled that when I was a kid, Mom sometimes showed me her scar, said I was an emergency caesarian, and hinted of an unplanned pregnancy.

When I hit puberty, Mom warned me hard that boys mean pregnancy, so stay away. "It's the woman who pays," she used to repeat. "Don't end up pushing a baby carriage!" It wasn't banter; it felt anxious and scary.

I tried to ignore it all, like the weather, but suddenly in that 2008 hospice it hit me: I'd always had some underlying feeling of fear, because I knew:
Mommy doesn't like me.

What child grows up afraid because "Mommy doesn't like me?" Don't all children think Mommy likes and loves them?

Hey, when I was a kid, I'd never been through childhood before. I didn't know I wasn't supposed to feel that.

All I knew was: Mommy doesn't like me. She told me so herself, early and often. I just interviewed five older relatives for the *Inner Child Workbook* who confirmed it.

My Wasted Life

Now in 2008, I reasoned that Mom was terrified of death. No matter what she said, I decided, what Mom needed was a huge amount of love. I tried compassion as best I could. I sat with Mom for hours. "It must be scary to be here," I said, "Let me hold you and support you emotionally."

"I don't want you to hold me," Mom said. "I don't want you anywhere near me. I sat on the living room couch and cried after I got off the phone with you every Sunday for 30 years."

"Is this a good time to focus on bygones?" I persisted. "I've had a rough time with my divorce and losing my home. I could use emotional support, too. Can't we do that for each other and just be mother and daughter?"

But no. Now the years of phone hang-ups were about to be explained.

"I'm not interested in emotional support," Mom growled. "Your sister helps people every day. What have you done with your life? You have a brilliant mind and we gave you everything. It's your own fault that you married Larry.

"It was a wasted life, a wasted life! You deserve what you got. Emotional support doesn't mean a thing. The only thing which means anything is money. If you care about someone that's what you give them."

Did I imagine this? I wish. I also wish I'd taped it, but who brings a recorder into the hospice with their mother?

Not only did she say it; I believed she was right. I even called my sister to ask desperately, "Is it true, is it true, did I really waste my entire life?" "Of course not," she said, but was too preoccupied with Mom to discuss it.

To a kid, Mom is God. God must be right, so I must be Bad. I'd felt that all my life.

I must have led a wasted life. Mommy doesn't like me, so I must be worthless.

It's Not My Coat

On days like that (most days) my cell phone kept me alive. I placed a lot of calls from that hospice to friends in California and Virginia. When my sister couldn't help, I was reduced to calling Ice Queen Rita. "Is it true, did I have a worthless life?" I asked in panic.

Dr. Rita always refused to talk by phone, but under these circumstances she agreed. God is merciful. Rita gave me one of her textbook examples, this one with lasting value.

"No one cries for 30 years for someone else; that's nonsense," Rita said. "Your Mom projects her psychological problems onto you and you take it on yourself.

"If she's so miserable, then she's the one with the failed life and she's crying for herself, not you. She should have gone to medical school herself, not tried to break you over it. Why should she make you a pariah for marrying anyone? This is *her* psychic garbage and you've been assuming it for years.

"It's like an ugly hairy coat that comes in the mail that you didn't order. You open the box and it's a horrid shade of vomit yellow-green, with stuff sticking out of it. Your mother says, 'I ordered it for you, this coat is You! You must try it on.' You try it, she has you walk around in it, but you hate it. You hate the style, the color, it doesn't fit at all—but she makes you wear it.

"It's time for you to take off the coat and say: 'Mom, *this is not my coat.* I did not order it; you did. I think it will fit *you* better; please wear it yourself.' Tell her to wear it. Let her be responsible for her own resentments and complaints.

"This trip is an opportunity if properly taken. This is not your coat. You've got to take it off and emotionally separate from her. Do not tear yourself to pieces. Do not listen to the self-critical voices in your head; those aren't your voices—those are Mom's voices. Step back. Take a walk. Take deep breaths."

I'd known for years that my self-criticism sounded awfully like Mom's criticism. "It's Not My Coat" is a great story; I use the phrase to this day.

But logic didn't calm my heart for beans. I was still alone, terrified and in a state of clinical shock. Plus, Rita still wasn't doing emotional support.

She ended with her mantra, which always gave me a migraine. "You must talk to the Inner Child and tell her 'Mom was ridiculous, you don't treat a daughter like that.' Just disengage," she concluded.

I was alone in Miami, 1,200 miles from my sister in New York, 3,000 miles from Rita and my friends in California, sleeping in Mom's retirement condo surrounded by people on walkers, completely isolated from Planet Earth.

Go tell Daniel to "just disengage" from the lions. That's a sick joke when we're stuck in the lions' den; the result is chop meat.

"Why didn't you walk out?" asked my chiropractor Dr. F. years later. "Why didn't you say, 'Mom, you're mean, I'm leaving'? Your family could have hired help." "Because you're sane and I wasn't?" I asked.

Survival Instinct

Yet we all have survival instincts—strong ones. Trouble was, my instincts for self-preservation had been overwhelmed since childhood by events beyond my control. Now in that hospice, it felt so overwhelming that it was like living in a nightmare during the day, all day, every day.

Often it felt as though Mom's critical voice was so loud in my head, that her voice had *become* the inside of my head. I had waking and sleeping nightmares about Goya's *Los Caprichos,* etchings of people grabbed by monsters and birds with huge claws. All I wanted was for Mom to let go her claws from my brain.

One day watching Mom nap, I was dimly conscious of a horrifying gut reaction from deep in some prehistoric part of my mental sub-basement. Up came a horrible idea: something which is inflicting so much pain upon my sister and me requires the raw animal response of fight or flight.

"This is a creature in total misery," I thought. "It can't find enough meaning in life about which to feel peace, so it's going out inflicting hurt because that's the only way it can know it exists. This is a golem, a hurtful thing, and it's about to be sent to New York to make my sister miserable. I must defend my baby sister!"

Horrified at my own upsurge, I ran from the room and out of the hospice. To keep my immune system alive I'd been jogging daily. Many palm trees narrowly escaped my assault on the grounds of Mom's condo that night as I jogged off this animal fury until I limped inside and fell asleep senseless in my gym clothes.

Parts of me deep within had the gut instinct that emotional pain this intense must mean that I was about to be killed. We all have a survival instinct to fight back. Luckily my higher faculties prevailed.

I decided I had to bring some calm to Mom's soul. I went in one morning and insisted on loving her. I sang to her. I held her hand. I rubbed her back. I used the fact that she was about to be kicked out of the hospice for failure to die on schedule as a selling point.

"Linda's finding you a place in New York," I said. "How am I going to get to New York?" Mom demanded. I talked her through how we would get her into a wheel chair, onto a plane with oxygen, I'd sit with her on the plane, and Linda would meet us at the other end.

Suddenly Mom regarded me with a baleful look and moaned, "I'm sorry I separated you from the family."

I felt moved and teary, but I was too far gone into the emotional pain pit to feel any relief.

I was alone and out of my mind with isolation and grief. I had to use the computer for business and one evening I just found myself on Match.com.

Wasn't I more ready for a mental hospital than a dating website? In retrospect, that's a big "Yes."

Years later I heard the saying at Al Anon about the guy who's been sober for months, who suddenly "just finds himself" with a drink in his hand. That's how I "just found myself" on dating websites.

Nobody warned me. Dr. Rita said I was doing fine. She said I was well enough to work, and to drop my own therapy to fly around the country nursing others.

I thought my problem was a huge deficit of romantic love. I had no connection in marriage, then I got a taste of it from Dan that blew me away. I'd accepted starving as the norm, then discovered that there's food out there.

I couldn't stand returning to nothing and no one in California after weeks of this living Hell.

"I hope to meet a productive man who has worked in transportation, construction, engineering, the military, science, or any field which gives him the satisfaction that, at the end of the day, he can look at his work and say: 'Today I created something to make the world better'," said my Match.com profile. It also mentioned my singing.

"I'm a productive guy," one engineer wrote back. "I like to be active, play racquet ball and bicycle. I also have this music connection and found it fascinating that you perform music. Got to go practice the piano! With a song in my heart," he signed off. A prospective accompanist, no less. We spoke by phone about everything from Schubert to Schopenhauer.

Another night there was Bob the Air Force man. We had the same science degree and interest in world affairs. "I just read your profile and was impressed," he wrote. "We seem to have a lot in common. Appreciated what you wrote in your profile and have never seen it put quite that way before." We hit it off by email and then by phone.

Mom passed away in Florida the Sunday before Thanksgiving and my brother-in-law booked me to New York. I packed up what I could carry of our parents' belongings and made arrangements for the furniture, while taking calls from Match.com.

Mom's funeral was held in New York in my sister's upscale church on Thanksgiving eve. Again Linda and her family said all the words. When they were done, again I got up and sang, this time Mom's favorite, "Moon River." Again everyone cried and almost applauded.

Again I had no tears. This time at least I knew why.

I'd been scheduled for months to sing in the Handel's *Messiah* given annually at the Nixon Library in California on the Sunday after Thanksgiving. "I've kept my life on hold in Florida long enough," I told Bob; "I'll be back for the concert."

"You can't be alone in California right after your Mom died," he said. "Let me take you to dinner afterward."

And you, dear reader, know what happened next.

Notes

1. Gerson, J. (Undated). In the need-fear dilemma, a child "both needs the mother for comfort, but something in his history with this mother has instilled fear and distrust."

4

Hit by a Truck

4.1 Kathy and Bob. (Rosie Barana)

Thanksgiving 2008 was a transcontinental emotional blur. On Wednesday I was singing at Mom's funeral in a dingy sleet near Manhattan, almost dead with grief. On Sunday I was back in the California sun, singing in the Nixon Library's White House Ballroom all lit up for Christmas. The concert was moving, I wore a long gown, and the gentleman who appeared was everything that Dan was not.

Captain Bob was an Air Force officer turned FedEx pilot who arrived in epaulets. He'd been in two wars, moved armies on cargo planes and fed cities, where Dan had shot only defenseless deer.

Bob was thoughtful and intelligent, where Dan was not. Bob was a family man who loved his ex and children to distraction, which Dan had not. Bob believed in marriage and declared his intent to re-marry, while Dan would holler "Run!" at the groom whenever we saw a wedding party.

Bob even came by his southern drawl honestly; he was from Alabama.

Off he whisked me to the proverbial candlelit dinner with the proverbial piano music; we talked into the night by the proverbial fire amidst the holiday lights. I was toast. Again.

"My best friend met his wife on Match.com," said Bob, and began to tally where we "Match." We both loved books, music, and ideas. We both worked out and loved the outdoors.

Soon Bob gave me a hand-crafted bookmark with an 1840's quote from Emerson, "The Compensations of Calamity." Tragic events can develop our souls, it says; we may find new bonds "more friendly to the growth of character." Who in her right mind wouldn't think I was a candidate?

But I wasn't in my right mind. Neither was poor Bob. It went very well at first; too well.

Then he simply disappeared.

Two weeks later he called. We had dinner but now all he talked about was his wife and her betrayal.

Then he disappeared for two weeks. Just as I was crying myself to sleep, he called, we had dinner, and he talked about his wife's betrayal. Then he disappeared for two weeks. Just as I was crying myself to sleep, he called, we had dinner, and he talked about his wife's betrayal.

No, my brain was broken, but my computer isn't. He just kept doing that; it was always the fourth date. It became 20 fourth dates, spaced out (and I do mean spaced out) every two weeks for one full year.

"He's still crying about his wife? Run!" said my divorce counselor. "He can only hurt you. I've seen it a thousand times. Run like hell. Now!"

"A broken heart is like a flat tire," I read. "Imagine that instead of repairing the flat, you just start driving. Soon you will have destroyed the tire and be riding on the rim.

"Transfer that into relationships. You drive your heart into a new relationship though you have done nothing to complete what was left emotionally unfinished by the ending of the last one. You're not available for a new one.

Now you're riding around on the rim of your heart like a flat tire, parking in someone else's driveway," headed for a blow-out. (1)

Clear enough. People who are focused backward on old relationships are in no shape for new ones. If you meet them dating, run, or they'll drag you into a blowout. Plus if we have pain from our own prior relationships, we must heal it before starting new ones.

Did I listen? Sure, and here is what my thinking brain wrote:

Why Get Hit By a Truck? - December 7, 2008

You're an emotional train wreck, you hurt too much.
You're not ready for prime time; no one will take this on!
You can't look for love when you need it so badly.
Users will smell it and use you as prey.

Good men will smell it and back away;
Precisely a decent man won't want the responsibility,
Of hurting you if it doesn't work out.
And he's entitled to have it maybe not work out.

You can't hide, there's no point in trying,
You must fix yourself, or you can't return to flying.
It will always end in trying to heal the child who's sick,
With some guy's d—k.

"But the loneliness hurts too much!" you cry.
Yes, yes, the pain gnaws at me, eats me inside,
But does it help to run out into the street,
And get yourself hit by a truck?

Mourn your parents and the loss of your life,
And don't put the weight of that on anyone else.
Don't drive on the rim of your flat tire,
And park your car in someone else's driveway—

Or you will get hit by a truck.
You've already been hit by two cars (both parents),
And two trucks (divorce and one bad rebound).
Looking to add a jet aircraft?

Head vs Heart

It was Ye Olde Head vs Heart Conflict. Since the Ten Commandments ca. 1500 BC, many of us have only grasped the concept of right vs wrong after being hit on the head with stone tablets. Yet what the head thinks is right, is often not what the heart craves. Our emotions are ferocious enough to drive us out of our minds.

This led for millennia to acting out, pestilence, genocide, and pickles such as Sodom and Gomorrah. In Rome ca. 100 BC, having ten divorces was not uncommon in the elite. If Moses hadn't hit them on the head, the Hebrews might have spent more centuries sacrificing virgins to golden calves.

Ultimately rules can't be imposed on humans from the outside, because the heart is simply more powerful. We've got to grow up our emotions.

But how could I actually *do* that?

I needed a concrete program to "educate my emotions" so my heart would stop getting me hit by trucks and turned into sacrificial roadkill for golden calves. That's the purpose of therapy, I discovered much later.

But in 2008, Whu Nu? My first two therapists didn't. What I needed, they said, was more head logic and bigger stone tablets. They had no program to educate my emotions and didn't care how much it hurt.

Darkness fell. The loneliness felt like a wild beast eating a hole in my heart 24x7. The therapy death sentence to sit home alone just made it worse. No human soul can take isolation like that.

So occasionally I'd date, but couldn't get interested in anyone but Captain Bob.

"What am I doing wrong that Bob doesn't connect?" I agonized.

Nothing, actually. In fact, it was Bob who couldn't connect. He had a bad case of attachment disorder and there was nothing I could do about that but run. Yet I didn't. I really was right out of a cloister.

Instead, I vowed to listen compassionately to Bob's woes for as long as it took. I went to church, prayed, and combed the Bible, the self-help shelves, the Buddhist literature and the Hindu Yogic scriptures on compassion. In early 2009, I wrote him a blank check on my soul:

Lettuce - January 10, 2009

Dear Bob,

Your experiences you've told me like to broke my heart. You've given unconditional love to your family for so many years, picking up your daughters' rooms and leaving little chocolates on their pillows, and that is what they'll remember: "Daddy loves me." Your beloved wife returned such generosity with treason, on top of which, you offered to give her your heart a second time, and a second time you were betrayed. Even the stones would cry out.

The books I've been reading on the human mind are clear, that the path to true happiness lies in understanding the other person. The only way to do this is compassionate listening. Here's one sage's description:

"When you plant lettuce, if it does not grow well, you don't blame the lettuce. You look into the reasons it is not doing well. Yet if we have problems with friends or family, we often blame them. Instead, suppose we simply learn how to take care of them? Then they will grow beautifully, like the lettuce... No blame, no reasoning, no discussion at all. What we need is understanding. If we understand, and we show that we understand, the situation will change...

"To understand, we must learn the practice of compassionate listening... If you sit quietly and listen compassionately to a person for one hour, you can relieve a lot of his suffering. Listen with only one purpose: to allow him to express himself and find relief." (2)

I've decided to have a try at just listening to one Super-Dad.

You've been hurt so badly that there's only one cure: you need unconditional affection and joy. You need someone to come to who makes you feel understood, relaxed, and appreciated. Period. You need someone to just listen with compassion. You need someone to water your lettuce.

I would like to give you this—and there is nothing I want in return.

Everyone else has imposed on your time to the point that you are toast, and you have no time. I will not. I want nothing from you—except to be the person you come to when you want to be happy.

There may be women in this world who are so different from your wife that you can't even imagine it.

—Kathy

"I like that!" Bob emailed back. Sure. Everyone likes blank checks.

Sometimes I feel like a poor writer because Bob ain't gettin' much character development in this book. Then I remember that in a year of dating, I never got to see enough of him to see a character.

"Experts warn women not to be blindly driven by the pain of divorce," I joked to Bob, "but to look into men's characters to check that they're not an alcoholic, gay, or a vampire.

"I'm counting on FedEx to screen out alcoholics and I know from experience that you're not gay. But actually, I've never spent a day at the beach with you or even seen you in daylight. So I'm not sure about the vampire part." We both laughed, but it was true.

My heart, however, didn't listen to my clever head. Bob's stories of moving armies were so potent. His wife's betrayal was so tragic. His Dad stories were so heartbreaking; how lucky his daughters were to have such a loving, sensitive Dad. His Southern drawl was so hot.

After I took his calls, I'd get emotional relief for two days. Then Bob would go into radio silence and in two weeks I'd be in such panic that I felt compelled to take his next call.

It was No Exit. For a year.

The Marianas Trench

I did notice that my emotional pain had somehow shifted seamlessly from the Dan bucket to the Bob bucket. Embarrassing, no? Is she 14? Then there was the bone-crunching intensity of the pain, which went on for days at a time.

"Pain? Naturally!" said everyone. "You've lost a lifetime marriage, both parents, the Dan affair, your East Coast support system, and a stable job, all at once." I read about an emotional crisis scale which assigns 100 points to each such life crisis and warns that when we're over 300 points, we must expect functional breakdown.

That put me at 600 points. I should have checked into a clinic like Byron Katie, but it was on her health insurance, not mine.

It was all so over the top that I had to have answers, and then I remembered the pain in the hospice with Mom.

Did my life-long Mom issue bear some relation to the bizarre extent of my current anxiety?

I'd always felt panic around Mom and couldn't think of her without a guilty anger. It felt like Mt. Everest: how does one approach something of this magnitude which has loomed since the dawn of memory?

I got a CD on anxiety and meditation by a Harvard MD. Our fight-flight response is physically time-limited, he reports. A caveman mobilized in fight-fight killed the saber-toothed tiger fast or was killed; either way, he was not in stress mode long.

Today, however, we live under 24x7 stress of phones, texting, traffic and so on "as if the saber-toothed tiger never goes away," he said. (3) I was too frantic to meditate, but that tiger image struck a nerve.

"That's me!" I said. "I exist in a permanent state of panic, and the saber-toothed tiger was Mom. I've been so terrified of her for so long that I'm under a tiger attack in my head 24x7."

Again, I'd already identified many self-critical voices in my head as Mom's voice. Why should I feel bad that I don't have a husband or a mansion? I need them to have Mom's approval. Why should I feel panic about my divorce and lack of children? Mom called me a failure. Why do I feel guilty about my finances in 2008 when everyone's in trouble? Mom warned me all my life to avoid financial insecurity.

It hit me that anything I could think of to feel bad about now, might go back to Mom's criticism and demands on me as a kid.

"Aha," I thought, "good news! It's just Mom's voice in my head.

"That means I can think my way out. I'll just stop listening to her because, uh, she's dead, what she says is nonsense, and it's just my imagination. Then I can feel good all the time."

Nice try, thinking brain, but you can't heal the heart. Only deep people support can do that, I learned later.

Rita didn't do support, so I sat alone and tried to think my way out as she instructed. But the more I thought about Mom's voice in my head, the worse the pain got.

"It's like dredging the Marianas Trench," I told friends, "the deeper into the Mom pain I get, the more pain there is." Down and down I went into a bottomless pit of nausea.

The Incubator

Then I heard from my sister that I'd been incubated for weeks at birth, and from an aunt that I was never breast fed. In late January 2009 I took these factoids to Dr. Rita. She made a guided imagery tape, instructing me to walk to the incubator to comfort my infant "inner child."

She never told me how damaging incubation is to an infant. Babies require intense personal touch and holding for their brains and nervous systems to develop. Left in a box, a baby goes into a physiological crisis which can kill it. It's so serious that today hospitals have programs to remediate incubation. (4)

But when I was born, or even in 2009, Whu Nu? Not Rita.

To her it was simple. "You must experience the pain left in your body from infancy," she announced. *Alone.* It was Bring It On, with Rita as George Bush Jr. on the aircraft carrier before jetting back to Washington, leaving me alone in the Gulf, er, Trench.

I could feel directly, deep in my gut, that incubation had been terrifying. "Get in touch with your shame," Rita said.

"What shame?" I said again. "I just go direct to *panic*." She ignored me.

I didn't know it then, but "panic" is precisely what babies do when they are not held by a loving, attentive adult. Stress chemicals overwhelm that baby's brain and it goes into clinical shock.

Why does this half this book revolve around my compulsive urge to be held, by Dan, Bob, or anyone? My physiology was screaming for exactly what it needed as an infant.

There was nothing wrong with my body. There was something wrong with my therapists.

Here, then, is The Incubator Tape:

Rita: You're out of the womb and in an incubator, you're not being comforted, not being touched, and you're very, very small. Imagine yourself as an infant totally detached from what sustained you. Imagine how scary that is.

Kathy: I just start bawling if I connect with that, I go to pieces. It's this little screaming id, crying and crying because nobody ever came (sniffling).

Rita: You've got to let yourself feel all that. The only thing a baby has is its cry; the baby knows that if nobody comes, it will die. The baby doesn't know it's being monitored. But this time when you go back and feel the pain of that infant, you the adult will be there for it. Imagine you walk up to the incubator. What are you going to do with the baby?

Kathy: Pick it up and hold it.

Rita: And what are you gonna say to the child?

Kathy: I love you?

Rita: Right, I love you, look at the wonderful beautiful you.

Kathy: I just do this until I stop crying? It's gonna take weeks, months?

Rita: Depends on you. What else would you like to do with the child?

Kathy: Hug it, hold it, rock it... I love swings...

Rita: You can sit in a rocking chair, you can sing to it, make it warm. The most important thing is touch: hold, caress, kiss. So hearing you talk to it, sing to it, hearing the love in your voice, feeling your touch, your total acceptance—that's what you have to *do for yourself.* If you had an infant, that's what you'd do.

Kathy: I don't know, I've never had children!" (Falls apart.)

Rita told me to go home and listen to this tape, alone, until I'd felt all the pain.

It shoved me into total meltdown.

I was pulled under water down into the Marianas Trench, then down into the earth underneath, into an even deeper trench. "Up all night, can't sleep, can't eat," I journaled. I couldn't identify an adult or a child, just a sea of agony.

Next day instead of going to the beach, I couldn't get out of bed and developed alarming chest pains. "It's so painful to be ripped out and thrown away in an incubator!" I wrote. "Never since I was born have I been held; every ounce of my being goes berserk when I think about this. That's why Dan was so overpowering."

I was in such hell that I wanted to strangle my therapist.

Rita didn't connect the incubator to my lifetime loss of attachment, or even tell me that I needed attachment. She also refused to give me attachment. Today that's called "re-traumatization," re-wounding the deep wounds of childhood.

For three months I worked it, and all I got was broken sleep, waking in a sweat from nightmares. "Nothing but a pit of abandonment at my core," I wrote, "a huge parade of Kathy-I-Don't-Love-You dinosaurs. Repeat dreams that I'm alone in the snow watching families but I don't belong."

By late March 2009, Rita and I were both sick of it.

"Congratulations," she announced, "You've gotten to the bottom! You can't go any farther back than the incubator. There is no more pain. You're done. You can get on with life and start dating."

Are you doing a double take? Googling the statute of limitations on irresponsible therapy? You're smarter than I was.

I didn't feel like I'd gotten to the bottom of anything.

The agony I felt was bottomless, never-ending, and growing.

I've tried everything to deal with my Mom issue, I thought. I tried to change my thinking and fell into the Marianas Trench. I tried therapy and fell into a Marianas Canyon under the Marianas Trench.

Feeling the Mom pain made me feel worse, and therapy made me feel "worser."

Something in me snapped. "It's just not happening for me," I decided, to quote Dan.

Therapy was time-consuming, painful, expensive, and pointless.

Why not quit and return to finding a mate?

Notes

1. James & Friedman (2006, p.30).
2. Thich Nhat Hanh (1991, p.78).
3. Weill & Kabat-Zinn (2001).
4. Loewy et. al. (2013).

5

Thirty-Eight First Dates

5.1 *Dating up a storm. (Rosie Barana)*

The pain was so bad that I would have been dead at my own hand if not for my pal Steve McWhan.

In August 2008, my divorce counselor told me about a local choir which sang the big pieces I love by Mozart, Beethoven, and friends. Some rehearsals were an hour away so in September, I emailed the whole 120-person choir asking to carpool. Steve saw it by accident in his junk mail which he rarely opens. His office was right by my place, so he replied "yes" to save gas money.

Two weeks later I was writing a business plan for a nuclear reactor and recalled that Steve's an engineer. I rang and asked him to review my document. He was so surprised that we got to talking. That was the first surprise.

Later we learned that both our marriages ended the same day, July 4, 2006, when I left home and Steve's wife left him—on opposite ends of the country. He'd been married 25 to my 27 years.

Steve had a girlfriend now and I was crazy for Dan and then Bob, so we quickly agreed to keep it platonic.

Anyway, Steve's not my type. He's from a long line of Scots back to the Norman Invasion, a cheerful fellow except when his freckles get sunburned. His uncle patented the McWhan Cell for chemical storage and Steve was raised to uphold the family honor. Whenever he's called "Steve McQueen," he retorts that McWhan was the original 12th-century spelling.

One night as Steve dropped me off after chorus, the Disneyland fireworks began to boom as they do every night. "I've never been to Vegas or Disneyland," I joked. "We had an annual Disney pass and took the kids twice a week," he said. "This year it's free on your birthday; when is that?"

"May 4," I said. His face fell.

"My wife died on May 4," he said. "Didn't she divorce you?" I asked. "First she divorced me, then she committed suicide," he let slip.

Steve was in enormous turmoil, I soon learned, a devil's cocktail of bottomless sadness and guilt, as if he were responsible. "If only I'd been a better husband," he would say, with a grief-crazed look like a fugitive. It was all he could do to make it to work and chorus.

The pain in my chest was getting worse, no matter what I tried. The failure of therapy felt like the end. It felt like I'd played my last card.

Many times I wanted to kill the flood of pain the only sure way.

Seeing what suicide had done to Steve, however, took away my last out.

What would it do to my sister?

So now we have:

1. My shrink says I'm cured and ready for dating.
2. I'm dying of loneliness "3,000 miles from nowhere" and Bob's worse than no company.
3. I can't even kill myself. I'm stuck frying alive in Hell.

Broken Picker

Then my friend Rosie gave me a book on dating by a local psychologist. If love isn't going well, he suggests we examine *ourselves,* to see if we have a broken "People Picker."

"He says that the daughter of an alcoholic walks into a room full of people and is 'turned on' by the one man who's an alcoholic," she giggled. "He used those words at my church!"

Absurd, I thought. After watching her Dad beat her Mom, she'd run like mad.

No, the book explains; we gravitate towards what we experienced from parents, like ducklings follow momma duck. No matter how painful, what we learned early has a powerful *draw,* inaccessible to consciousness thought, which gets us into trouble.

"We go to what we know," said Dr. Matt. "It's called 'repetition compulsion.' "

The book doesn't mention that 50% of us suffer these attachment wounds as kids. I heard the author say that later. But it's all about the prevalence of people who have troubling relating. (See the Appendix for the science.)

"You made one choice for a mate and it was bad," the author tells a gal divorced from a ten-year marriage. "Isn't it obvious that your 'people picker' is broken? You are 0 for 1. But now you think you're ready to make another lifetime commitment, using the same broken people picker you used to pick the last one? No, no, no!

"Go into divorce recovery. Get therapy. But do not go dating to mate." (1)

I thought about the alcoholic's daughter and it hit me:

How did my Dad relate to me?

I always felt so bad for him because he was so tired when he got home, but finally I had to admit: Dad was not emotionally available to me.

Do I have a pattern of men like that? During 30 years with one man, I didn't have the data to know.

Now I took a body count.

Larry wasn't available. Dan bragged that he was militantly unavailable. All Bob thought about was his wife; he certainly wasn't available. It takes three pointed heads to make a plane, I joked glumly: Larry, Dan, and Bob the pilot.

Counting Dad, I was 0 for 4 with emotionally-unavailable men.

Strive for Five

Stop dating to mate, the author said, and start "dating to relate."

Learn to relate to new types of people outside your pattern, by meeting many different types. Ditch the ones your broken picker found, and don't settle for the next few. Get out and meet large numbers of people over many months.

"Lady," he told one gal, "if you don't want to marry the FedEx man, you had better go out!" (2)

"OM Gracious I am literally dating the FedEx man," I nearly screamed.

"Strive for Five," the author said. He told clients to talk to five new people of the opposite sex every week.

It was bold, it was counter-intuitive, and people in Hell want ice water. I was tired of my failed life, failed therapy, failure with Bob, and here was something radically different and PhD-approved.

Wait; I've just spent 30 years in a convent and I've got a lousy record with men. Now I'm going to meet a slew more? I needed a "guy adviser." Again I rang Steve and we made a "no-dating" pact so he could be my adviser.

Wading back into the dating shark pool, I began gaming the on-line system with irrational exuberance (as Alan Greenspan would say). On Day One I signed up for Match.com, eHarmony, Chemistry.com, Plenty of Fish, and Craig's List (years before the killer).

During March, April and May 2009, I not only talked to more than five men a week by phone; I went on 38 first dates in 13 weeks.

View of the Canal

I averaged three dates a week, sometimes three a weekend, and took notes afterward. The results were so absurd that it became a Sandra Bullock-style comedy routine whose joke was always on me.

Something was seriously awry, not only with my internal people picker, but also with the external "guy market." I found a lot more disconnecters out there than humans.

The first problem was honesty.

"Last Saturday I met a guy whose online photo looks like Baryshnikov," I told Steve, "but he showed up looking like Khrushchev."

Next, a nuclear physicist invited me to the best restaurant in Newport, but arrived looking like a geriatric patient barely able to walk.

5.2 *Where are the humans? (Fox/Lucasfilm)*

Then a real estate mogul turned up to report that he'd just quit his job to become a professional gambler, and asked me to move to Vegas with him.

The second problem was requirements. Huh?

I spoke to a BS in math (like me) who was a tri-athlete. It went beautifully until he asked if I were a tri-athlete. "I'm in good shape," I said, "but no." He sighed. "Sorry, I only date tri-athletes," he said.

I got a call from a man who sails. It went well until he asked me to come to his boat every Saturday for the next ten weeks to practise for his next race. I'm an avid sailor, I said, but couldn't make such a commitment so fast. "I need crew," he said, "and I need a lover. I want a woman who can do both."

A bright attorney spoke by phone about "making friends first" and other high principles. We were having a great talk over dinner until he asked if I liked sashimi. I ate too much in Japan, I said, and don't eat much now. "What about New York?" he said, "I'm considering moving there." I lived there 30 years, I said. He announced that we weren't compatible.

"They've got a script and they're auditioning," quipped Steve. "You've got to meet their requirements or else."

In fact, each one had zanier demands than the other.

After we had a great phone chat, another gent arrived for dinner in a ponytail and tattoos. Tattoos are important, he said; he'd traveled the world to find the best artists in Borneo. "How many tattoos do you have?" he asked. "Gosh, I wish we'd discussed this by phone," I replied. I didn't meet his requirement.

I even discovered that California men speak a different dialect of English.

Back East, "whatever" means "Sure, as you prefer." In California it means "go to hell"—or worse. In Washington DC, NSA stands for National Security Agency, but in California apparently it means "No Strings Attached," as in, well, sex. I always thought VD was an illness, but California men use it to reference Valentine's Day. Disconnects like these did lead to some highly-amusing results, but hey, this is a family book.

Oh well, I shrugged, it's about numbers–large numbers.

Some days I had no time to take notes between appointments. I began phoning Steve so he could audiotape my reports as I drove from one date to the next.

I reported on the aerospace exec who wrote me a long email and invited me to cocktails. When I arrived, he didn't look up from his phone for ten minutes. He finished his text, gave me a blank stare, proceeded to detail all his troubles on the job site, and then left.

I reported on the IPO financier who taught yoga and how we hit it off by phone discussing banking and health. Then when we met, he asked if he could keep his gold bullion and guns under my bed.

I reported on the charming medical equipment CEO, a nice guy who, however, neglected to lock his car trunk—so that my purse was stolen. I was in such bad financial shape that I couldn't manage losing my phone, wallet, license, and all my keys without the stress showing. He was annoyed.

I even met three men who dated me, then returned to their wives.

One was major league ball player. At evening's end, he told me that I was so sweet and innocent that I reminded him too much of his ex and the love they had. He said that I had inspired him to return to her and mentioned her name; she was a movie star.

There were also reports not for Steve's ears.

The owner of a large auto company spoke at length about inviting me to travel the world together, then stated, "Just so you know, I'm looking for a companion for sex only, no commitment."

An IT executive asked me to Huntington Beach Pier for dinner. He called enroute to change the location to the Marriot, then changed it to his hotel room. When I demurred, he went back to work at 7 p.m.

A Newport banker told me after dinner that "I'm going to want to sleep with you by the third date, but I don't believe in monogamy." Those two ideas back-to-back are less than inspiring but he was oblivious. He announced that the banking business was better in Australia, so he was moving there. "Can you come?" he asked.

Then there was the burly owner of an upscale salon who, while we were out dancing, entered the restaurant ladies' room to grab me and kiss me by surprise. "I live in the moment!" he laughed as I shooed him out.

Eventually I did a statistical review of the 38 men; several had more than one issue so it doesn't add:

Zaney requirements: 8
Khruschev/too old: 5
Never married: 8
Married 3+ times: 5
Party guy: 5
Sex only: 6
Returned to wife: 3
I fell asleep: 2

Yes, I literally fell asleep at dinner on two dates who were watching the restaurant TV.

"This morning I got an email from a guy who saw my sailing photos online. He has a great sailboat—in New Zealand," I finally wrote Steve. "Maybe that's my problem: I'm in the wrong hemisphere."

"Or the wrong planet," Steve laughed. "It seems like Earth is a dive where Martians troll for dates. 'Hey baby, wanna come to my place? I have a view of the canal.' "

"Yeah, I'm starting to feel like Luke Skywalker wandering into the bar with the aliens in *Star Wars*," I moaned. "Am I the only human out here?" Our email exchanges began to look like this:

From: Steve McWhan; **Sent**: Tuesday, April 6, 2009
Subject: What is Tatooine? (Figure 5.2)

On what planet was the *Star Wars* bar? Chalmun's Cantina is a bar in the fictional city of Mos Eisley on the planet Tatooine. It is the haunt of freight pilots and other dangerous characters of alien races... and a band of musicians named Figrin D'an and the Modal Nodes.

From: Kathy Brous; **Sent**: Tues, 06 Apr 2009
Subject: Re: What is Tatooine?

I think I sang with the Modal Nodes back in 1771... Is it called Tatooine because everyone there has tattoos? Maybe I should go back to the convent...

Can't Run from Home

By my birthday in May 2009, failing on so many dates wasn't funny. Steve still thought I should see Disneyland. We did go and I slapped on a smile but felt suicidal inside.

Bob never noticed my dating; he just called twice a month to wring his hands about his ex. Every encounter made his unavailability more clear, but the worse my new dates went, the more I feared to dump Bob. "He's unobtainium," said Steve. That's an engineer's joke about materials they wish they had, but which physics says can't exist. (This was before *Avatar*.)

Bob had a meltdown on Mother's Day that tore my guts out. His entire family, kids and in-laws, he said, went to his wife's new pad to celebrate with her boyfriend, leaving him home. "My parents are dead, I'm an orphan," he groaned. "They left me alone; they even took my dog. One day I'm head of a house full of people, the next they're all gone."

Tragic. How could I not console him? But Bob was driving on all four flat tires and having blow-outs with me. One night he announced that he was going to die for his children.

Steve wasn't impressed. "All parents feel that way but we don't shoot our mouths off," he said. "That's like bragging about having opposable thumbs." I didn't know; evidently I had no thumbs.

Then Bob literally made me vomit. On May 20, I was due to sing a concert I'd been rehearsing for months. On May 14, Bob caught a stomach bug on a long flight and was so sick he couldn't pilot the plane home. Three days later he said he was fine and kissed the bug over to me. Two days after that I nearly had to be carried out of the dress rehearsal and spent concert day on my knees in the bathroom. Bob was back on radio silence.

Then there was Alan. I'll always remember my high school boyfriend Alan because he had the right diagnosis.

I had to write about Alan for an exercise in a dating book in late May. He was a pianist who introduced me to Beethoven and shared my passion for airplanes. We'd visit JFK to wander the TWA terminal for fun, intoxicated by diesel fumes and dreams of world travel.

Alan was also in therapy at 17. As for me, at 16 I already had a highly-developed sense of fight-flight. Fighting was unthinkable so flight was my default; I was obsessed with getting away from home.

"No one can run from home; it's impossible," said Alan somberly one day. "You'll never be happy until you make peace with home."

I was carrying around some major hurt inside and until I addressed it, I'd feel bad wherever I went, he said. His prime suspect was Mom.

Trouble was, Mom seemed to be a fact of life too huge to change. You don't like the weather, you move, I thought.

It took me 35 years to get it.

I graduated high school a year early and ran to college on scholarship. I finished college early, spun a globe, and found the farthest place on earth from Long Island, New York that I saw: Kyoto, Japan. I stuck out my thumb in Boston, hitchhiked to San Francisco and boarded a boat for Yokohama.

On the Toronto to Denver leg, in fact, I air-hitched.

I read that company jets might take respectable-looking students, so I put on the only nice dress in my backpack and found the Toronto small craft terminal. "Would you have room for me on your flight to Denver?" I asked a group of innoculous-looking suits. They did, and behaved like perfect gentlemen rescuing a stranded niece all the way.

Later I detoured from San Diego to Guadalajara on an old wood-burning train, its smoke rising over the mountains, then camped with other students on a peninsula surrounded by ocean. The locals grilled iguana on the beach, so delicious I still crave seconds, and the water was phosphorescent at night.

"I'm very stable, but every 30 years I act up," I joked in 2006, arriving in California again. "At 20, I went to Japan; now 30 years later I've moved cross country. Wait and see what I do at 80; maybe a moon landing?"

Yet in May 2009, the fact was inescapable: no matter what I did, I couldn't find a good "Match."

Alan must be right: I'll have try again to face my Mom anger before I can remarry. I decided to ditch dating as I had therapy, and wrestle the Mom Pain to the ground.

Wait, didn't I just try that and get a drubbing in the Marianas Trench?

Yes, but that's because I tried to think my way out.

Well then, thinking no mas! I vowed to hunt 'til I dropped for a way to fix my sick emotions.

"And now, for something entirely different," as Bullwinkle says.

Notes

1. Cloud (2005, p.32).
2. Cloud (2005, p.27).

6

Flatten Me

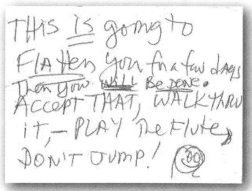

6.1 Flatten me. (Kathy Brous)

Steve was in a sea of emotional pain, too, since his wife's death. I urged him to get the *Grief Recovery Handbook*; I saw it googling "grief" in 2008. I thought it was about death, Steve's issue, not mine. I needed a mate.

But Steve, ever the engineer, was determined to deal with emotions scientifically. Now he bought the book, looked inside, and got a copy for me. "This is a program to retrain the emotions," he announced. "You need it, too."

Thus began our three-year saga with the GRH, as Steve dubbed it. We wanted off the emotional pain train and bad.

So many people suffer pain from the past: death, divorce, or any loss that hurts. Yet our culture teaches that there's nothing we can do about emotional pain. Just wait, we learn growing up. "Time heals all wounds."

This is a damaging misconception, the GRH warns. Often people who do nothing still hurt badly 10, 20 or more years after a major loss. We're taught "six myths" in particular which make it impossible to release pain:

1. Don't feel bad. (Don't feel. Feelings are bad. Stuff it.)
2. Replace the loss. (Get a new spouse, like you'd get a new cat.)

3. Grieve alone (Feeling sad is especially bad. Go to your room.)
4. Just give it time. (Just sit; air will spring into your flat tire.)
5. Be strong for others. (Your feelings aren't important. Stuff it.)
6. Keep busy. (Distract yourself to help stuff it.)

In fact, no action on this list eases emotional pain. (1) Instead these myths impel us to stuff our pain down and carry it inside for years. It's like polishing an infected toenail neatly, only to find later the toe has rotted underneath.

When we stuff it inside, as time passes, "crud" builds up around our hearts, they say. "Grief is negative, and cumulatively negative." (2)

In "Pay Me Now or Pay Me Later," GRH authors John James and Russell Friedman compare the heart to a car engine. An old ad warned that "failure to change the oil filter led to a buildup of crud, which eventually destroyed the motor," they say. "If you spend a little on maintenance now, you might save a tremendous amount replacing an entire engine later."

When we stuff it, a "buildup of emotional 'crud' around the human heart" also "tends to cause us to limit or restrict interactions that require an open, loving heart." (3) We become unable to really relate to healthy people, so we isolate or find unhealthy relationships.

After a lifetime of crud buildup, a serious tragedy like death or divorce can also trigger suppressed pain from the many previous hurts that we never knew to grieve. Now our heart's imploding inside, but it's so hard with crud outside that we can't feel what's happening, so we go into a tailspin.

To heal emotional pain, first we must recognize the power that old ideas like these myths have, and realize they are false.

Second, we need new ideas, starting with the decision to act. "Waiting for time to heal the heart without taking action, is like waiting for air to jump back into a flat tire," they write. (4) We wouldn't just wait. We'd change the tire or at least phone the auto club. With damaged emotions, don't wait until you feel better, they warn. You'll never feel better unless you act.

Third, we must practice these new ideas. We've been practicing the old myths so long, they're deeply etched into our brains. To override them, we need a program to repeat new ideas over and over, and over time.

Action Program

The GRH, as its subtitle says, is such an "Action Program" to heal emotions. It outlines detailed steps which are concrete, extensive, and time-consuming—that is, credible and scary as hell.

First we make a chronological Loss History Graph listing every major loss in our lives. This shows which relationships entailed the most losses. Then we pick the most painful relationship—say it's George—and make a chronological George Relationship Graph of losses specifically related to him.

Next we put the incidents on the George graph into a text list and sort them by importance. We turn this into a Grief Recovery Completion Letter to George (hereafter "Grief Letter"). Then we read it aloud.

We repeat those steps separately for each individual regarding whom we feel significant pain.

This was going to take a big bite out of our lives. Complicated? Overwhelming? Sure. But wait—there's more!

We also need a Grief Partner who's had a loss and wants to work these exercises. We need to meet them weekly to read our work to each other. We do this for as many weeks or months required until we feel we've been "seen and heard" by another human being, enough to relieve the pain. GRH does advise those who can't find a partner to work alone if necessary, but say that partnership brings the best relief.

Steve and I felt that finding a partner was key. We couldn't work together; mourning some things with the opposite sex was too much. We needed a gal for me and a guy for him.

We soon learned that finding a Grief Partner was only slightly less difficult than finding a marriage partner or a unicorn. "Unicorn hunt" became our buzzword.

I checked at community groups and the local hospice for others in mourning, while Steve asked around at the office and in choir. It soon became clear, however, that people don't like to admit to bad feelings. "I'm too pressed for time" was the final excuse. Most people were not willing to "get into grief" at all, let alone systematically.

After a two-month search I spoke to my local hospice director Greg at end June. I'd been at his bereavement meetings, but feared to discuss my divorce because I had no kids, or to discuss Mom's death due to my anger.

Hospice pamphlets describe the death of a family member with whom relations were poor as "complex grief" and say it's especially difficult. GRH calls it the "loss of a less-than-loved-one" and notes that it's rough. "People are crying that they miss their beloved parents, so I'm afraid to upset them," I told Greg. "I don't fit in even here."

"You are not a freak," he replied. "You just have complex grief."

Finally I asked Greg, as a professional, to hear my grief writings.

Interesting coincidences began. In December 2008, I'd sung Handel's *Messiah* at a community college. I knew it well enough that all the sopranos followed me, except when I sat down during breaks and dissolved in a pool of tears. One lady took pity, gave me her email and invited me to her women's group. I blanked that out for months.

Finally in March, I emailed Sherry Dexter and attended her meeting at a church in Irvine on March 18, 2009. There I sat each Wednesday and said, "I'm in a lot of pain and I need to work on this *Grief Handbook*. Could someone be my Grief Partner?" After three months Sherry couldn't stand it anymore and in late June, two days after I spoke to Greg, she volunteered.

Suddenly I had two people to hear me.

Lifetime of Loss

On July 3, I took a room in Laguna Beach for the summer and began my Loss History Graph of every major loss I'd ever had. Just for starters. This would be too much to take without the beauty of the ocean for comfort.

The exercise blew me away; it revealed an entire life of loss. Losses went as far back as conscious thought and just kept coming. The handwritten graph was supposed to fit on one page, but I needed two pages and only my worst losses in my tiniest scrawls would fit.

My first memories were swallowing that penny at four and the other early losses described in Chapter 3. Then came more. When I was five my best friend fell off my swing, broke her arm, and was never allowed to see me again; I was crushed. At nine I cracked a lamp and was ostracized for weeks. Cowering under school desks during the Cold War, I felt far more terrified than the other kids.

Then came the JFK assassination; I sobbed in my room for weeks and couldn't stop. Finally Dad came in and said, "That's enough." They didn't like it when I cried.

Other than that Dad didn't appear on the lifetime graph. "Never home; never told the truth that Mom was crazy, not me," I wrote in the margin.

Alan left me when I was 17, saying I was too crazy. He was right. At 18 my first college boyfriend Jim ditched me and I was so devastated that I cried and hid in my dorm for a year. No one, led by me, could figure out why my crash was so big; it felt like the earth had fallen out from under me.

At 19, I met my second college beau Larry; then at 20 fled to Japan, wound up in med school, returned home at 25 and was excommunicated. The loss of not being able to see my sister was mind-boggling.

Then I married Larry and had 27 years of loss. There was no room on this initial lifetime graph for my marriage losses; I'd need a separate Larry Loss Graph later.

Leaving the East Coast I had to add the loss of my house and home, my friends, my long singing career, my beloved pianist (one of a kind), and all my finances in bankruptcy. Next came the losses in two rebound affairs.

My jaw dropped as loss after loss spilled out, covering every inch of two 8 x11 pages until there was no white space.

"My heart's like a car which never got any gas or oil, but I kept driving a Grand Prix race to the moon and back a few times," I journaled. "Now I open the hood and my engine crumbles onto the asphalt in a pile of rust."

"Unwanted pregnancy accepted all of this, desperate for any validation," I scrawled. "Tried to prove you had the right to exist, contrary to the ongoing drone 'you shouldn't exist.' "

July 8 was my first grief meeting with Sherry. When I got to the JFK assassination, I began to bawl.

"It's OK to cry," she said quietly.

That knocked me over. I was speechless. No one had ever said such a thing to me in my life. Wasn't crying the ultimate sin? It was a watershed, so shed water I did. I bawled for 20 minutes while Sherry held my hand, and kept bawling for the next three years.

I will always love Sherry Dexter for what she did for me that day. It was the most profound emotional release I'd ever had. It got to where I'd cry at the sight of her and became a running gag between us. Two years later when Sherry showed up at one of my concerts, I caught a glimpse of her in the third row and began to bawl.

On July 15, 2009, my calendar says, I finished my Loss History Graph and read it twice, to Greg at the hospice at noon, then to Sherry at 4 p.m.

My First Letter

Next we ask "which relationship hurt the most?" to see which Grief Letter to write first. I'd been with my ex twice as long as with my parents.

Mom, on the other hand, was clearly the most painful relationship.

On July 20, Greg and I agreed to start with Mom. "You can't get around the grief; pain is why you are here," he said. "The only way out is to walk through it and feel. You still need to do this because you've spent so much time doing other things to avoid it.

"So now: grieve. It's going to flatten you for a few days. Then you'll be done."

Looking at the Mom-related items on my lifetime Loss History Graph, there sure were a lot. All those times Mom came at me like a critical tiger; all those critical voices in my head. I copied the items by hand onto a new "Mom Relationship Graph," and then more Mom incidents came spilling out and were added. On July 22, I read this Mom Graph to Greg at noon, then later that afternoon to Sherry.

Next I typed up the incidents on the Mom Graph into a computer document titled "Mom Recovery Components." The GRH has us sort these into three categories: Amends (where I need to make amends), Forgiveness (incidents I need to forgive), or Significant Emotional Statements (I love you, I hate you, etc.).

Next I had to turn this data into my "Mom Grief Letter."

First come Amends for anything we regret doing or not doing: "Mom, I apologize that..." Second come Forgiveness items for each hurt: "Mom, I forgive you for..." describing whatever caused us pain. We likely won't feel forgiveness quickly, says GRH, but they insist that if we take this action first, "feelings follow." Third, in Significant Emotional Statements, we communicate key emotions still unsaid.

This opened a trap door to a flood of terrible pain, heavily accumulated "crud" around my heart, a poison cocktail of fear and guilt. How can I write such things about my own mother? For days I stared at the sun or moon on the ocean beyond my balcony and wailed, "It's so lovely here; how can I feel so horrible?

"It's just one letter," I thought. " 'It's going to flatten you,' he says. You'll feel lousy forcing yourself to remember how bad it felt with Mom. But it's finite, and when you've finished this Mom Grief Letter, you can read it and you'll be done."

I drew the self-portrait cartoon in Figure 6.1 with the scrawled words "Flatten Me!" and this tag: "Don't jump—Just play the flute and keep walking. Then you **will be done**." That refers to the finale of Mozart's *Magic Flute* in which the hero plays the flute while walking through a wall of fire. It seemed preferable to jumping off my second-floor balcony.

I didn't mean to do it. It was all an accident.

A Grief Recovery Letter is supposed to be two pages, but my first letter took me six.

I finished the Mom Letter on July 27, 2009 and read it to Greg and later to Sherry, then next day a third time to Steve. I included quotes from books on attachment which made me very emotional, hoping to read these until I no longer felt so bad about them. Below are samples.

Mom Grief Letter - Excerpts

Dear Mom,
I've been struggling with how to speak to you since your passing.

Amends

Mom, I apologize if I got too smart too young, got obnoxious, talked back and hurt your feelings.

Mom, I apologize for cheating on my homework in kindergarten and trying to erase the B to put in a higher grade.

Mom, I apologize for refusing to practice the piano.

Mom, I apologize for running away a lot: hiding in books, hiding in my room dancing, running early to college, running to Japan.

Mom, I apologize for all the later years I was rarely able to remain calm when speaking to you and lost my patience or my temper.

Forgiveness

Mom, I forgive you for sending the message that I was unwanted so often that I wondered as a child, "why did you have a child if you didn't want one?"

Mom, I forgive you for being mean when I cried. I was incubated so I was terrified that no one would respond.

Mom, I forgive you that you didn't hold me and love me when I just wanted more hugs and more love—whether I was crying or not, whether I got the A or not, whether I graduated med school or not.

Mom, I forgive you for often being hysterical, so I felt responsible for making you upset. I forgive you that it was like a saber-toothed tiger kept coming, so I lived in panic.

Mom, I forgive you that I wasn't allowed to be a child when I was a child, or be comforted and feel safe, or be able to let go and relax and breathe safely. I forgive you that there was so little trust.

Mom, I forgive you for making me work, work, work so hard for every little scrap of love that I felt like Oliver begging.

Mom, theory says that "a child has a compelling need to look into the face of its mother and see reflected back, eyes that say "You are wonderful" and a smile that says "You make me happy." (5) Mom, I forgive you for instead looking at me like I annoyed you.

Mom, I forgive you for telling me at four that you loved me because I'm your daughter, but you didn't like me, you liked my playmate.

Mom, I forgive you that I had to become the "Girl Named Sue"—"I grew up fast and I grew up mean/my fists got hard and my wits got keen/I knew I'd have to fight my whole life through."

Mom, I forgive you for painfully ostracizing me for weeks over the lamp I broke and your ring that I lost.

Mom, I forgive you for humiliating me in front of the family and running me down in public.

Mom, I forgive you for being critical and hanging up nearly every time I phoned for 30 years. Mom, it used to rip at my gut.

Mom, I forgive you for the weeks of hostility while you were in the hospice and I was there to care for you.

Significant Emotional Statements

Mom, I always had the unrealized dream that we'd mend fences, forget the past, and you would finally say, "I accept you as my daughter."

Mom, I wish we'd had better communication and connection.

Mom, the *Grief Handbook* says to grieve the loss of a normal child's hopes and dreams. I don't know where to start.

Mom, I'm sorry that I never had the normal dream to go to Disneyland with our family; we didn't value such impractical things.

Mom, I'm sorry we couldn't have more family trips.

Mom, I'm sorry I didn't have the normal dream to raise children.

Mom, thank you for the bluebird mobile I had as a kid.

Mom, thank you for having Linda and when I said "Gimme" the day you brought her home from the hospital, thank you for letting me hold her although I was only four and a half. Thank you for letting her play with me and my friends and to always love each other so.

Mom, thank you for reading me poetry as a kid, so I knew those poems beginning to end and recited them for Linda at night.

Mom, I wish I'd told you how much I loved those walks in the park with the sun shining through the trees on the brook.

Mom, thank you for taking Linda and me with the sled in the snow to buy Christmas trees and for trimming the trees.

Mom, thank you for all the musical recordings which Linda I sang beginning to end and we still sing with her family.

OK, Mom, I'm glad I could be thankful. The beauty and the pain are so mixed up, but it can be excessive.

Rest softly, Mom; Good rest. Ruhe sanfte; Gute Ruh. Peace be with you at last, and bluebirds, too.

Goodbye, Mom.

Then all I could think of was a line from Keats. "Beauty is Truth, Truth Beauty. That is all ye know on earth and all ye need to know," I told Greg.

I stumbled downstairs, collapsed on a lawn chair in the hospice courtyard, wept half an hour, and fell asleep for two hours in broad daylight. Then I called Steve and said, "I just buried my Mom."

Notes

1. James & Friedman (1998, p.26-35).
2. James & Friedman (1998, p.56-57).
3. James & Friedman (1994).
4. James & Friedman (2006, p.30).
5. Wexler (2004, p.3).

Get Off the Carousel

7.1 Around in circles. (Benutzer:KMJ)

That Mom letter nearly killed me, I thought, but I've followed the *Handbook* so I've forgiven Mom. "I need a grief-cation," I told Steve.

We assumed that to face our pain, we had to drive the grief process. That is, we imagined we were in control, so I could stop any time.

But on July 30, I was back in emotional pain so bad that I couldn't eat, sleep or even work, for the first time in my life. It felt like "romance pain." All I could think of was writing long emails to Bob.

"Lose my job? This is insane," my thinking brain journaled. "I've felt my deep Mom pain. Doing that was supposed to stop these wild emotions.

"Why do I still feel so bad?

"Wait; some books say problems in adult romance can be a projection of feelings for the opposite-sex parent. Is my problem with men actually a problem with Dad?

"I need a Dad Relationship Graph and a Dad Letter, and now—because this hurts!"

The idea that we can't control the grief process shocked Steve and me. Apparently a container ship of stored pain still lurked in my nether regions. I faced my Mom pain, only to have a new layer of pain come up about Dad?

Why didn't my divorce seminar tell us about grief? Why didn't my therapists teach me to grieve? Why aren't we taught in school?

A Dad Letter also raised another problem: Dad didn't appear on my lifetime Loss History Graph. That meant I had no data for him. I loved Dad deeply, but had no idea what else I felt.

I queried my subconscious for a week; nothing. Finally what came up was music, again.

Why did I sing "You'll Never Walk Alone" at Dad's funeral? It just popped into my head, the first time I'd heard it in 40 years. Linda and I grew up dancing to that LP. Then Dad dies and up from childhood bursts *Carousel?*

The song meant at Dad's funeral what it does in the film: Dad will always be with us. Billy the carousel barker dies, leaving his wife Julie to raise Louise. As a teen Louise can't fit in with the other kids, so Billy descends from Heaven to give her a star. As he disappears back to Heaven, Louise and Julie sing "You'll Never Walk Alone," happy that Billy loves them in Eternity.

Then I remembered another *Carousel* brain burp. One January 2009 morning after Bob left my place, I awoke with Julie and Billy's opening love duet "If I Loved You" in my head, another song I hadn't heard in 40 years.

"Where did this come from? Despite its sadness, it feels good," I journaled back then. "Don't cry when Bob leaves; he's just going to work, like Dad had to go to work, like Billy had to go. Dad, like Billy, always returned to me, and so will Bob.

"Bob's such a good man, just like Dad. Feel his pain, feel compassion and suddenly you realize: 'If I Loved You' feels good because Dad didn't abandon me; he did love me! Bob loved me last night! Relax, everything will be fine."

How poetic. What faith! What psychological insights...

What horse manure can be spun by a mind in wild denial with a lot of pre-school Daddy buttons to push.

My CoDependent Life

Egads, I've spent months going in circles on a carousel, trying to win Bob's love as he disappears literally into the heavens, round and round. Result? I'm always left alone.

"When a codependent dies, someone else's life flashes before their eyes," they say at Sherry's woman's group, Co-dependents Anonymous (CoDA).

The term "codependent" began with the sober wives of alcoholics. Studies showed these gals had parents who drank or were otherwise emotionally unavailable, so they re-stage their childhood drama with a man so emotionally unavailable that his head's up a bottle. He's dependent on the drug, and she's "codependent" on it. She's so focused on the mess in his life, that she can't feel her own pain badly enough to leave.

Now I put in a DVD of *Carousel* and watched as my myth of love dissolved into a psychiatric nightmare. Everything I'd written was 100% bass-akward.

I was a certified codependent. I was so fixated on Bob's drama, that I couldn't feel him ruining my life. "Billy can't communicate, can't relate, period," I journaled now. "He lives off Julie, knocks her up, then leaves.

"Julie is the ultimate codependent. 'Time and again I would try to say, all I'd want you to know,' she sings, but she never speaks up."

"Larry?" I used to say of my ex. "He's the man parked in the space marked 'husband,' but performs none of the functions thereof."

Now I remembered Julie's song, the one I sang for years: "What's the use of wondrin', if he's good or if he's bad/Or if you like the way he wears his hat... He's your fella and you love him/That's all there is to that."

"I've got a codependent template for love and it's nuts," I journaled.

"You'll never walk alone? Baloney; you are alone! Billy's gone. Poor Julie, trying to stand by Billy; he can't communicate–in fact, he's dead. Now, *that* is unavailable."

I remembered real trips with Dad to the carousel in the next town when I was four. "I longed to belong with Dad among the pretty lights and horses, but he didn't even notice me," I wrote. "He was busy jumping for the gold ring. I rode on his horse and it terrified me when he jumped so high."

What, my pattern again? Yep: Dad wasn't available; Bob isn't, either. Dad, Larry and Dan had one foot out the door; Bob hardly comes in the door. Again I was 0 for 4 with emotionally unavailable men.

"I don't need to get over my fear of the carousel," I wrote; "I need to get *off* the carousel! It's a squirrel cage of work, work, work for love that goes nowhere fast."

The GRH says that Relationship Graphs should also list aspects of relationships that never happened, unrealized hopes and dreams, and things left unsaid. (1)

That's why my Dad Relationship Graph is mostly empty: *so much never happened*. Until I list and forgive what I missed, it will keep hurting.

Suddenly I had several items for my Dad Graph. Out poured my unrealized hopes and unspoken thoughts.

"Dad, why didn't you protect me from Mom?" I scribbeled. "Why didn't you hold me when I cried? Why didn't you ask why I was crying or what hurt?"

By August 12, I'd completed the Dad Relationship Graph and Dad Recovery Components, and read them to Sherry. On August 16, I turned these into a five-page Dad Grief Recovery Letter and read it to Sherry on August 19. Some samples follow.

Dad Grief Letter - Excerpts

Amends
Dad, I apologize that I didn't thank you for working such long hours nights and Saturdays.
Dad, I apologize that I didn't see you as a human being with strengths and flaws, but saw you as something wrong in my life.
Dad, I apologize that I didn't insist on seeing you more during later years, but I didn't see how with Mom around.
Dad, I apologize that when you died, I couldn't cry, but I cried rivers for Dan.

Forgiveness
Dad, I forgive you that you let Mom lock you away from us every night.
Dad, I forgive you that you never said "Mabel, what you're doing is *wrong*."
Dad, I forgive you that you didn't just say: "Mabel, stop torturing the child!" when I was under attack.
Dad, I forgive you that you didn't hold me when I cried. I forgive you that you didn't ask what hurt.

Dad, I forgive you for always having one foot out the door. I forgive you that you often didn't notice me, and I did have to walk alone.

Dad, I forgive you that like Billy in *Carousel*, you had no words to express how you loved me.

Dad, I forgive you that you didn't object in my twenties when Mom excommunicated me.

Dad, I forgive you that I don't need to get over my fear of the carousel–I need to *get off* the carousel.

Significant Emotional Statements

Dad, I need to stop crying to men and complete my relationship to you. My Dad image is where the real trouble with men is buried.

Dad, I always dreamed our family would be happy together instead of arguing.

Dad, I wish we had more family meals together, then my ex never came home, so I've eaten alone for 30 years and still eat at the computer.

Dad, thank you for teaching us to ice skate.

Dad I always hoped to communicate better and more with you.

Dad, it's really hard to say goodbye because I'm not sure if my relationship with you may take more weeks or months to understand. More may be buried 'way deep; I may be a lot more numb than I can imagine.

Dad, I'm so sorry we didn't communicate well. Dad, I love you. Goodbye, Dad.

General Theory of Love

"That was quite a Dad letter," said Steve. We all thought I was done with grief.

I felt better for a few days, but then felt worse. Again.

Concerned, Steve wondered if science would back up the *Grief Handbook*. He got a book on the brain called *A General Theory of Love*. It confirmed the GRH in spades, so naturally he dubbed it "GTL." It showed that I was even sicker than we realized.

I never meant to get into brain science. But therapy was a disaster, romance was worse, the GRH had revealed an inferno in my soul, and Steve's tragedy removed my suicide out. That left me two choices: a convent or brain science. I listened to Schubert's "Die Jonge Nonne" quite a bit, but my body wasn't buying.

That's how I began mainlining brain science.

Modern America has declared war on emotions, GTL begins. That's damaging because "emotions have a biological function—they do something for an animal that helps it to live." They cite the 1960s "triune brain" model, recently confirmed by brain scans. It shows that mammals have three distinct brain regions, with physiologies almost as different as the lungs and kidneys. (2, 3)

First came the primitive reptilian brain stem, an outgrowth of the spinal chord. "Reptile" controls basic survival functions like breathing, heart beat and body temperature.

Second, mammals developed a limbic brain, wrapped around our reptilian brain. It prompts us to care for our young, not eat them as reptiles do. "Limbus" invented emotions like love, which release feel-good opiates like oxytocin. It also creates anger and other negative emotions to release feel-bad stress chemicals, so we know when we're being hurt. Hopefully.

"A body animated only by the reptilian brain stem is no more human than a severed toe," notes GTL. "Reptiles don't have an emotional life." (4)

Third came the frontal cortex, best developed in primates, which wraps around the others. "Frontal" allows thought, language, and future planning.

I was told growing up that emotions are bad, so this hit me hard. "Emotions are good? These voices in my head saying 'stuff it' are wrong?" I wondered.

In fact, says GTL, emotions are who we really are. I was shocked. I always thought that "I" was all my head talk.

But my emotions are a mess; now what?

Aye, lassie, there's the rub. Our three brains are "stove-piped" together haphazardly, scientists say, to keep us alive long enough to reproduce. They mis-communicate frequently and the stress this causes often makes for lousy quality of life after age 40. (5)

Our thinking Frontal brain isn't even in charge. "Ideas and logic mean nothing to two brains of three," says GTL. Reptile and Limbus steer Frontal unseen and unbidden. "We... imagine ourselves... our own masters, when the truth is that our masters are sleeping. One wakes within us, and we are ridden like beasts." (6)

Yikes. My heart won't obey my head because Limbus and Frontal don't speak the same language. My thinking brain says "dump Bob," but my limbic emotions overide it—and that's wired in. I'm screwed.

Mammals need the love of a mate to live, adds GTL; without love, we die.

Yo, I'm dying for a mate; my body's been screaming that for months. Where are these lovey-dovey mammals when I need them? I meet only reptiles who treat me like prey.

Limbic Resonance

Then my frustration became terror. The very development of the brain after birth depends on the mother communicating mammalian love via deep eye contact, reports GTL. They call it "limbic resonance."

Oh, No. Not Mom. Not again.

Yes, they insist.

A baby is born with little limbic brain function and needs "face time" with the mother to develop it. "By looking into his eyes... a mother can reliably intuit her baby's feelings and needs," GTL reports. "(W)ithout limbic regulation from the mother or some human caretaker, his vital rhythms collapse and he will die." (7)

If a mother freezes her face, her baby goes into a tailspin, as shown graphically in the "Still Face" experiment. (8) I can't imagine Mom looking into my eyes, period—let alone to figure out my feelings and needs. Science sez that means my brain was fried in infancy?

"The lack of an attuned mother is a shattering injury to the complex and fragile limbic brain of a mammal," GTL affirms. (9)

My gut sank. A photo captioned "Isolated rhesus monkey" showed a baby monkey "curled up in a lump," dying without a mother. (10) My body screamed in pain at how familiar it felt. I had the urge to curl up and die, too.

I fought for 30 minutes, then did collapse sobbing in a heap. It was impossible not to connect this to Rita's incubator tape and that horrific Mom Letter.

I phoned Sherry to read the book passage, then Steve. "Gosh, I hope you don't feel like that baby monkey," said Steve. "I *am* that baby monkey," I moaned.

I was a dead bunny, er, monkey, and I'd barely begun to research.

There's only one way to heal such childhood damage, GTL concludes: therapy. This typically takes five to ten years, at the cost of a college education.

Now you could hear me cursing in New Jersey.

"The limbic brain takes mountains of repetition" to retrain, they say. "Neurons that fire together, wire together," and mine were mis-wired since birth. "No one expects to play the flute in six lessons or become fluent in Italian in ten."

Healing requires repetition, repetition, and more repetition.

Now, *that* I could feel. Emotions don't change just because the thinking brain wills it. "Ideas and logic mean nothing to two brains of three." I knew that languages and music demand repetition and time to learn. Even if you held a gun to my head and said "Speak Romanian," I couldn't do it.

But GTL insists that only therapy can get this right. We must attach to a therapist to learn new ways to relate. Safe in this new relationship, we must repeat these new limbic patterns for years. We must rewire instincts about relating, bad old neural patterns baked in during childhood. Only by repetition of new neural patterns can we override the old. (11)

Right then, of course, Bob called. We had dinner, he cried about his wife, and now he had severe chest pains which scared me no end. "Ah want to remarry," he repeated, "but mah hands are tied."

Didn't I just write that Bob is as unavailable as my poor Dad? Yep.

Did I run? Nope. My real masters in Reptile and Limbus rode me like a beast.

Then Bob disappeared again and the pain went ballistic. Naturally; he'd hurt me again. But I couldn't face that fact or I'd have to dump him.

Instead, I decided the pain was more Dad Grief still lurking inside, so on August 24, I watched Verdi's father-daughter opera *Simon Boccanegra* for clues about Dad.

I never got past the opening credits at the Met.

The Larry Layer

The starburst chandeliers at New York's Metropolitan Opera hang just above the orchestra, then during the overture are retracted up four stories to the ceiling. Opera lovers see that and feel it in the chest: a firestorm of emotion is about to hit.

I saw it and a voice in my chest cried: "Larry never let me be a woman!" Then I was weeping violently.

Huh? Larry? Larry who?

I never think about Larry. He hasn't crossed my mind since the day I met Dan in August, 2006.

Now here he was, out of nowhere: Larry, the man parked in the space marked "husband."

I went through a ream of tissue, then ran for my notebook. "Whoa, that's non-linear," I journaled, "where is this coming from?"

Why do I still feel so bad?

Yikes, another layer's coming up all by itself: the marriage layer.

In the 1980s, hoping to break his rollerblade habit, I took Larry to the opera and he got hooked. In New York we were at the Met regularly, making friends in standing room and sharing many emotional moments.

Larry even bought me the official Met necklace with a miniature chandelier pendant.

7.2 What, more layers? (Kathy Brous)

Now I recalled a 2008 dream from a part of my mental sub-basement which I never would have known existed, had not my alarm woken me. I found my notes. I'd dreamed I was making a dozen runs through a collapsing building to an arcade on the other side. Why?

I had to buy someone a coat. No, wait; I don't have enough money for a coat, but a shop there sells linings. I've got to buy one before the arcade shuts down forever.

For whom? At first it's too much to bring up.

Then suddenly I knew: it's for Larry. I'm afraid Larry will be cold without a lining for his coat. It's going to be cold around Washington after the 2008 financial crash when all the public services shut down.

I still loved Larry. Un-bunny-lieveable.

Now the old saw "I was afraid to cry because once I started, I'd never be able to stop," proved annoyingly accurate. I had never grieved Larry.

But look at the impact of those chandeliers. Look at that dream. Who knows what feelings for Larry got shoved down and buried during 30 years?

I wrote a Mom Letter, then tried to stop, but got hit by a new layer of Dad Grief. So I wrote a Dad Letter, then tried to stop—but now I'm whacked by another new layer: Larry Grief?

Grief comes in layers? (Figure 7.2)

"Sure; it's called 'breakthrough grief'," said my chiropractor, a therapy veteran. "When we release some layers of pain, more layers come up—because they can. It happens all the time."

Grief Handbook sez: emotional crud is cumulative. It builds up around our hearts in layers over years until we can't feel through the thick crud.

Have I got to drill back through all the layers of buildup to remove it?

One thing for sure: I did love Larry. I loved him deeply and he broke my heart over and over for decades.

But how could 30 years of love and agony be so completely blocked out?

"You may not have been able to feel it because it's buried under deep layers of numbness," said Sherry. "My family doctor says we go all numb when we're hit by emotional pain too intense to bear.

"He says we sometimes need to get under our numbness the way surgeons debride a burn victim. They remove layers of dead skin to reach skin that's alive and can grow. We feel enormous pain in the layers being taken off, but healing can only occur when we get down to a layer which is alive."

It hurt to remove those Mom and Dad layers, but the crud still felt as deep as the layers of the Grand Canyon.

The Yellow Letter

On August 25, I began a Larry Grief Letter. "It's not a Relationship; It's a Disease," I titled it.

That's what I muttered to myself for years, crying in the bathroom about Larry's latest doings. On Sundays he'd make appointments with tennis partners instead of me; he'd cancel vacations; he'd let me down financially. It was so consistent that even back then I got it: this is an illness.

"Started Larry graph; wanted to die," I journaled now. "First Mom, then Dad.

"And now: My Life.

"Oh, No. I can't do this again. Flatten Me III. No one should have this much hurt a third time."

Then I found my notes on a large yellow pad for my last in-person meeting with Larry, dated November 2006, and my blood ran cold.

"Don't ever say this is about money," my Yellow Letter began. "I'd have supported you until the cows came home, if you'd treated me like a man should treat a woman. I was so in love with you that I worshiped the ground you walked on, but you didn't even notice I exist.

"Now I have nothing to show for 30 years of breaking my butt... You've already taken most of the value from the house... Like you used up the value in me."

Back in 2006, it repeated several times: "*you didn't even notice I exist.*"

Yikes: didn't I just write that to Dad?

"You taught me something even worse," my Yellow Letter ends. "You taught me not to trust humanity.

"I'm making the decision never to let anyone hurt me again. I'm making the decision to wall up my heart, never let anyone touch my heart again. If even you can't be trusted, who could be trusted? I was rock solid, but you took me for granite."

Egads, I used a steam shovel to "wall up my heart" back in 2006. Rock layers again. I did such a good job, I forgot there was a construction site. I was no better than Dan.

How could 30 years be blocked out? I could find only one word: *fear.* I couldn't feel the depth of Larry's betrayal because it shook my faith in the whole human race. That terrified me to the core.

"Face the fear head on," I wrote now.

"Grieve Larry; make it real. Just keep reading the Yellow Letter out loud. Force myself to remember: I loved Larry; I gave it everything I had. Experience the full love, the full hurt!"

On September 1, Bob left town for Labor Day. My pain went through the roof. I went sailing, then stood alone watching the sun gleaming on Newport Harbor.

All my life I've thought that if I didn't feel good, I was stupid, so I've gone to a lot of effort to feel good. I suspect I'm not alone.

But now I got radical. I resolved to give up feeling good altogether.

Got pain? Well, then, let us feel the pain: Larry pain, Dad pain, feel all the pain there is until I'm sick of it. I finished my Larry Graph and read it to Sherry September 2. I sorted it into Larry Components and read them to her September 9.

The loss of my entire adult life was slamming me in the solar plexus.

I vowed to read the Yellow Letter and Larry Components as often as it took to sink in. I'd pull over while driving home and read them to myself in grocery store parking lots.

On September 16, I finished my Larry Grief Letter and read it to Sherry, with items like these below.

Larry Grief Letter - Excerpts

Amends

Larry, I apologize if I got too upset about how often we had to move. I never felt safe in my parents' home and was paranoid about not having a safe home.

Larry, I apologize for when I reacted with panic to all our financial adversity.

Larry, I apologize for holding you responsible for everything that happened. I should have taken responsibility and gotten myself out much sooner.

Larry, I apologize that I didn't react like a normal woman and say, "This isn't a relationship—this is a disease; we need counseling."

Forgiveness

Larry, I forgive you for estranging me from my family, then leaving me alone. "No one should be left alone as long as I've been left alone" keeps repeating in my head.

Larry, I forgive you that I loved you to worshiping the ground you walked on, but you didn't even notice I exist.

Larry, I forgive you for always having one foot out the door; for not coming home at night; for leaving me alone during the holidays.

Larry, I forgive you for running up huge credit card bills on top of our mortgage and utility bills, forcing me to work two jobs.

Larry, I forgive you for browbeating me into the last refinance to pay your bills.

Larry, I forgive you for abandoning me emotionally, for beating all the fire out of me until when I left home in July 2006, I felt as if I were dead, and I thought in fact I'd soon be dead. So when I left I did crazy things and I'm lucky I got out alive.

Significant Emotional Statements

Larry, when Bob asked recently if I still love you, I denied it. But in fact I have no idea.

Larry, my feelings for you are buried under deep layers of crud like the endless rock layers in the walls of the Grand Canyon.

Larry, this numbness and sense of crud piled high and deep is very painful.

Larry, Dan and Bob owe me nothing, but you were my husband and you committed to love me. Larry, I must grieve the loss of that hope.

Larry, thank you for coming to my concerts and knowing the words to all my songs even in German.

Larry, thank you for going with me to the opera and for getting interested in opera.

Larry, thank you for buying me the Met chandelier pendant.

Goodbye, Larry.

Hole in My Heart

Hours later that same day, a CoDA member passed me Robin Norwood's *Women Who Love Too Much*, the "Codependents' Bible." I couldn't put it down until dawn.

"Millions of women" are obcessed with "impossible men" who can't relate or attach, she writes. Dozens of fearful case studies of educated, successful women in awful relationships showed me my own life on every page. (12)

These women marry men who are workaholics, sports fanatics, or have something else to do instead of relating; men who quit working to live off their wives; alcoholics or drug addicts; men who are already married or secretly gay.

They somehow consistently find a man who is married to someone or something else.

But I was stably married to my college love for decades! We were educated and from squeaky-clean suburban families. Larry never drank anything but orange juice...

Yes, but Larry always had something better to do. The moment we married he began staying at the office past midnight. Then he quit working; while I paid the bills, he spent the equity in our home. He became a rollerblade and tennis addict, gambled money on local politics, and had a heavy Internet addiction.

Dan was married to his farm. Bob said he wanted to re-marry, but within months announced that he couldn't. In effect, he was still a married man.

Yeah, I was 0 for 4 with emotionally-unavailable men.

In fact I've had nothing but married men—and now I'm sleeping with a married man. My history is no different than any of these ghastly case studies.

This is an addiction like any other, Norwood warns: "we use relationships as drugs... literally fixing with a man." Without him, "we go into withdrawal: shaking, pacing, obsessive thinking..." That's me.

But why? Fear.

Such women all had parents who were emotionally unavailable or abusive, leaving the child in fear. Fear drives us to re-stage our painful childhood so we can "go back and fix it," because we can't live with it.

Then came the death sentence.

Addiction to relationships kills as surely as alcoholism, Norwood demonstrates. As kids, stress gunned our adrenaline. Now we gun our adrenaline with men, to avoid feeling our childhood pain. It's like "whipping a tired, overworked horse," she says, until the adrenaline addiction kills us.

"It is not *like* a disease… it *is* a disease," she writes (italics in original). We develop deadly levels of ulcers, anemia, eczema, diarrhea, insomnia, high blood pressure, and terminal depression. (13)

"It's not a relationship—it's a disease." I said that for years.

Unless I quit, I'll be dead like any addict or drunk in the gutter.

But wait; there's more.

If we quit, we must face "the terrible emptiness within that surfaces when you are not focused on someone else," Norwood concludes. "Sometimes the emptiness will be so deep, you will almost be able to feel the wind blowing through the place where your heart should be.

"Allow yourself to feel it, in all its intensity… just by holding still and feeling it, you will begin to fill it with the warmth of self-acceptance." (14)

Isolation Row again? Why should feeling emptiness make me feel full?

I'd felt an empty "hole in my heart" ever since I could remember; it felt sickening.

My first memory of TV was about a documentary on a baby's heart surgery. As the camera showed a scalpel in bloody tissue, the announcer intoned, "Here is the hole in Jackie's heart." I could never forget the sight or my terror at his deep voice.

Now the moon on the ocean came beaming through my window and I felt the urge to share it with Bob. But then I looked over my balcony and saw the giant letters on the asphalt at the corner below: S T O P.

"Just S T O P," I thought. "Just get off the carousel."

I tried sitting alone a few days, but it plunged me into the blackest depression.

Scariest Place in the World

Mom Letter, Dad Letter, Larry Letter… now what?

I'm trying to heal, so I'm facing my pain. But the more pain I face, the more comes up.

Why can't I get to the bottom of this? Why is there always another layer of tears to this onion?

Why do I still feel so bad?

I'm an adrenaline addict, that's why.

Desperate, I attended an Al Anon meeting September 19, which would have freaked my family to the gills, if I had any family or gills left. There I borrowed a CD by Kevin McCauley, MD on addiction.

McCauley calls our reptilian brain stem "the scariest place in the world." It's like a snake, he says, which does three things: kill, eat and fornicate. When threatened, it shuts off our frontal thinking and limbic empathy, and puts us in fight-flight. That's useful under short-term stress like a tiger attack.

Long-term, unaddressed trauma, however, chronically elevates stress chemicals until Reptile reads almost any stress as a survival threat and screams, "Relieve this before I kill something!" At this point the brain experiences alcohol and drugs as the only source of enough feel-good dopamine to numb the pain.

Then McCauley said the scariest thing I'd ever heard:

"Certain brains are hyper-sensitized to stress," he said, and prone to addiction.

When a mother is stressed during pregnancy, her stress chemicals damage the baby's reptilian brain. The baby's brain develops an ingrained tendency to go into fight-flight at even minor stress and this can continue for life. (15)

I was an unwanted pregnancy and Mom was anxiety personified. She was so flooded with cortisol that it probably caused us both that near-fatal infection.

Oh, No. My brain stem was fried in utero, **fried since the sperm hit the egg,** and now I could feel it.

I read my notes on this to Sherry, a nurse by trade, and her eyes grew wide.

"We talk about this happening to babies at the hospital," she said. She felt it; I could see the fear in her eyes.

"You know how when you cry, your whole body shakes?" she added. "Most adults tear up at the eyes; they don't cry that way. *That's how an infant cries.*" Whu Nu?

At the end of the day: it all resonated, and I was terrified.

So when Bob calls, I answer. He's the only thing that can pour on enough dopamine to ease my brain stem because it was born fried.

I'm a basket case. Who can live with *this*? I want out!

But then there was Steve... and he still removed my last resort.

I was stuck in living Hell, so down and down I went into the pain. It's not for nothing that Dante represents Hell as a downward spiral.

Notes

1. James & Friedman (1998, p.119).
2. Lewis et.al. (2000, p.22-25, p.37-38).
3. MacLean (1990).
4. Lewis et.al. (2000, p.23).
5. Siegel, RD. (4-15-11).
6. Lewis et.al. (2000, p.33).
7. Lewis et.al. (2000, p.75-6; p.85-6).
8. Tronick (2007).
9. Lewis et.al. (2000, p.87-89).
10. Harlow et. al. (1965).
11. Lewis et.al. (2000, p.187-9).
12. Norwood (1985, p.26-195).
13. Glatt (1958); Norwood (1985, p.196-213).
14. Norwood (1985, p.254).
15. McCauley (DrKevinMcCauley.com)

8

Why Aren't You Crying?

I redoubled efforts with support groups. I joined Christian groups, Buddhist groups, yogic groups; I hurt too much to let the verbiage throw me. I learned German to sing Beethoven and Italian to sing Verdi. Now I'd learn any language to get healing.

Alcoholics Anonymous (AA) promotes attending "90 meetings in 90 days" to heal addiction. I met Sherry on Wednesday afternoons, then attended CoDA Wednesday evenings at the Irvine church. Local psychologists Henry Cloud and John Townsend had a Monday meeting there, too, so I joined. Tuesday nights Steve and I compared notes after choir.

8.1 Yellow letter grief. (Steve McWhan)

Now the pain was so bad that on Thursdays I added DivorceCare, a program for mourning a lost marriage. I read my Larry Letter September 16, began DivorceCare September 17, then started Al Anon September 19. I was at six meetings a week.

To heal emotional pain, Cloud and Townsend said, we need regular time sharing our feelings with "safe people"—platonic friends, small groups, therapists, pastors. Not dates. (1) Just as the GTL brain scientists wrote: "face time" is the only way to heal emotions. That's why we read to Grief Partners.

But Steve and I had far more pain than a few friends could handle, so we tried everything to find more listeners. We invited people to coffee, workouts, and picnics. Steve joined the bereavement series GriefShare and a men's group. I held dinners and even organized a DivorceCare pajama party.

Sadly, most folks were in too much denial. One night I walked into DivorceCare in tears. "Why are you crying?" everyone at my table asked.

"I'm divorced!" I said. "Why *aren't* you crying?"

Physical Knife

The experts on the DivorceCare videos, however, had enormous insights. Divorce is "the most painful thing you can put a person through," they say. It's not only a loss of love as with death; divorce adds rejection deep enough to damage our very identity.

"There's no way you can survive this kind of pain and live," one divorcee says; "it feels like a physical knife."

Marriage makes us one flesh, they say, a sexual and emotional bonding too powerful to be neatly torn on a dotted line. In divorce that one flesh is brutally ripped apart, leaving "gaping emotional wounds... Parts of you go with the other person... You lose a part of yourself forever."

I felt precisely as though I were being ripped apart.

"I haven't only lost my marriage. I just realized that my *parents* divorced me!" I exclaimed one evening. I'd been trying to figure out for months whether I belonged in DivorceCare for divorce, GriefShare for death, or both.

Nobody wants to feel this much pain, so we medicate, the video experts say. This includes alcohol, drugs, and food abuse, and also dating, workaholism—any type of diversion.

Romance feels like the best painkiller, says Dr. Jim Talley, but it's "like having a broken foot. Take a shot of Novocaine and you can walk... but one day you look down, see bones sticking through your skin and realize you've done a lot more damage... than if you had put a cast around it."

Stop medicating, they conclude. "You can have extreme pain by doing it right, or excruciating pain by doing it wrong," says Talley. Over 70% of second marriages end in divorce because people jump into romance right after divorce, when they can't think.

"Pain is the body's natural healing mechanism," insists Laura Petherbridge. "Don't abort your healing. Lean into the deep pain. *Just let it hurt.*" (3)

So I did—and it felt like open-heart surgery without anesthesia.

Trouble is, to do that we need people support, like a child hurt at school comes home to wail to a compassionate mom. That's why folks get sober at AA: members listen compassionately. It's better pain relief than booze.

Yet Steve and I found that most others feared our pain. Most people couldn't take my horrific letters for more than a few weeks.

Chasing the Arsonist

I did have one insight that September. One day I was moaning that Bob was fixated on his ex, constantly writing her letters. Then suddenly I saw that I was doing the same thing. I kept focusing on Bob, writing him emails.

Oops. I'm as fixated on him, as he is on her!

Now I recalled Buddhist scholar Thich Nhat Hanh:

"If your house is on fire, the most urgent thing to do is... put out the fire," he writes—not chase the arsonist. "If you run after the person... your house will burn down." (4)

It's just as foolish to focus our emotions on others, he says. Instead, focus on *putting out the fire in our own heart*. By breathing to calm down, looking into our emotions and embracing our own feelings, the pain will subside.

Wait; the *CoDA Handbook* also advises us to sit and try to feel our own feelings, not focus on others. Talk about two totally different sources.

Focus on the fire in my own heart? I'd have to know what I feel!

Can't I please feel something just on my own, forgetting Bob?

Fine; next time I'm upset at anyone, I'll practice ignoring them and try to focus instead on what I'm feeling.

Opportunity knocked days later when divorce-related papers from Larry arrived to be signed and overnighted back. As I left UPS, I collapsed in my car in the parking lot.

Imagine the energy it took to force the word "Larry" from my mind, then quadruple it, but slowly I did.

What am I feeling, just me, verboten to think of anyone else? Well... I feel depressed and terrified to be alone.

Damn Larry leaving me alone all those years. Oops—No Larry! I said, slapping myself. It's "what do I feel, just inside *me?*"

OK, OK, I'm depressed and miserable, lonely and terrified to be alone. I want to go home, cry, and never get out of bed, but I can't because I'm too terrified to be alone.

"Depressed, miserable, lonely, terrified." I sat in the car repeating that, and it was no longer practice. *I was in it:* "I feel depressed. I feel miserable. I feel lonely and terrified." It came down to "lonely and terrified," repeated over and over.

There was a lot of full-body infant sobbing; my torso went into spasms and my back banged involuntarily against the car seat, hard. The fear got worse, the knife-in-my heart loneliness got worse, the sobs grew until I was gasping for air and choking.

Then slowly it subsided, and it was... over. I looked absently at the UPS receipt in my hand. Only $6.95, I thought. Time to hit the gym.

Oh: the terror and pain have faded. I feel better. Amazing!

This was the first experiment I ran on my body, calling myself "Froggy on the lab table." "Experts aren't helping, thinking doesn't work," I'd say, "hmmm... let's make an incision in the heart and see what happens." I also had to hold the forceps and scissors.

But I had a new theme: "It's what am I *feeling*, not what is He/She/It *doing.*"

Run It Backward

On October 1, I hadn't heard from Bob in ten days and felt nauseous. I drove to my inland shack to fetch a few items. As I was folding one of Dad's shirts, Dad's broker called about money (every coincidence in this ridiculous book actually happened). Good news, yet I began to sob.

Again came a ghostly little voice from deep in my chest. "Dad, you've left me money but you're gone, and I have a hole in my heart," it said. "Dad, I wish you'd given me your time instead of money. If I had a healthy heart, I could have made and kept my own money."

Ghostly voices from my sub-basement for the second time in two months, as with the Met chandeliers? That woke me up. Suddenly a brutal passage from Norwood made sense and I ran for the book:

"Millions of women… choose to take as partners men who are cruel, abusive, emotionally unavailable, or otherwise unable to be loving and caring," she writes, due to "a childhood during which overwhelming emotions are experienced. She does not want to feel her shame, fear, anger, helplessness, panic, despair," so she focuses on trying to fix a man's behavior. (5)

OK. When I feel pain, what if I try to go back and feel my "shame, fear, anger, helplessness, panic" from childhood? When I'm in pain about the present, what if I change the subject to my past?

Run it backward. Stop trying to control people in my present; just feel the pain from my past.

I forced myself to forget Bob and focus on Dad.

I sat down with Dad's shirt, staring at it, thinking about the broker, what an expensive shirt it was, how I'd never seen Dad wear it because I never got to be with him.

It was easy for the little voice to take the wheel: "Dad, I wish you'd given me your time instead of leaving money. I still have a hole in my heart."

I sat there feeling the contrast between living, breathing, hugging love and a dead bank account. I remembered Mom saying, "Emotional support doesn't mean a thing. The only thing which means anything is money."

Sitting breathing deeply, the pain receded and I began to feel relief. In an hour I no longer felt so bad about Dad, and guess what?

I wasn't upset about Bob anymore.

"Maybe there's two kinds of pain," I journaled, "bad pain and good pain. If I focus on others, I feel worse and worse in a pain down-spiral which is endless. That's bad pain.

"But if I focus on my own feelings, I have to actually feel them, so I feel worse at first. But if I can stick with it, eventually I feel better. Miraculous! That's good pain. Is it because I'm feeling the feelings through?"

The Sherry Corollary

That evening's DivorceCare video was titled "Facing My Anger." In divorce, betrayal and hurt "go all the way to the core of a human being," said the experts. "The main source of the anger is rejection."

Anger per se is fine, they insist. "It's an indicator that something's very wrong. It's our response to anger that counts." It's acting out anger that is deadly dangerous. One clip showed a woman smashing her ex's stereo, then reaching for a gun. I felt ill.

Passively holding anger inside isn't much better, they add; "it becomes a bitterness that will ruin your life."

We must feel our anger, they insist, without acting. Just feel it and let it go. Confess anger to friends, clergy, professionals, people with whom we feel safe to share ugly feelings. But don't tell the antagonist; they're not safe. (6)

Invaluable wisdom, but I couldn't feel any anger. I just felt depressed and lonely again.

On October 7, I sat down with Sherry.

"Mom Letter, Dad Letter, Larry Letter, why don't letters stop the pain?" I asked. "I peel the pain onion, but all I get is another layer of pain. Since that anger video I've felt depressed and nauseous, but I can't feel any anger."

"My doctor says depression is anger turned in on ourselves," she said. "That video is right. Don't deny or suppress your anger. Give voice to it. Yell to me, yell to God; He can handle your anger!"

Then Sherry had a scary idea.

"If you didn't feel relief from your Dad letter, maybe there's so much crud on your heart that repeating 'I fogive you' isn't enough in your case," she said.

"What about expressing your feelings? You've gotten mileage from that. Maybe change the letter from 'Dad, I forgive such and such' to 'Dad, I feel angry or sad' about it?"

That meant a Dad Grief Letter #2, Flatten Me IV. I took the printout of my first Dad Letter and over each "I forgive you," wrote in by hand whatever I could feel about it.

"Dad, I'm so sad because you couldn't connect, so you brought home money," I wrote. "Dad, I feel miserable because you expect me to be happy with money but you're not here.

"The limbic emotional brain takes mountains of repetition to retrain," I repeated. "No one expects to learn Italian overnight; we need practise." So I read Dad Letter #2 over and over. I read it to Sherry, to other CoDA gals, to Steve, three times a week for six weeks.

One day sitting with Sherry, there came a river of anger.

"Dad, I'm so angry that you never stood up for me when Mom attacked me," I read furiously. "Dad, why couldn't you just hold me a little while?

"Dad, I'm so angry you never said 'Mabel, what you're doing is *wrong*.'

"Dad, I'm so angry recalling the *Carousel* scene when the kids taunt Louise. 'I hate you!' she bursts out, 'I hate *all* of you!'" Seems I'd identified with that for decades and finally now I could feel it.

"I hate **all** of you!" I yelled to the planet at large. That was a first. Sherry's eyes grew wide.

Voicing this much anger was cracking something open. Suddenly the crud on my heart began to move. The more anger I voiced, the more it felt like huge techtonic plates were moving in my chest, as big as the Earth's crust moving in an earthquake.

The more I repeated "I hate all of you," the more my internal crust moved and the bigger the space I could feel between the plates.

Wow, that's how I felt last year, pumping Dan's tin can full of actual bullets. I've been angry for years but didn't know it.

Days later Citicard called to say that they'd put a $1,200 fee on my Visa and I flew into a rage at the operator—as if a working mom in South Dakota were to blame. After it was resolved and we rang off, I felt awful.

You can't call back a Citicard operator to apologize, so I called Steve to confess. "Can't feel my anger? Nonsense, I'm ready to explode whenever the phone rings!" I said. "I must be furious at Mom, Dad, Larry, and Bob."

"Chasing the Arsonist" and "Dissing the Citicard Operator" became our new catch phrases.

Months later, on December 2, I was reading to Sherry for the nth time, when in the middle of my four-page rant suddenly I didn't feel angry or miserable anymore.

Out of nowhere, to my shock, I suddenly felt forgiveness—and love.

I recalled a dream from the night before. "Please," I asked God, "can I receive acceptance from You?"

"It's OK, Kitten," He said. "You're on the right track. Go easy on yourself."

"That's what Dad used to say," I told Sherry, tearing up. " 'It's OK, Kitten.' He called me 'Kitten.' I hadn't thought of that in 40 years. This must be what real forgiveness feels like."

I reported to Steve how Limbus my emotional brain had shifted inexplicably out of pain and anger, to love and foregiveness.

"I read over and over to my wife 'Lena, I forgive you,' but it still hurts like crazy," he said. "Yet when Sherry has you repeat your actual feelings, you get relief from them. The Sherry Corollary! What a boost to our tool kit."

Steve's always ribbing me about my math degree. Math is based on theorems, core ideas proven over centuries. Corollaries add something new to theorems. The GRH provided our basic theorem: our thoughts must be heard. Now we had the Sherry Corollary: our feelings must be felt, too.

The Predator

On December 30, 2009, with no word from Bob since before Christmas, something inside me snapped. Loving Bob was a sentence to a life alone on weekends and holidays.

It was such a carbon copy of life with Larry that I finally choked on it.

"No More Larry Life," I vowed. No more bonding with Bob. I never so much as kissed him (or anyone else) again.

On January 5, Bob called; I just let him talk and for once that was useful. He cried about his family's 1999 Millenial New Year's Eve party, and how proud he'd been to have built a large home so everyone could come inside to a warm fire. He lived to protect his wife and children, he said, but ten years later now his life was over.

I'd never heard a man speak of protecting a women that way in my life.

Three mornings later, suddenly like a football hitting me upside the head I was in full-scale flash-back to the hideous abortion I had in 1982. As if it were happening now, I was spread out on that table in the Manhattan clinic to which Larry took me, by city bus and with a stiff upper lip.

I went through that whole ugly first Larry Letter without even a thought of this. How could I? It must have been such spirtual and physical agony that I buried it six feet under, below a ton of crud and crust.

"What did I marry?" one of my internal voices piped up.

"Compared to this Protector image, I married a p-p-p-..."

It took me five minutes to spit it out.

"I married a *p-p-p-... a p-p-p-... a Predator.*"

I had to hear the concept of Protector to realize what Larry had done. Larry was so unsafe, the scraps of Bob that his wife threw out look like protection in comparison (not that Bob would protect me). There followed a long entry in blank verse ending like this:

With that same lightening strike it hit me:
The man I married lacked all such capacity.
It was so unsafe to never have a fireside for my children,
It was so unsafe that home was where he killed my children.

I saw the image of a man who treats his wife like a woman,
Where my husband treated me like a man.
It took three days to put words to it:
My husband was a Predator.

On January 12, I started a new Larry Predator Letter #2, "Flatten Me V."

"I've had a revolution in thinking that's got me puking metaphorically," I emailed friends. "Forgiving Dad for real in that second Dad letter apparently broke another dam. Now up comes a deeper layer of Larry grief.

"I've realized that I'm the woman who called into one of John Townsend's radio shows, asking if she should set a boundary with her husband. 'What happened?' asked John.

" 'He shot me in the head,' she replied.

"John said that he started to laugh, then started to cry. 'Lady, you need guarding,' he said. 'Get the police, lawyers, get people around you.' (7)

"That's how I feel: like I've taken a gunshot to the head," I wrote. "Suddenly it hits me that I married a Predator who took my entrails out. That included an abortion which has been entirely buried in my sub-brain."

I wrote Larry Predator Letter #2 in "Sherry Corollary" form. Each item began: "Larry, I *feel* XYZ"—and there was a lot of XYZ:

Larry, I feel so sad that until I read about "safe people," I had no idea there even was such a thing as a safe man, because I lived in such un-safety with you.

Larry, I feel deep grief and fear at how you took me down for an abortion like taking an animal to be spayed.

Larry, I feel convulsive grief as deep as Hell that you never protected me.

Larry, I'm vomiting up decades of never being treated like a woman.

I took this new horror and read it twice a week for months to whomever would listen.

Track Your Anomalies

In December, I lost my beach pad lease. On January 3, I lost my inland shack lease. That same week I finally lost my Virginia health insurance. Now I had to sign my life away by taking a desk job with a health plan.

In February 2010, I found a job in Anaheim and a condo the same week. The job felt like an act of God. The CEO asked how I'd learned the foreign languages on my resume. "Singing opera," I replied.

"Sing some opera!" he commanded. I let it rip with Madame Butterfly's aria and people clapped all over the office. I demonstrated guts, so he hired me.

The condo was another godsend. I searched for weeks near major freeways but found nothing, and was pushed farther and farther south. Finally my desperate realtor sent me photos of a place an hour south of Anaheim.

"Dana Point? Are you crazy?" I said, but had no choice. I got the condo at half price because the bank that foreclosed on it wanted out. A week later I realized: I'm a 12-minute walk from the ocean. I've landed by accident at the beach.

"Track your anamolies; that's where you see the hand of God," said Townsend in a talk I attended. (8)

Yet the pain kept coming. Changing my external circumstances did nothing to ease the internal angst.

"This is my mausoleum; I'm going to be entombed here," I moaned about my condo. "That's why I rented that inland shack for three years; I kept hoping to meet a man who'd take me home. Moving in here alone makes the truth unavoidable: I don't belong to anyone."

I felt like the 14-year old in Avril Lavigne's video singing, "Won't somebody come take me home?"

No one would.

So instead, I loaded the two-inch mini SanDisk mp3 player that Steve got me for Christmas with over 80 songs, from *Carousel* to Linda Ronstadt to Verdi's *Don Carlos*, anything associated with Mom, Dad or Larry.

I used music accidentally to access buried feelings for my first Dad Letter, repeat-playing *Carousel* until I felt emotions for Dad. After discovering yet another layer that I never knew existed, Larry grief, I got sick of crust. I began to deliberately use music as a crust buster.

This revealed a special healing property of music.

Emotions take mountains of repetition to retrain? Music is great for that; recordings are the same every time we play them! I read the Larry Predator Letter three times a week to friends. I listened to music that Larry and I had shared for two hours a day commuting. Then I hit the gym or jogged playing Larry songs, singing and pounding out the hurt with every rep.

The response from my subconscious was huge. More and more buried Larry pain surfaced to be dealt with, for weeks. It had been a long 30 years.

Weekends Sherry or Steve would visit to read letters, then we'd walk to the beach.

Steve and I were hiking Salt Creek Beach in early March when suddenly I jumped.

"Remember the Larry Yellow Letter?" I said. "When I came to California in 2006, this was my favorite beach, and that's where I wrote it! Over there by those rocks." I whipped out my old clamshell and flashed a picture dated September 23, 2006. We were looking at the same rocks.

"This was Nirvana then; I couldn't even imagine living here," I said.

"Track your anomalies; you got pushed back to the scene of the crime," said Steve. "This has to help bust your crust, to come here often, to a place where you really felt that Larry hurt."

Many Saturdays we walked to those rocks. I'd read out a Larry Letter, then stand in the ocean and bawl as the awful truth and the magnitude of the loss cracked my heart open. (Figure 8.1) I wrote Larry Grief Letters #3, #4, and #5, read them again and again, then bashed it out exercising with my mp3 cranked up to Larry music. For five months.

Funeral for My Marriage

In May, another godsend arrived in another book.

"If grief is the answer to so many of life's problems, why don't we have grief parties?" wrote John Townsend. "We do; they're called funerals, gatherings where we can be sad and begin to process our grief...

"We cannot let down and let go if we are not being held up," he said.

"This is why I tell people that God put tear ducts in our eyes. Grief is a relational experience, and your pain has to be seen eye to eye with another person. Someone should be looking at us when we are crying, and we should be looking at him or her. Then we know that we are not alone and our tears are seen and heard." (9)

"I need a funeral for my marriage!" I shouted.

A funeral? That's where we can really "let down" our defenses and "let go;" we can fall completely apart in public and flat out wail about our loss. People will come around us and literally hold us up. They will hug us, take care of us, and see our tears. Then they'll feed us a good meal and a stiff drink.

How safe I would feel there to release a huge amount of hurt!

On May 19, I emailed Townsend's quotes to ten friends, inviting them to a funeral for my marriage. I wanted to read a final Larry Letter, then burn it and other documents, so I found a park in Corona del Mar with barbecue grills. I asked everyone to sing something simple.

This was only one event; this they could manage. After juggling schedule conflicts we settled on July 18. Now I had a deadline.

I stepped up reading letters. Finally I arrived at Larry Letter #6, Flatten Me VI, and it was awful:

Larry, I've never been afraid of death, but now I'm overwhelmed at how the failure of love feels like death itself. Losing the immortality of my love feels like losing the immortality of my soul, which is death.

Larry, I hurt so bad when I hear people talk about a soulmate, because you refused to be my soulmate.

Larry, I feel enormous loss, thinking that I could die without ever having been really loved.

Larry, I feel despair because this means that I may die without ever having lived.

Larry, I feel deep disappointment and sorrow because only love can outlast death, but you have taken my love from me and left me only emptiness.

Steve was writing a funeral letter for Lena, so we began reading grief letters to each other in his minivan, in a parking lot half way between our offices. All that padding and neck support let my body sob and bang so hard against the seat back that I dubbed it the Grief Van, or alternately, my padded cell.

On June 28, we were reading again. All I expected was more "Flatten Me" pain:

Larry, I feel hurt because no one should be left alone as long as I've been left alone.

Larry, I'm so angry that you parked in the space marked "husband," but never acted like one.

Larry, I'm angry and frightened that it wasn't until you got physically violent that I saw what you really are.

Halfway through the five-page letter, my voice trailed off...

"I don't feel angry anymore," I said quietly. "I don't even feel like reading any more of this letter.

"I think I'm done with this." My jaw dropped.

Steve was shocked, then pleased. "Until now, I had no idea how we could know if this grief process was working," he said. "How do we measure when we're done? Seeing you get tired of the anger and hurt shows how."

On July 18, I was ready for the funeral.

I put on a simple black dress and the Met Opera chandelier necklace that Larry bought me. I brought my papers and a boom box to play accompaniment so we could sing. I reached the park, set out my things on a table, and then I saw my friends coming.

Without a word from me, they were all dressed up in black, ladies in hats and veils, Steve in a black suit, many carrying flowers. My knees went weak. "Just like a real funeral," I muttered. "They're taking me seriously." It was incredibly moving and we hadn't even begun. This was the program:

Funeral for the Marriage of Kathy & Larry - July 18, 2010

Amazing Grace (Traditional) - Delia
Du bist die Ruh (Schubert) - Kathy
Widmung (Schumann) - Kathy
Thoughts of My Homeland (Hyeon Chae-myun) - Sumi and Kathy

Grief Recovery Letter #6 to Larry - Kathy
Burning of divorce decree and financial documents

Lacrymosa (Verdi's *Requiem*) - Steve
Balm in Gilead (Traditional) - Harriet
Swing Low, Sweet Chariot (Traditional) - Sherry

I briefly read Townsend's quotes that we need a funeral to be held up, so we can let down; we need people to see and hear our hurts and tears. Then we went right to the music.

I sang two love songs that I'd sung to Larry for years. By the middle of the Schumann ("You my Soul, you my Heart, you my Joy"), I was bawling for every hurt of my lost love.

Without a word three women rose, came to my side of the table, and put their arms around my shoulders to literally hold me up.

It was right out of the story Sherry tells about elephants. "When an elephant gets sick, if it falls down, it will die," she says. "So the other elephants stand next to it and physically hold it up until it heals."

"We also die without human support."

Steve told the story to his GriefShare group. "I'm from South Africa, and it's true!" the pastor said. "I've seen elephants do this."

It was true. All I could do was literally sink onto my friends' shoulders thinking, "thank you for being my elephants."

It was wonderful. It was perfect.

It was a huge shot of the extra support I'd always longed for. I also learned that day that group support is stronger than individual support.

Again I felt my heart move wildly, like crust and plates in an earthquake. I sobbed awhile, then we went on.

My choir-mate Sumi and I sang a Korean song of homesickness.

Then I pulled out Larry Grief Letter #6, all five pages. I wasn't angry anymore, so I soon reached the end:

Larry, I'm glad there's a continent between us. I hope never to see Virginia again.

Larry, I'm going to take your photo off my phone now and burn the documents from our marriage, while my friends sing Verdi's *Requiem*. Then I'm going to burn this letter.

But when I was asked recently if I planned to burn a figure of you in effigy, I was surprised. "No," I said, "my anger is spent." I've honestly forgiven you.

So Larry, I can say goodbye now and be OK. I'll continue to wear the Met pendant because I love the Met and I want to enjoy happy memories of our nights at the opera.

Good night, Larry, and goodbye.

God be with you.

Steve had the charcoal going so burn I did. Reading the copy of our divorce decree cost me tears, but into the flames it went. The Yellow Letter copy I instinctively tore up ferociously before tossing in the shreds.

I opened a heavy satchel and out came financial documents, boxes and boxes of checkbooks with our married names. The more I hauled out, the more we all began to laugh. Now we had a bonfire going and we were having a good time.

Just at the right moment Steve whipped out a bag of marshmallows with flawless deadpan, and distributed skewers. You had to be there; it was one of the funniest things I've ever seen.

We ended with Harriet's "Balm in Gilead" and a group version of "Swing Low, Sweet Chariot." Then off we went for the wake and a bottle of wine.

Whu Nu funerals could be such fun?

Notes

1. Cloud & Townsend (1996).
2. Townsend (7-27-09).
3. Grissom & Grissom (1994).
4. Thich Nhat Hanh (2001, p.24).
5. Norwood (1985, p.139-142).
6. Grissom & Grissom (1994).
7. Townsend (7-27-09).
8. Townsend (2-13-10).
9. Cloud & Townsend (2004).

My Inner Cat

9.1 Linda, I want my family. (Kathy Brous)

You'd think I could take the rest of the summer off. But no.

On July 23, my sister and her sons made a surprise trip to LA to check out colleges. I was fine touring with them for two days, fine returning to LAX, fine taking their bags from my trunk, fine for the hugs goodbye.

But as I opened my car door, I saw their backs and luggage riding up the escalator to disappear into the terminal, and up came another little voice:

"Linda, I don't want you to go!" it yowled in my chest. "Linda, I want my little Brice! (One Brous, two Brice; that's her nickname.) Linda, you were all the family I ever had.

"Linda-I-want-my-family!"

I collapsed on the wheel in full-tilt meltdown at the airport curb. I couldn't drive; I couldn't even see, but I had only minutes to leave or the drug-hunting airport police might take me in. Off I drove in hysterics out past the 32-foot-high letters "LAX" with their 100-foot towers of light that tell you exactly where in the world you are.

"We're alone in LA," the voice said. "What are we doing out here drowning in people who never heard of us?" California dream? Now we learn that parts of me consider LAX the place I fly *out of* to get to people who know me back East. I felt an umbilical cord being ripped out of my gut: no more Brice, no more New York, no more Dan, no more songs with my pianist.

I swerved into the first gas station I saw and turned the key. "No. More. Home," the voice repeated in my chest. "Before, I was nowhere; now I'm 3,000 miles from nowhere. Lord, I'm one, Lord, I'm two, Lord, I'm three, Lord, I'm four, Lord, I'm 3,000 miles from my home…" I bawled for ten minutes until it attracted the local pan-handling brigade. I drove off, pulled into the next station, called Harriet (a world-class music scholar and professor no less), and cried to her for another 20 minutes. Then I still couldn't drive, so I called Steve to "talk me home" as if he were air traffic control.

When I sobered up later I knew: my last Larry letter may as well have been written to my sister. Just replace Larry with Linda: "Larry, I hurt because I wanted a family. Larry, I hurt because I wanted to belong." "I cried so hard I nearly choked," I told Sherry. "Loss of family."

Wait. Did reading Larry letters over and over for a year just strip 30 years of crud off my heart? We thought that would debride my soul down to "healthy tissue" which could heal.

Instead, here's more break-through grief. Did I just dig down to pain from before I met Larry at 19? Have I hit yet more layers of damaged childhood tissue?

One thing for sure: grief from a much younger me was coming up.

Journey to the Center of My Brain

It's always been there; ever since I can remember, the pain's been there. No one should be left alone as long as I was left alone. On July 28, I woke at 5 a.m. in a nightmare out of nowhere about the "primal scream," seeing that shrieking face, with the words repeating in my head: "I was the abortion." I'd heard vaguely of the 1970 book *Primal Scream* and the painting on its cover, but images of that contorted face are widespread.

I stood up, then collapsed back onto my bed in a fetal curl with a loop in my head of the image and the words "I was the abortion."

I was due to cook at the company picnic but I couldn't even walk. Later I had to leave myself two excruciating voicemails to record a question so frightening that otherwise I'd have blacked it out:

Was I feeling the pain felt by my aborted baby—or my own pain?

I had an abortion at 32 and suppressed the memory ever since. "Don't end up pushing a baby carriage," Mom used to warn, and in my terror I played God and took a life. I committed another sin, after a lifetime of Mom saying that everything I did was bad. I never questioned my *mens rea*, the guilty conscience of a criminal mind. All I could do was shove down the event and the emotions.

Until my letters to Larry.

"Larry, I feel deep grief and terror at how you took me down for an abortion like taking an animal to the vet to be spayed," I just wrote. I was too frightened to have children because childhood was so painful, I often thought; I can't visit that upon an unsuspecting child. Must I now write a "Letter to My Aborted Baby?"

No. Actually it felt like "abortion" was something that was done to me.

I thought about it madly. What did I feel about the abortion?

Did I feel guilt? Sure, but I was born feeling guilty. Did I feel bad about my baby? Sure, but I was born feeling bad about everything I did.

I couldn't go back to sleep, I couldn't wake up, and I sure couldn't function, but slowly the lunatic nightmare rant "I was the abortion" began to make sense, and hard.

I dreamed that Mom wanted to abort me *in utero* and some level of my physiology knew it by the acid bath my cells experienced in that hostile womb. As I lay mentally screaming I knew: I wasn't wanted to be born. I didn't belong to be. My existence was not in question; the answer was, "No, you shouldn't be. Throw the bloody tissue out." I was psychologically and emotionally aborted, and I could feel that primal scream.

"So I killed my baby," I journaled. "I couldn't have a baby, because I was the baby that had to be killed."

That was why I couldn't grieve my baby and why my real reactions were not guilt or remorse, but terror and panic. I could feel the panic of being in a lethal environment about to be killed. I'd have to walk through that, before I could feel anything about my poor baby. That morning as I lay in fetal position, unable to rise, with all that hung in the balance—my job, my health insurance, my home—all I could think of was: I was the abortion.

Eventually fear gunned my adrenaline to where I dressed and drove 90 minutes to the picnic, put on a chef's hat and a smile, and grilled 70 lbs of chicken for 110 people. But I was frantic inside.

Without invitation, my sub-brain was barfing up pain from infancy to age four. The *Inner Child Workbook* said that I flunked infant bonding and its Rx was to lie on the floor smearing myself with applesauce.

I needed better answers on bonding. Fast.

A CoDA friend gave me a book on how we develop from birth, *Changes that Heal* by Henry Cloud. He had the real story and his Rx ain't applesauce.

Bonding is the ability "to relate to another on the deepest level," he writes, "share their deepest thoughts, dreams, and feelings with each other with no fear that they will be rejected."

I couldn't even imagine it. "Who would want to do this with *me?*" I wrote in the margin. "Bonding is a basic human need," he went on, "Without relationship, we can't be truly human… Not only do we not grow, we deteriorate" and become chaotic inside. That was me; isolated and chaotic. (1)

At birth, we go "from a warm, wet, dark, soothing environment… into a cold, dry, bright, harsh environment," Cloud says. "We are in shock. One look at the face of a newborn gives a picture of this total isolation… Then the mother takes the child and begins to hold him closely and talk softly… Emotional bonding has begun." God makes birth scary because "you've got to scream and dial the number," he says.

My legs shook. Terrifying, yeah, that I could feel.

But hold closely, talk softly? Gibberish. I couldn't feel any such thing, just terror. Up it came again, the terror of being stuffed in a glass box. Cloud writes about the pure panic of never having bonding as an infant and feeling a bottomless pit of panic and rage inside.

"It's not your fault," he says, like Robin Williams in *Good Will Hunting*. (2)

When a baby is held and cared for, he says, it grows "***emotional object constancy***." The child stores up "memories of being comforted" by mom. "The child takes his mother in and stores her inside," then "is able to experience himself as loved constantly, even in the absence of the loved one."

"Nonsense!" I wept again.

Then Cloud went over the top. "We don't need alcohol, street drugs, or sex. We can live very well without them," he concludes. "However, we really do need relationships" and bonding to live. We can get bonding as adults from "safe people," he says. (3)

"Live without sex?! You're nuts!" I shouted, throwing the book at the wall, cursing. I'd stopped relations with Bob, but he was still calling and I was starved for touch, a lifetime's worth. I didn't want to hear science call it optional.

That was the first of four times that I put *Changes that Heal* away for weeks. I'd read another 60 pages, then throw it against the wall again.

CTH, as Steve naturally dubbed it, took me two years to finish, compared to two months for Goethe's *Faust*.

Oh, well; any book you haven't thrown across the room at least once because it smashed your world view, probably isn't worth a long shelf life.

The Id Within

Next was a trip booked long ago to my sister's home in New York for her son's 18th birthday. On August 4, I was stuck on the transcontinental flight with an infant crying two rows away for five hours. But, track my anomalies.

My reaction to babies crying has always been fear, panic, and if no one soothes it, nausea. I'd feel bad for the baby, but at some point all I felt was my own terror. I knew on some level all my life that this must be because I'd been left to cry a lot as a baby. Fighting off nausea, missing sleep and hearing that baby yowl, a few hours in it struck me:

It sounds exactly like my tomcat Tom hiding under the bed when he was sick, yowling. "Whah, whah, whah," cried the baby, then in my mind it morphed to "yah, yah, yah" and then "yow, yow, yow," exactly like a sick tomcat.

Yikes, I thought, *I can't find an inner child because what's inside me never got to be that old.* Dr. Rita demanded an inner five-year-old, but what's inside me never got to be five.

It never got old enough to become a person. All that's inside me is a screaming infant id, days old, yowling in sheer pain. All I've got inside is an "inner cat." Tom. My "inner cat" Tom.

God Almighty, I'm a lot sicker than anyone ever imagined.

Tom slept on my shoulder for 18 years. We also had a female cat named Pinky who stayed up late with Larry; cats are attracted to the opposite sex pheromones. So I wound up with a furry cat for a husband.

One day in Virginia in 2004, we took Tom, who was stiff, to the vet. Larry dropped us at the curb and drove away. "Your cat is dead," said the vet. "That will be $95.00."

Flash forward to San Clemente Pier in the glorious California sunshine, June 2009. Since 2004, I'd been to Asia on business twice, worked several Pentagon contracts, and kept performing. But now my marriage of 27 years to Larry was dead back East, too. I'd pulled up my life and my scalp by the roots and moved 3,000 miles to get warm out here. After a perfect beach day, I let a friend grab a table for drinks while I found the restroom.

I didn't return for almost 40 minutes. On my way back, I saw a stray cat eating fish trash and collapsed on a concrete stanchion at the foot of the pier. I couldn't stop bawling despite the public mortification, and all I could think of was: "I miss my kitty. I want my kitty. I want my kitty right now."

Soon I began using the word "fur" in a way that my cats inspired: to describe what mammals do for each other. Mammals have fur, unlike other beasts, but how they use it is more interesting. At first I was "re-furring" to the way cats snuggle and get fur all over us—not just our clothes, but our hearts.

Tom snuggled furiously and Pinky was no slouch, either. She sat on my lap at the computer until she was 17 and died in my bathrobe. Fur is what all the Internet photos of cats—without which some say the Internet wouldn't exist—are about.

Then I realized that when cats "fur," they create direct emotional connection. That means people can also provide fur to each other. When people can't get enough mammalian emotional connection and affection from other people, cats become the go-to source.

Dogs have plenty of fur, but cats are more blatant. Cats want love and they want it now. They don't over-think it. They go right for getting their needs met. They open their eyes and jump you and as soon as they get into a nice furry position they feel safe, so they fall asleep. (4)

Joe the Electrician

Now in 2010, with no real cat, no husband, and no inner child, I landed at JFK in a panic and was pulled into a whirl of parties. On August 6, my sister's crowd set up a picnic on the sandbar south of Long Island where we grew up. Terrified by the turmoil within, I walked alone to the jetty at the end to see the sun on the ocean and Manhattan beyond.

As a child I fled here nearly every day of every summer. I recalled gazing for hours as a kid at the beauty of the sunlight on the waves, wondering why I felt so awful amidst such wonders. As I climbed the jetty now, rows of silver airplanes were still taking off every five minutes from JFK and soaring out past me over the ocean, just as long ago. My misery was complete: divorce, my parents' deaths, and now those big silver birds.

Bob flew the LAX to JFK route; when I was in California, he often called me from JFK. I was soon longing to be swept up by him onto one of those big jets. "How many years has Bob been taking off here?" I wondered. "Was I meant to be with him ever since I saw these planes as a kid?"

As I sat there draped in a towel, I remembered Mom, how I didn't belong in my family, and my nightmare that I was the abortion. I began to bawl for the sheer misery of feeling so out of place, yet again, so many exhausting decades later.

Climbing down, I was greeted by a man who was playing with his son along the jetty.

"I couldn't help notice you were crying," he said. "Can I help?"

"My Mom just died and I'm not in my right mind," I said.

With that, he began to weep. "Oh, no, *my* Mom just died, and I can hardly bear it!" he said.

We stared at each other. Like everything else in this ridiculous book, this actually happened.

"My name's Joe; I'm from Freeport. I'm an electrician," he said, non sequitur.

"I'm Kathy; I used to love the fish restaurants in Freeport. I'm from here but I live in California now," I said.

"I love my Mom so much, I can't believe she's gone, I can hardly function!" he cried, tears streaming down his face. "I think about her all the time, my kids miss her, but I had to be strong for my family at the funeral last week so I didn't cry... Now I'm having trouble controlling myself."

"Try to remember the name of this book: *Grief Recovery Handbook*," I said, head talk kicking in.

"Would you like a hug?" he asked suddenly.

That sure changed the subject, and the answer was beyond question.

"Yes, if you don't mind my get-up," I said, referring to my bikini and towel damp with tears.

Then Joe the electrician from Freeport, a total stranger, holding his son's hand in his left hand, put a strong right arm around my shoulder like a perfect gentleman and hugged us both to him. The three of us hugged and cried a long time, until we couldn't cry anymore. All I had was the towel; neither of us had pen, paper, or device. I tried to get him to memorize my email so we could write, then I had to go.

Walking back five minutes later I ran into my sister. "You'll never believe this," I said, telling the story. "I thought walking there might be good for you," she said. We hugged and cried some more.

That evening Bob, knowing that I was in New York, called me from California. Infuriating. I couldn't do a thing about Bob the arsonist, but I could journal about the Mom pain burning in my own heart.

I recalled a question John Townsend took at his February talk from a grieving man. "My wife passed away," said the man. "I have three children age six and under, and some nights they're just crying 'I miss Mommy.' Where do I go?"

"I am so sorry," said John, shaken. "The best antidote for a child that's lost a mother, is a mother. An aunt, a grandmother, a neighbor... Under six, a child is on life support... When they say 'I miss Mommy,' it means, 'There's a

Mommy hole in me!' They need warm women around them—neurologically, developmentally, physiologically—double time." (5)

Now I scrawled on a stray paper at midnight:

I have a Mommy Hole in me,
I didn't know that I had needs;
I came to the ocean to escape rejection,
I came for the beauty; it made me feel loved.

Loved by Someone who put all this here for me.
Wonder at the beauty, wonder at the pain,
Wonder why whatever happens,
Still the pain remains.

Kids have a Mommy hole in them?
I've got a Mommy hole in me.

Parts of My Brain Are Dark

On August 9, I was back commuting in California, working on a concrete pour at Seal Beach Marine Base. It didn't look to the Marines or to me as though I had anything wrong with my high-performance brain.

Driving, I put on "Getting Love on the Inside," a 2002 Henry Cloud CD. "Humans are neurologically designed, physiologically designed, psychologically, emotionally, and cognitively designed, to be in a relationship where you are loved," he began.

Bonding, again.

"Babies can't sooth themselves," he said. Really? Whu Nu?

"Adults must calm them, and the minute we put them down, they start crying again.

"But after adults do that a million times, the gap for how long they can tolerate not being held gets wider and wider," he noted. "They are taking our love from the outside, and it's becoming part of them on the inside... The love of other people somehow goes inside us, and becomes actual equipment that we take in and walk around with on the earth." (6)

Emotional object constancy again; now Steve was calling it EOC. I felt sad. All I had was an inner cat. Then Dr. Cloud tripped a wire:

"It's like a programmer writing software on a disk: then your computer is able

9.2 Nearly drove off the overpass (Kathy Brous)

to perform," he said, but if no one gave our limbic emotional brains that software as infants, we can't function.

"We can now do scans of the brains of older kids who were not held or soothed, and there are parts of the brain which are dark," he added. "There's nothing growing in there, because nothing was planted; neurologically there's literally no brain activity."

I nearly drove off the 91 Freeway's Anaheim overpass in Figure 9.2 at 70 miles an hour. It hit me in the gut the minute he said it:

"Parts of my *brain* are dark!"

I didn't discover the PET brain scans in the Preface (which start this book) until 2013, but eventually I did learn that Cloud was right. Parts of my brain just weren't firing.

Steve says that we all have opposable thumbs? No wonder I feel like I have no thumbs. I never got the software to function.

"We need to know that *someone bigger than us, loves us,*" Cloud said, to get that software. Then we feel "connected to God, connected to each other, and connected to ourselves." That last point means we can actually feel our own feelings.

Yet today, "modern man has moved the fig leaf from the genitals to the face," he said, quoting philosopher Rollo May. "People are free with their sexuality, but there's no way they're going to let anyone look into their soul."

Yikes. My parents did divorce me. Look into their soul? No adult I knew had time for a child to do that.

When we don't get love, Cloud went on, we build up "hardness of the heart."

"Like the crud build-up in GRH," said Steve. "The more crazy Lena acted, the more I poured on the love, but it was like trying to water a plant in the desert. The soil had a crust so thick, the water couldn't get in."

"Yeah," I said, "The grief letters cracked the crud on my heart; it's so thick and now there's such turmoil, it feels like the earth's crust is moving."

Wait–I'm missing all that software, so of course I feel lousy? I always thought that we all feel lousy as kids, then we grow up and find someone to love us. That's wrong? If I'd gotten the software, I'd have felt fine all along?

I felt bad all my life, but I was supposed to have felt good all my life?

Can I just download the software now and I'll feel better?

The Loss that Is Forever

Just then I had to read a certain business book. At my small local library, business and psychology were on the same shelf. I noticed *The Loss that is Forever: The Early Death of a Parent* by Maxine Harris and *Motherless Daughters* by Hope Edelman. Not for me, I thought; my folks died so recently. But I tossed the books into my car trunk.

Weeks later on August 24, the night before they were due, I glanced at the books and the bottom fell out again.

In case study after case study, I was shocked to recognize the same awful feelings I'd had all my life but never dared discuss with anyone.

"The language of adult loss is totally inadequate to capture the panic, pain, terror and confusion of a grieving child," writes Harris. "The flood of feelings is likened by some to a tidal wave... Survivors of Hiroshima lived through horrors that were beyond words. So parental loss is spoken of as a catastrophe beyond words... nothing in life remains untouched; the catastrophe is absolute."

Loss always felt catastrophic to me. The smallest daily loss of a slip of paper plunged me into panic. The loss of a relationship made me nauseous.

There was no denying the resonance shaking me as these case studies reported the identical feelings.

"With no mother, the child experiences terrifying insecurity," Harris says. "Nothing is safe, predictable, or secure. The rules for how to behave, who is to be trusted, are totally altered. The fundamental world order is shattered; chaos governs events."

Me again.

"The loss felt inside seeps out and engulfs everything. 'I couldn't make sense of it, as though I were the only survivor of a bombing,' one woman said. She referred to the "hole in my heart." (7)

It's physical. I've often had that unexplained feeling of suddenly falling into a hole. All my life I've been awakened from sleep by the feeling of dropping so abruptly from a great height that I was choking. In my 30s the doctors wired my up body to test for sleep apnea, but found nothing. In 2009 I realized that I had "no standing point" because that hole under my feet could open up and swallow me at any time.

One day in her late 20s, writes Edelman, "as I reached the middle of the crosswalk, I looked up and saw the midday sun" reflecting off large windows. "Like a size-twelve workboot kicked into my gut I felt it, and I clutched my stomach, unable to breathe. The light turned green and cars started honking; a few drove around me... I couldn't speak. I couldn't move. All I could think was, 'I want my mother. I want my mother, NOW.'" She was 14 when her mom died. (8)

The word "Boston" flashed before my eyes in big red letters.

"My God, that was me in Boston!" I thought. I spent the summer before graduating college alone there, wandering the streets barefoot. Six months later I fled to Japan. Yet now I could feel what was at the bottom of the "hole in my heart"—and when I heard Edelman yowl "I want my mother, NOW," I could feel that, too.

Suddenly I was *in* Boston, age 20, barefoot and suicidal. "I want my Mommy, *now!*" I howled.

It was inescapable: I had somehow lost or never had a Mom, and maybe not a Dad.

A month later my library closed for two years' construction; I'd only been there that once since moving to the area. It's a miracle I ever saw those books. Track my anomalies.

When this picture came together I realized why I had "no standing point," and talked about it for the first time ever. After that, the lifetime nightmares about falling from a great height stopped and never returned. It wasn't sleep apnea. I'd been falling through that childhood hole.

"I've done six awful letters: Mom (Flatten Me I), Dad (Flatten Me II & IV), and Larry (III, V & VI)," I journaled. "Must I write another Mom Letter?"

In fact, I needed a funeral for Mom to grieve these awful "motherless" discoveries. So yes, I needed a new letter.

On September 8, I began Mom Grief Letter #2, Flatten Me VII, and scheduled a funeral for November 27, 2010.

Notes

1. Cloud (1993, p.68-70). Actually Cloud was talking about attachment.
2. Damon, Affleck & Williams (1997). Take it in: Youtube.com/watch?v=UYa6gbDcx18
3. Cloud (1993, p.46–64).
4. I'm missing the fur, *Medium.com/@KathyBrous/im-missing-the-fur-1c80a85ae537*
5. Townsend (2-13-10).
6. Cloud (2002).
7. Harris (1996).
8. Edelman (1995).

10

In God Like a Fish

10.1 La Jolla Shores. (Kathy Brous)

How would I survive months of this new "motherless" pain and then a Mom Funeral?

I had to find more people support and new ways to download all that mammalian software I'd missed.

I longed to feel that "someone bigger than me loves me," to feel EOC inside. That's why I dove into the safe people program at the Irvine church. But I was too damaged, so instead I mostly felt terrified of the church undertone which kept repeating "you are bad." It was Mom's drone and I knew it from birth: "You're a rotten kid."

"In the absence of relationship, we experience condemnation," says John Townsend, and "a good deal of negative, critical self-talk." (1) I sure had an absence of relationships and I sure couldn't take any more "condemnation voices." I'd learned to fear condemnation since the sperm hit the egg.

On September 24, I completed Mom Grief Letter #2, a horror show about my lifelong feelings of terror and isolation, and then the "motherless" discovery. I wanted to read it repeatedly, well before Mom's funeral, to get sick of it as I had my Larry letter. I read it to anyone who'd listen two or three times a week for the next two months.

"I've got a letter" became my theme. Sure, with so much hurt inside my texts are perfectly awful. But once I have a letter to read about these feelings to people, experience shows that the feelings come "up and out." Eventually I get relief.

God Inside?

Next, hunting for new software, I accidentally discovered meditation. At a business conference.

There an entrepreneur spoke about "human software engineering" (really) and distributed a book on how to heal "conditioning." That's an old yogic term for false unconscious emotions and beliefs imprinted from birth by family and culture. It often creates childhood pain too big for a child to handle. Such pain is repressed and sits within us as adults as a constant stream of anxious thoughts. (2) I checked and the literature confirmed it.

Get underneath thought and quiet the mind, the yogis say, and we discover that God is inside us.

As when a pool of ruffled water grows still, we can see the shiny coin at the bottom—so when our minds become still, we can look within and see the face of God, they write. (3) To quiet thought, the yogis developed hatha yoga stretching poses, mindfulness meditation, and chanting, Vedic traditions since 5,000 BC. (4)

"Way down in the bottom, you can find the love of Jesus in the bottom of your heart," say the gospel singers. (5)

After a lifetime of panic buttons in my chest, I craved that stillness.

God is inside me? Oh, Someone Bigger than me loves me! I want that, I really want that, my insides howled.

I found a yogic group that hosted chanting and meditation. On October 1, I drove an hour to their San Diego Center. Their mantra from ancient scripture, *Om Namah Shivaya*, means "I honor the Divine within me."

"The limbic brain takes mountains of repetition to retrain," I thought. "If I long to feel God is inside me, why not repeat that He is? Why not repeatedly honor that, so I can stop repeatedly condemning myself?"

Next day back to San Diego I drove for more chanting. I got singing CDs of the mantra and an epic Vedic poem, then booked a Motel Six to stay and chant everything next morning.

Another healing power of music: emotional regulation.

The brain is a rhythmic organ, I later learned. The reptilian brain stem develops first, the rest of the brain from it, so Reptile propagates its fears through the entire brain, says Bruce Perry, MD. If Reptile is badly distressed, it painfully disables our higher emotional and thinking brains. (6)

Only "rhythmic regulation" can calm that brain stem, he reports, "patterned, repetitive rhythmic activity: walking, running, dancing, singing, meditative breathing." Music can relieve pain because it works at the deepest levels.

Back then I simply felt it, so I found a weekly yogi meeting near my office.

Tuesday nights I'd stand there chanting Sanskrit hymns to God. "Jyota se joyta jagao: Light my lamp from your lamp," we sang. "Mera antara timira mitao: Remove the darkness from my heart." Soon it would morph into "Jyota se joyta jagao, I've got a lot of Me OW! I hurt so bad, God, please remove this 'Me Ow' from my heart!"

Just in time.

Mom's hatred resonated through me that Fall to where I felt stripped of life. Every day I woke in terror. "Of course I feel bad," I'd tell myself, "I'm missing all the software I need.

"If I'd gotten good software as a kid, I'd feel fine. So: download good software!" Then I'd chant the epic at home. Commuting to work I'd sing to "Jyota" or "Arati" ("wave a light") for another hour.

My fear needed mountains of retraining, so this went on daily for two years. Whenever I hear those chants, I can see the I-5 and I'm back in 2010. They often honor the "Self," the divine within us.

"Download Self respect from *Om Namah Shivaya*," I wrote. "Honor your Self and re-honor your Self, until your brain starts to grasp what being honored feels like."

I didn't want to ditch my Judeo-Christian tradition, so I also stuck with the Irvine church and talked up meditation. "I need a lot of repetition." I'd say. "Could we sit together repeating 'Be still and know that I am God' and meditate?" No luck.

My yogi friends, however, were delighted to repeat it endlessly—and that's the point. We need repetition.

"No one, lead by me, has ever honored me, let alone seen anything divine in me," I journaled. "I've been told I was unwanted tissue that shouldn't exist. All that anyone, especially me, saw inside me was trash; that's what anxiety panic feels like.

"That's why I need to hear it short and clear: 'God is inside me.' "

So I repeated *Om Namah Shivaya* for dear life. I needed to hear those three little words over and over—so over and over, I sang with my mp3 and bowed to the divine within me. I bowed at meetings, in the car, at the gym, at home.

I bowed to the ocean. I bowed to God's face reflected in the sunlight on the ocean, then danced in the ocean singing *Om Namah Shivaya* for hours.

"My mp3 is my pacemaker," I told friends. "It keeps me alive." The two-inch mini player was always on me.

Hide the Key

I'll always be grateful to the yogis for helping me feel safe enough that Fall to prepare the Mom Funeral.

In one yogic parable ca. 400 BC, the Creator assembles the animals and says, "I have a Divine Key that I want to hide from humans until they are ready. It unlocks the realization that I am inside them." Various animals offer to bury it in the mountains, under the ocean, in remote places where humans never go.

"No," says the Creator each time; humans will go there and find it.
"Give it to me," an eagle said then. "I'll fly to the moon and hide it."
"No," said the Creator. "Someday they'll go there, too."
Finally an elderly, blind mole suggested, "Hide it *inside* them."
"Ah!" said the Creator, and it was so.

"God is My Protector," I journaled:

People either grow or damage our souls,
Limbic resonance especially ain't neutral,

One picture or audio is worth a thousand words,
And bad software is bad software.

Good software is the only cure,
It's the loving voices you should have had.
Whether you get under the crud, or get snowed under by it,
Depends on how much good software you download.

After a month chanting "I honor God within me," in late October, I was back in the San Diego motel awaiting the chant next day. Singing along with my mp3, I tried to ignore the students partying outside and the misery of being alone in that dive on a Saturday night. Chanting the ancient song of suffering and transcendence, my body shook as I felt a lifetime of pain shoot through it.

Then I recalled another yogic teaching:

"Thinking that we are without God, is like a fish thinking that it has never seen water.
"Our life is in God. In God our breath moves in and out." (7)

Wait. I've been reading grief letters for 18 months. My heart was full of crust and those letters cracked it open.

And now, evidently, it was open enough to feel my longing for God. Reading about "God inside," now I felt the need in my chest. Suddenly I was scribbling madly:

What would you not give to let go all this pain?
Can you even imagine the hurt you've sustained?
Do you know how much love you should have received?
Can you feel it from God and begin to heal?

That's what God gave me, when the bottom fell out and He brought me into that sleazy motel room. Now it was repeating in my head endlessly:

I am in God like a fish is in water;
In God my breath moves in and out...
I am in God like a fish is in water;
In God my breath moves in and out...

"A strange calm comes; I feel really vulnerable, and vulnerable feels good," I journaled.

"I want to connect real deep. I've debrided off enough dead layers of my soul to feel through the hurt.

"I've gotten down to living skin, my need for Someone Bigger. It feels good because chanting touches my living layers and fills the need."

Next morning I soaked up the chanting, then walked slowly along the nearest beach at La Jolla Shores. The wet sand was shining in the sun, reflecting rows of palms as in the photo above. I picked up my long faux sari and waded into the water.

"Can you even imagine the hurt you've sustained?" I repeated. Seeing the enormity of God's face reflected in the light on the ocean, after chanting about Him endlessly, I could feel He was bigger than my pain. I threw up my hands and yowled until all the pain I could feel that day was released.

"There was so much love that you should have received." The idea that I deserved love began, somehow, to feel good.

Suddenly I felt loved, validated, and appreciated.

Suddenly the love felt bigger than the pain. I was astonished, it felt so good. What is this? How did it happen?

Repeating that God is inside me, I begin to believe it.

Then I was chanting "I am in God like a fish is in water!" until I was drunk with happiness, singing and splashing in the waves like a silly fish, wandering endlessly down the long shoreline. I don't even remember driving the hour trip home.

Message in a Bottle

On October 30, friends took me to San Onofre, where we hiked down a spectacular canyon to a long pebbled beach surrounded by cliffs. Sitting on the pebbles with my feet in the water watching the sun dance on it all, Beethoven's "Song of Atonement" came up on my mp3. I hadn't done it in ten years and began singing away into the waves.

When I performed this long ago, I had no idea what pain was.

When I sang, I used to feel that "spark of God" from Beethoven's "Ode to Joy," as if God and Ludwig were doing the singing inside me. I just had to get out of the way and it poured out. It felt wonderful.

Now I could feel the suffering in the slow opening lines, "Lord, hear my cry." But then after a long lament, suddenly the piano breaks into a peal of joy. I used to wonder why and now I saw:

It's the deeper joy that comes after we've actually felt the pain and told it to God, so we get real relief.

The way I actually felt my anger, told it to Sherry and got relief.

It's as if God left me a message in a bottle that just floated in off the ocean. When I sang this years ago, He was preparing me for today's pain. Now I'm in it, and when I hear this, I can look back and feel, "Oh, He warned me. He was with me then and He's with me now."

He even began to seep into my dreams.

"God Spoke to Me but It Gave Me Indigestion," I headlined an email to Sherry and Steve on November 4.

"Truth is stranger than fiction," I wrote. "Last night after an evening of meditation and prayer I fell asleep exhausted. At 3 a.m., I awoke with a dull clenching pain in my chest. I wondered if it were heartburn or worse.

"Now the masks, the denial, and the Bob anesthetic are gone, and I am left with cold reality: I'm 'home alone' with Mom. I felt the pain in my chest grow worse.

"Yes, the service for my Mom's death is in three weeks, and I am following my program. No matter what desires come to medicate myself with men, I focus every unpleasant feeling on Mom and her rejection. Night before last I pulled over for gas, opened my phone, saw Mom's photo, and sat there crying for an hour at how bad it hurt to look at her.

"Here I am alone again with the Cookie Momster and she is the voice of the Pit: 'I'll get you, my Pretty, and your little dog, too.'

"Just as I wondered if my heart would physically break, it hit me:

"But you're not alone now. You've learned that these negative voices in your head are mostly Mom's voices, just bad neural patterns, bum software accidentally installed.

"Now you're honoring your Self, separating your Self from those critical voices. Now you know that you aren't bad, and you're growing good software from your friends."

"Then came a loud voice:

" 'I also come with the System!' it said.

"I was wide awake and quite astonished.

"For the first time in my life, God was speaking to me, up close and Personal.

"In case anyone had doubt, His voice was backed by the solo violin soaring above high C to open the 'Benedictus' from Beethoven's *Missa Solemnis*.

"Then the pain in my solar plexus got worse. Much worse. I was alarmed. All these decades of anxiety can not have been good for my cardiovascular system.

" 'I also come with the System!' said the voice insistently.

"OK," I replied, "I've been praying repeatedly to You to please remove this pain from my heart. If my heart is giving out and it's time for me to see You and that's how You plan to remove the pain, I'm ready."

" 'I also come with the System!' " said the voice.

"I gambled that it was only heartburn, got up, took two anti-acids, grabbed my mp3 player and returned to bed. I did a lot of slow, deep breathing to relax what I hoped were purely psychological spasms.

"I turned on Beethoven's 'Benedictus' and began sobbing uncontrollably. And yes, California, these were Good Tears. Tears of deliverance, tears of gratitude, tears of un-comprehension but who cares.

" 'I also come with the System!' " God repeated, and as I gave myself over to the music, the pain stopped.

"As long as I fought the Mom pain, it just got worse—but when I stopped fighting, threw up my hands, and turned everything over to God and Beethoven, I got relief. Whu Nu?

"So thank you for all the good software!"

Flatten Me VII

Yet as the funeral approached and I read my letter over and over, the motherless children's images of tidal waves and Hiroshima reared up and filled my head, bigger and badder than ever.

"Memo to Self: Hiroshima," I emailed Sherry. "Stop medicating with Bob, and I feel the real pain inside: Mom hates me. They don't want me. I don't belong. All I've got inside is my inner cat Tom, just yowling.

"Take away the anesthetic, and the surgery is excruciating.

"Well, then: Hiroshima. You can't expect to avoid screaming.

"The only way out of this baby pain is to take a nice, leisurely stroll through Hiroshima. Got to feel down into all that Mom pain, if I want to release it.

"So, bonzai, baby: Flight 666 now departing for Hiroshima."

I did a lot of late-night journaling that month.

" 'Pain is the thing that makes us drop what we're holding, so that we can embrace the love of God,' says C.S. Lewis," I wrote.

"Oh yeah; pain is the Manufacturer's Alarm System.

"God put it in us to tell us what's bad for us. If we drink scalding liquid, or stay with a mean person, or suffer the death of a loved one, our body reacts with pain. If we deny the pain, it grows. But if we feel the pain as we are designed to do—just let the wind blow through the hole in our hearts—we feel better. At some point. This mourning undoes the muscle knots of pain. In a few days or weeks or months. Eventually."

On November 6, I was driving home down the 57 Freeway from the annual *Messiah* rehearsals, devastated that Bob wouldn't be at my concert this time. I put in a CD of Dorothy Maynor singing Handel's "O Sleep, Why Dost Thou Leave Me?"

"O..., O... Sleep..." it began slowly, in notes sustained forever, Maynor wailing softly. "O sleep, again deceive me: to my arms, restore my wandering love." As she stretched the "wah—ndering," my heart stretched with longing for Bob, who was always wandering away.

It was so emotional that I had to pull over and find a pen. Out poured two pages of hand scrawls.

Sleep?

"All those years, Larry, when I had to sleep alone," I wrote. " 'Billions of people sleep in pairs,' I used to tell him, but he never would.

"Then after Dan fell asleep, I couldn't, dreading how he'd look right past me next day. Now driving the 57 where I first followed Bob home, then he only came to me at night and left, never staying until morning.

"Now I see why I collapse in my car until midnight or find another book to read.

"I'll do anything to avoid going to sleep, alone, anxious, and unregulated—after a life alone with no human beings at night to regulate my broken biorhythms. (8)

"And dreading—O Sleep—when I do lie down, the nightmares, the broken sleep, the unending, willful neglect. Waiting and waiting in vain, because since I was born, nobody ever came.

"Two cars, two trucks, and a jet airplane. Flatten Me VII."

Arriving home I wrote:

You can break the grip of this beast.
But make no mistake: you're not done yet,
There is yet a vat of pain to face, O Sleep;
And many terrifying dreams, O Sleep.

Pay Mom Now—or carry her around Later.
What would you not give to pry these rocks off your chest?
A finger? A toe? One lousy month?
I've got a letter. I *can* break the grip of this Beast.

I began playing Maynor's "O Sleep" from my mp3 every time I read my Mom Letter to anyone. It always brought up a ton more of emotion. Then I'd work out to it and let the sobs wash through my body.

Tram into Mordor

Now I also knew what I had to do at Mom's funeral. It involved her ring.

Mom ostracized me for weeks in fifth grade after the small gold ring she gave me slipped down the drain while I washed up at school. The guilt felt awful. Later I found a husband who didn't buy me an engagement ring, so to look respectable at work I wore costume rings from K-Mart.

In late August, I'd chosen one resembling Mom's ring to wear for a few months, to remind me every day of what I was doing, then be thrown away.

"Ring?" you say, "sounds familiar."

Exactly.

The modern image for Hiroshima, of course, is the fiery landscape of Mordor.

I've got to spend the next month walking barefoot across Mordor to drop Mom's ring into Mount Doom.

That's what it already felt like; I already felt like a small animal in a landscape of sheer terror with a long way to walk down a very dark path full of fiery pits.

Soon I was chain-downloading graphics of Mordor from the Internet. The pictures of tiny hobbits hiding from ferocious orcs felt oddly familiar. That's how I felt; helpless and surrounded by oversized monsters.

I've had repeat nightmares since age two or three about the wolf in Disney's *Peter and the Wolf*. It's six feet tall and fills my bedroom doorway at night, then enters and bites the back of my neck. I wake up screaming.

Mordor was an apt metaphor for some serious psychological issues, another knock-off of Dante's *Inferno*. Dante says it's a huge funnel into the earth with its widest ring at the surface. Down it spirals beyond sight until the worst sinners fall into the apex: Satan's jaws. I was hoping not to get that far down.

"I can't handle this pain; I want out!" I kept thinking. *But then there was Steve...*

Again I was stuck in living Hell, and down and down I went.

Oh, well. Got pain? Flaunt it.

I drove around playing Mom's favorite song "Moon River" and the Judgment Day call from Verdi's *Requiem*. Several times hearing the Verdi, I hit my knees praying "Lord, please save my Mother's soul... Lord please save my soul that it was so hard to love my Mother. Lord, help me please. Please take away some of this pain."

I sent Sherry emails with photo essays on *Lord of the Rings*. "Here are Froda Baggins and her Grief Partner entering Mordor, surrounded by orcs," I wrote under one nasty drawing. "Just drop Precious over here into the volcano... Or is this Match.com they're entering?"

In another email with a cartoon mockup titled "Tram into Mordor," I wrote:

"Me *OW*. Here goes the trip across Mordor. 'One does not simply walk into Mordor,' says a film character. So many jokes about that on the Internet. Here's an image: 'One does not simply take the tram into Mordor.'

"Nope. One crawls. Slowly. My knees hurt. My belly hurts.

"I'd rather take the tram. I want this to be done."

Funeral for My Mom

Now for the funeral on November 27. I had that photo of Mom on my phone; I took it in July 2006 while visiting my parents in New York. I drafted a one-page program and popped in the photo, then broke into sobs of grief and terror. Her smile felt icy and disgusted as she stared at me.

I didn't have the strength for many calls. I invited Sherry and Steve to a local park and put my boom box and papers on a picnic table. There was only one person on the program: me.

Funeral Service for My Mom - November 27, 2010

O Sleep, Why Dost Thou Leave Me (Handel, *Semele*)
Moon River (Mancini, *Breakfast at Tiffany's*)
Dies Irae, Tuba Mirum (Verdi, *Requiem*)

Dies irae, dies illa/Solvet saeclum in favilla/Teste David cum Sybilla
Day of wrath/Dissolves the world in ash/Told by David and the Sibyl
Quantus tremor est futurus/Quando Judex est venturus

Cuncta stricte discussurus
What trembling there will be/When the Judge is come
All strictly to discern
Tuba mirum spargens sonum/Per sepulchra regionum
Coget omnes ante tronum.
The trumpet miraculously showers sound/Through the tombs of every land
Calling all before the Throne

Grief Recovery Letter to My Mom #2 - September 24, 2010
Burning of documents

Wenn ich mit menschen (Brahms/Corinthians I.13)
Ma lassu ci vedremo (Verdi, *Don Carlos*)

"Grief is a relational experience, and your pain has to be seen eye to eye with another person. Then we know that we are not alone, and that our tears are seen and heard." —John Townsend

———

I began, of course, with music. I must be sick of these pieces after so many weeks, I thought, but today was different.

Today I had two compassionate human beings giving me limbic eye contact. Looking into their eyes as I heard the music, I felt seen, heard, and able to feel feelings that I didn't even know were down there.

Four bars into "O Sleep," my torso burst into full-body infant sobs. I'd been playing that song and reading my letter for weeks, but now, looking into my friends' eyes, I accessed far deeper emotions than I'd ever felt before.

Halfway through I read, "Mom, I need to forgive you so that after all these years of frantic searching, I can finally drop your ring."

I took off the K-Mart ring and without thinking, hurled it as far into the bushes as I could—hard.

Immediately a strong, cold wind came up, blowing everything off the table and making it impossible to continue outside. Steve had his van so we retreated there. I was shivering; the two of them, parents to the end, bundled me up in a blanket and we huddled inside while I finished reading.

Being up close with two caring souls who continued to regard me with serious eyes was even more powerful than sitting outside.

I had somehow developed a longing to see Mom in Heaven, so the final Brahms and Verdi songs were on the theme of 1 Corinthians 13-12: "For now we see through a glass, darkly; but then we shall see face to face. Now I know only in part; but then I shall know fully, even as I am known."

Mom Grief Letter #2 - Excerpts:

Mom, I feel shocked to discover that the horrible emotions in the parental death books were the emotions I've had all my life, unexplained feelings of terror and isolation.

Mom, I feel so scared to realize that on some level I had no mother, as if the mother required by my childhood neurons had died.

Mom, I feel so depressed to be missing all the warmth and mentoring a mother would give.

Mom, I feel so sad you didn't show me how to put on makeup or stockings or nail polish or other things mothers apparently do for their daughters.

Mom, I'm so sad you wouldn't help me fit in when we moved to the new school in fifth grade, even if it meant getting colorful shoes like my friend Alison. Mom, I'm so sad you didn't take me for shoes just for that.

Mom, I feel so scared that you never gave me the biological necessity of bonding. Then I spent my life with a man who couldn't bond.

Mom, I feel so sad that I was roadkill when Dan finally flooded me with bonding chemicals and my subconscious screamed "This was missing all your life!" With bonding I wouldn't have been so vulnerable.

Mom, I feel terror reading in the parental death books that "a child is unable to sustain itself alone." Without a mother, they say, "the loss felt inside seeps out and engulfs everything. "

Mom, I often feel overwhelmed by some unidentified loss so huge, that the smallest daily loss, even a slip of paper, throws me into panic. Mom, after all these years of frantic searching I've got to finally drop your ring and breathe free.

Mom, now the Dan masks and the Bob masks are falling off, and I'm forced to look at what has always been behind their rejection.

It's you, Mom, the original Rejection Monster. It looks like the Cookie Monster is coming, but it's got a knife labeled "rejection."

What's a monster with a knife doing in my room when I'm so little?

Mom, I feel devastated that I missed the movie: I went through my whole life without ever bonding, without a real marriage, without children.

Mom, I feel so sad that God may not grant me a soulmate on this side of the grave.

Mom, I feel afraid that I may die without ever having lived.

Mom, I feel so sad that I'm vomiting up 50 years of simple human needs which went unmet. My limbic brain always used to moan that I was lonely because I didn't have a real husband.

But Mom, the more I force myself, when I feel lonely pain, to forget men and instead focus on you and Dad, the more I know in my gut: I am missing a mother, a father, and a family, and that is what really hurts.

Now I will know why I'm crying when the holidays come.

Now I will cry every day about *what really hurts*—and that is how I will heal.

Notes

1. Townsend (2010, p. 52-3).
2. Stone (2008, p.27ff; p.160).
3. Muktananda (1981, p. xi).
4. Tilak (1903).
5. Stuart (2005).
6. Brous (4-11-14).
7. Muktananda (1981, p. 2).
8. Lewis et.al. (2000, p. 85-6; p. 170-2).

11

Move the Tale

11.1 Piglet and tigress. (Sriracha Tiger Zoo) (1)

The Mom Funeral, however, didn't stop the nightmares or the little voices. They got worse, and the voices began shifting back and forth from Mom to Dad.

"What's happening to me?" I yowled, "I didn't mean to do it.

"It was all an accident!"

I couldn't even remember many events, so I began making tapes on a pocket recorder given me by the Japanese Foreign Ministry at the 2000 Okinawa Heads of State Summit (really). Talk about personality collapse.

Days later (track my anomalies) I received this chain email:

Date: December 3, 2010; **Subject**: Pork Chops or Not?

In a zoo in California, a mother tiger gave birth to cubs, but they were premature and died. The mother tiger started to decline in health. The veterinarians felt that if the tigress could surrogate another mother's cubs, perhaps she would improve. The only orphans to be found were a litter of weanling pigs. The vets wrapped the piglets in tiger skin and placed them around the mother. Would they become cubs or pork chops?

The email photos showed the tigress nurturing the piglets as her own, a picture of total bonding. Seeing a tiny piglet sleeping on the tigress' head, its fragile legs dangling by her jaw, hit me hard. (Figure 11.1) "Piglet found a nice furry mom; she's not clawing him," I told my tape. "He feels safe with her." I wanted a loving mom so badly, I began signing emails "Piglet." (1)

But I didn't have a loving anybody; I had a tiger clawing me inside.

So I also craved protection.

I had the constant urge to contact Bob, but Sherry gave me a cartoon daily diary based on Norwood. "In Recovery, we no longer call up a man to tell him why we aren't speaking to him," it says. So I didn't. But it felt like surgery without anesthesia, over and over.

"Why wouldn't a child being chased by a beast want to run to a protector?" I woke up moaning into my tape December 5.

"If cave experiences are in our genes, then a child is programmed to sleep in a safe cave with mom, protected by dad from the tigers outside. But I was made to sleep in the Tiger's Cave, to be clawed at random, with no one to protect me. That has to be the worst experience imaginable for a child.

"I don't want to sleep in the Tiger's Cave anymore!" I cried. (2)

In short, as the Mom denial broke up, gnashing like ice in front of an icebreaker, I started to feel the real terror of the Tiger's Cave. Then the layer underneath it began to move, too. I wanted protecting and bad.

Do We Need a Father?

Up came more breakthrough grief about Dad.

"Enough; I needed protecting and didn't get it," I journaled. "Now I'm in the dark trying to figure out what I missed?" We had books about a child's first phase, bonding to Mom, but almost nothing about the second phase: separation from Mom to Dad.

I went to CloudTownsend.com and ordered every audio talk with "Dad" or "Father" in the title, such as "Do We Need a Father?"

Being a bookworm turned out to be a disease. Much of what happened to me occurred because when I want to know something, I get a book. Or an audio/video lecture recording.

On December 9, after four years in California, I took my car to the DMV and paid the late fees to get California plates. At nearly 5 p.m., a clerk handed me a screwdriver and told me to bring him my Virginia tags. I unscrewed the old plates, traded them for new and was left to install them myself in the dark, in a dress and heels. Kneeling on the cold asphalt, I collapsed in tears.

"There's still no one to help me after all these years here," I sobbed. "I came here searching for the dream of the warmth missing all my life, but no place on earth can provide it—because it's "Dad software" I'm missing, so I'm carrying that cold emptiness around inside me."

On December 12, a stack of Dad audios arrived. Another earthquake.

I was overcome to hear all the "software inputs" a Dad is supposed to give a girl, which I was missing. I'd never even imagined such a relationship could exist. For real, I had no thumbs. Every item felt like a bullet shot into my empty heart:

"Do you feel empowered to go out and live your talents and dreams?" asked Dr. Cloud.

"No," I muttered.

"Do you feel empowered to be fully present in an intimate relationship?"

"No."

"Do you feel empowered to try again when you fail?"

"*No*, I just feel terrified that I'll be ostracized, so I frantically keep trying!" I began to yell.

"Do you feel empowered to stand up to people?"

"NO!"

"Do you feel empowered to be on your own, away from your support system?"

"*What* support system?" I hollered. (3)

"Fathers do very specific things which are really important," Cloud continued. First, "infant research shows that the most important thing a Dad can do for the baby is to love Mother. Mom needs to be... loved herself to have something to give this little child." I sure couldn't feel that. (4)

Second, kids around age two must decide "I want to be a person" and separate from Mom, so Dad must be the child's "alternative attachment object." But if Dad is absent, passive or hostile, the child is stuck with Mom in an "enmeshment goo... Many women who didn't have a father to attach to, are attracted to an abusive man, a sadistic man or any powerful man," he said. Me again. "They need an aggressive pull to forcibly get them away from Mom. There's a reason for every illness."

Third, a Dad must validate a child's "gender roles." Yikes, what's that? "A girl needs to be able to go to Dad and ask 'Am I attractive?' " said Cloud. "Is he warm, does he treat her in a way which encourages her to seek that kind of man, a loving, strong type who respects her?" Respect? I couldn't imagine it.

When we don't get the software, people do anything to medicate their childhood pain so "the lambs will stop screaming" in our subconscious, he concluded, referring to the horror film. (5)

I didn't know it then, but Cloud was addressing the prevalence of childhood attachment damage. He didn't give numbers here; he just taped a whole lecture series on it. (Again, see the Appendix for the science.)

Thich Nhat Hanh speaks of bringing our "unwanted guests" like pain, sorrow and anger up from our mental basement to release them. Steve used to watch me cough them up when I read letters. "That was quite a hairball you just brought up," he'd say when I cried so hard that I almost choked like a cat.

After we heard Cloud mention lambs screaming, it became "ouch, that was a whole wooly lamb you just coughed up."

Sometimes the grief hairballs felt so big that we joked about the Stanley Steemer ad: "Did you ever clean up after an alpaca?"

The Boxer

As fast as I tried to turn this into a new Dad Letter, life happened faster.

On December 19, I woke up crying. "It's been a year since Bob touched me," I told my tape, "and I just want to stay in bed and cry all day. What's the point of all this murderous work? A year later, after a whole life without love, I'm no closer to human contact or to having a home."

Suddenly I heard Simon & Garfunkel's "The Boxer" in my head. " 'I am leaving, I am leaving'," I yowled, " 'I left my home and my family' at 17 and I had nothing! All I could do was run from the pain. 'Running scared, laying low,' that was me; horrible."

I brought it up on YouTube. Then I had to lie down, it hit me so hard.

"I ran from Long Island to Yale to see the boyfriend who left me," I said. "Then I just kept walking down the Interstate in the Connecticut snow, walking nowhere until Highway Patrol picked me up and sent me home. 'Lie la Lie' captures that horrible *just running*, period. 'Lie la Lie' is what we yowl when we gotta go! It hurts so much that all I know to do is *run* and sing nonsense syllables.

"Lie la Lie!" I sang, my body slamming the bed, "Lie la Lie!

"I've been cut until I cried out, in my anger and my shame, 'I am leaving, I am leaving!' " I sang. "I don't have the software to do Life! *I can't measure up.* I have no thumbs; I don't have what it takes inside. I can't!"

I hated this part, feeling the real emotions, but after it ripped through me I got incredible relief.

Here was another healing power of music: attunement.

I'd have an experience deep within that I couldn't put into words, then go find a song which resonated the same way. The music helped me put words to the emotion and not feel alone. Someone else had felt this, expressed it, and others had resonated. I wasn't such a weirdo.

When I couldn't express an emotion I'd feel lousy, but I learned that if I found a song that resonated with the feeling, I could identify the feeling. Then I'd have to feel it. So first I felt worse. But afterward I felt a lot better.

Years later I read that attachment experts actually use a musical term for this: *attunement.* When a parent feels what an infant or child is feeling, they "attune" to the child and help it ease the feeling. I latched onto music as a kid because people didn't feel what I felt, but the music did, so I felt better. I ran around at age four singing high scales to a Disney soundtrack. (I never knew it was Donizetti until I was 30.)

So, now what I felt was this:

A year later, actually, I'm saner, stronger, and closer to recovery.

I had to stop focusing on the Bob arsonist, which put me in an endless spiral of "bad pain." I had to focus instead on my own feelings, so they got worse awhile, but this was "good pain" because then I gradually felt better.

I had to stop giving myself to people who won't look into my soul. Enough disregard. Let them sleep with their disregard and see how satisfying that is. I've got to practice honoring myself 24×7, because I've been practicing condemning myself for a long time, as the yogis say. (6)

Flight Path

Then God weighed in again.

Months ago I'd been invited to a co-worker's engagement party. Now on December 22, it just happened to be at the hilltop restaurant overlooking the lights of Orange County where Bob and I often met. Pure misery: alone again at Christmas; she's getting married, and I'm an orphan without a life, staring at the city of the man who got away.

But track my anomalies.

Leaving later, I looked up and recalled: this place is smack on the flight path to Orange County Airport with a jet flying overhead every seven minutes, maybe piloted by Bob himself. I'll do anything to get this man out of my heart, I decided. I'm going to feel into my Bob garbage until I dig it out of me.

On December 23, I returned with my mp3 player full of Bob and Dad music. To a half-dozen songs from *Carousel* and "O Sleep," I added "Impossible Dream." Driving away from Bob's place I often sang that in tears, bewildered as to why he wouldn't love me, why my California Dream was evaporating.

Now I stood singing it to myself in the cold parking lot as holiday revelers rushed inside. I saw the planes stacked up to land and choked. Again I felt the powerful physical longing for Bob and–Oh, Now I Get It–the longing to be lifted up with great power by one of those airplanes.

Suddenly I was back on the jetty in New York at 14, watching the planes take off from JFK and soar out to sea.

Finally: to be lifted up into a Dad's arms and protected from the Tiger's Cave.

To be lifted out of the sea of pain which had engulfed me since the onset of memory, since the Disney wolf at my bedroom door, pain so immense that the only escape was to run to someone with power, "any powerful man," precisely as Cloud said.

That's what Bob has always been about: my dreams on that jetty that an airplane would lift me forcefully out of the pain. That's why I flew away to Japan and flew away to California. I'd fly anywhere to escape that pain.

Listening to the music now and watching the planes roar overhead, grief poured out of me. The more I felt the childhood pain, the less I felt about Bob.

Quite a breakthrough. Driving home I began to feel really good.

Then I got home and opened my mail. There was a Christmas card from Bob. After no contact in months.

Next evening, on Christmas Eve, Bob emailed to announce that he'd just had a biopsy for colon cancer and did not have long to live. Just like that; bang, bang, bang: the airplanes, the card, and the cancer.

Some Christmas gift.

"Oh, no, Bob's going to die without ever really connecting with me!" I cried. Science went out the window.

I fell into in a tailspin of weeping for 72 hours, mostly on my knees by my bed. "What a way to get rid of a man," I wailed. By Christmas night I was reduced to begging God to save Bob, singing "Kyrie Eleison, Christe Eleison" (Lord have mercy, Christ have mercy) from Beethoven's *Mass in C* all night.

On December 27 at 2 a.m., I began sending chain prayer emails titled "Please pray for cancer patient" to five dozen women from my support groups, who probably forwarded them to hundreds of people around the country.

"S T O P!" my Big Thinking Brain told my Obviously Stupid Heart.

"This was always going to happen. His heart was hard, hard, before you ever met him. There never was anything you could do. Look to creating your own emotional object constancy. 'Pain is the thing' to get you to drop what you're holding.' Drop him."

I re-read the yogic tale of the man who sat under a wish-fulfillment tree and could wish for anything; he got a beautiful wife, a mansion, luxurious food, and more. But one night he became fearful and imagined demons, so the tree manifested a demon before him. "He's going to eat me!" the man cried. So the demon ate him.

"We are in a similar situation," one swami writes; our minds concoct most of our suffering from nothing. (7)

"Forget Bob and go download good software," I journaled. "*Om Namah Shivaya*. Honor your Self and re-honor your Self. Download unconditional Self respect, then repeat. Go where you are valued. Get with the yogis and safe people, and be repeatedly honored until you can feel it."

"Stop Crying!"

The war between Frontal my thinking brain and Limbus my emotional brain consumed that whole Christmas vacation.

Out driving December 28, from nowhere a wave of sobbing decked me to where I had to pull over. I made it to Macy's parking lot on El Toro Road, and suddenly a little voice piped up in my chest, unstoppable:

"Daddy I'll never be bad again," it cried loudly. "Daddy I hurt because I don't understand why you think I'm bad!" I'm sitting bewildered in front of Macy's unable to drive, and this yowling from a strange planet is like another person's tiny voice, maybe five years old, and it's pouring out of my thorax.

"Daddy I'm crying because I'm lonely and my heart hurts. Daddy please don't tell me I'm bad because I'm crying, Daddy please don't tell me I'm bad because I'm crying... Daddy it hurts too much this pain in my chest. Daddy please help me, I don't understand what's happening or why but it just hurts too much this pain in my chest and I can't take it.

"Please Daddy, please. Daddy please make it stop.

"Daddy I don't want to sleep in the Tiger's Cave anymore, I don't understand what I did wrong or why this hurts so much but it really hurts a lot and it only feels better when I cry. So I can't help it, I just cry, my body just does that..."

What is this and why am I crying? I don't even know what it's about. I'd sung the lead in Verdi's *Joan of Arc* around 1996, but hearing voices going on like this in my own chest was a stretch.

Wait. Why couldn't I cry when my Dad died?

Because Dad always told me: "Stop crying!"

I couldn't cry because Dad didn't want me to cry. If I cried, Dad wouldn't love me. I might get the plastic slipcovers wet, a bad thing in the land of appearances. Dr. Rita, what an idiot! Saying that if Dad behaved like a stranger, naturally I had no feeling when he died. Poppycock. I had oceans of feelings, all deeply repressed–all pivoting around crying.

A child's brain is in the driver's seat and she's afraid to cry, and she's still crying to Dad about it.

That's why when Sherry tells me it's OK to cry or Steve sends me a teddy bear cartoon, it blows me away. It's OK with *them* if I cry. They even give me a bear to hold.

And I just wanted to sit in the car and cry for about a year. It started to feel really good. Sherry says Parenting 101 is that if a baby cries, it's your job to help it. Steve says that even with computers, if we input bad software the system sends back a cry for help and the engineers must respond.

"Thank you for letting me share," we say at meetings when we're done speaking. Well, thank you for sending your bear. Then I'm exhausted and suddenly the channel to that young place closes up.

Little voice? What voice? Gone like a Long Island clam scurrying under the sand. Did you see a clam? I don't see a clam, what clam?

I felt much better but wiped out, unable to drive. I fell asleep in the car for an hour. (I made a tape, or I'd have forgotten it all.)

Which Donkey?

Later that afternoon, to write a new Dad letter, I reviewed my emails to Bob from the last two years and was sickend by the reams of insanity. I poured out my gut but "he didn't even notice I exist." Again.

11.2 Move it where it belongs. (Keistutis/OpenClipart)

Then came an Aha Moment which saved my life.

Pain this insane, all those bizarre emails, triggers big enough to evoke mortal panic? Idiotic; Bob doesn't even know I exist.

No one I met only two years ago could possibly have caused pain this severe.

My Dad died in 2008 and I couldn't cry—but five days later I was crying buckets over a stranger, Dan? And I'll still doing it with Bob?

Feelings this intense have got to be about something *my Dad* did or didn't do. Not about a stranger.

The sorrow that it's a year since Bob held me? That's about Dad. The panic when Bob says he's dying? That's about Dad. "Bob's going to die without ever really connecting with me?" Dad died without ever really connecting with me!

From nowhere came the idea:

What if I move the tail from the Bob Donkey, to the Dad Donkey (sort of like the kids' game)?

What if I take the painful emotions I feel about Bob, pull them off Bob, and pin them on Dad? What if I move the whole story, "Move the Tale?"

How do I feel then?

I went back to Bob, the craving for airplanes to yank me out of the pain, the wail for protection from the Tiger's Cave. Then I pulled all those emotions off Bob and pinned them onto Dad.

When I used Norwood to "run it backward," I was forcing myself to ignore my feelings about Bob and focus instead on Dad. But when I ignored my feelings, I was partly repressing them with head talk. I was moving my head when I needed to move my ass, er, donkey.

Now I discovered that it's a lot more effective to feel my worst feelings about Bob, to get the emotions unblocked–and then move those onto Dad and feel whatever that brings up.

Up came torrents of Dad grief that I never knew existed.

Flood gates opened.

Suddenly I was looking at photos of my Dad and sobbing for him for the first time in the two years since his death.

Suddenly I could feel what I couldn't feel in 2008, when my inability to cry for Dad drove me into this grief ballpark in the first place.

"Now I've really got a letter," I thought.

From Christmas to New Year's, I wrote seven different drafts for a new Dad Letter, working furiously. I didn't go out; I was glued to the computer and the tissue box. It felt like grieving every hurt I ever took at every miserable Christmas in my life.

I emptied my folder of Bob's cards and letters, and found the "Compensations of Calamity" bookmark he gave me in 2008. "It's all got to come out," I wrote. Whatever feelings come up to make me cry for Bob, grab them and pin them on Dad.

"The worst thing that could happen to me would be if Bob proposed," I told friends. "Once we were married he would start to disappear, just as he always has. Just like Larry did. Larry pursued me for years, but once I married him, he disappeared.

"I've already given one lifetime to that! Another Larry Life? No way. Barf!"

On December 29, 30, and 31, I read my latest Dad draft to Sherry and then to Steve, three times. Samples:

Dad "Move the Tale" Letter - Excerpts

Dad, I felt so bad to hear that "the most important thing a father does is to show up."

Dad, what did we do that was so bad that you never came home?

Dad, we were stuck in the Tiger's Cave and it hurt; why didn't you get us out?

Dad, I feel so sad about the wild longing I felt for Bob when he talked about how much he loves his daughters and kept repeating "Daddy loves you."

Dad, I feel such a huge loss now that it hits me: I've never heard a man talk like that before, that's why it felt so explosive.

Dad, I feel so angry to learn now that I had a physical need as a kid to hear that from my Dad.

Dad, I feel so painful that my baby brain cried out from nowhere in Macy's parking lot, "Daddy please don't tell me I'm bad because I'm crying; Daddy it hurts too much, this pain in my chest..."

Dad, I feel so sad and terrified about the panic I felt that Bob might die, and the realization that this panic was really about how you died without connecting with me.

Dad, I feel so awful to realize that I was afraid to cry when you died, because I was afraid you'd be angry if I cried.

Fourteen days after his Christmas Eve hit and run, Bob called to say that his biopsy was benign, just a scare.

Ghost Father Wants Me Dead

I've had headaches, jaw pain, back pain, leg and foot pain all my life, cramps that made it hard to walk as a kid. My mother and her mother said it wasn't important, just hereditary; they had it, too. In my forties I developed migraines so fierce that I'd wake up mornings vomiting on an empty stomach.

But on Sunday January 2, I had the worst migraine and back pain ever.

There's no end to this hole in my heart, I thought. "Don't want to sleep in the Tiger's Cave?" I'm stuck there and no one's coming to get me out.

In fact, once I got past the denial and crud by "moving the tale" from Bob to Dad, I went into free fall with no bottom.

Why? Because there was no bottom. The "nothing there" was terrifying. No wonder I kept saying the lambs in my sub-basement were screaming.

That night I had a nightmare which woke me at 3 a.m. "Ghost Father wants me dead; he wants me off the planet," I cried to my tape. I didn't know if that meant Dad or even God. Schubert's fearsome song to Goethe's poem "The Elf King" was playing in my head.

A father rides at night with his child; the boy sees the Elf King behind every tree. The father says it's just the fog, but the boy hears threatening voices and his fear grows. The piano pounds out the spooky theme made famous a century later by silent movies. Finally the boy hears the Elf King threaten to snatch him by force, and dies.

"Father wants me dead" was the message my childhood brain got when Dad didn't accept my physical need to cry. To the baby, it felt like he wanted to shut me up. However untrue that was, my sick brain feels it still.

"Daddy there's a pain in my chest. Daddy why don't you come home?"

"In the absence of relationship we experience condemnation? You said it," I journaled. "So I tolerated more absence which Bob delivered. Now it feels like Dad's condemning me and God wants me dead."

Next day Monday the physical pain was so bad that I ran to see my chiropractor, told him the dream, and read him the poem.

Then I asked Dr. F. to hold my hand and tell me that God did not want me dead.

This was a man who had tackled his own demons over a decade of tough therapy and lived to report it. We'd been together sharing our stories for over a year, and he never shrank from my worst discoveries.

Now he took my hand and repeated exactly as requested, "No, God does not want you to die. And I don't want you to die, either! You need a real live person to tell you that in person.

"In fact," he said, "God wants to put his arms around you and hold you."

He also used to fall into these scary places when he pushed himself too hard, he reported.

"It's called 'overload' and it's common," he said. "That's why we have therapists: when we go this deep into the pain, we need supervision. Past a certain point, feeling the pain can damage the body."

" 'Don't overload the washer,' they say at CoDA," I groaned. "Your undies may come out smelling like your socks."

"Exactly like a washer," he said. "When I did feel overloaded, I'd go to a safe room, even a closet, and imagine God's arms coming around me and holding me, just like I want you to imagine now." He exuded compassion and it felt like confidence, so I imagined God's arms around me and it worked. Then he gave me the back adjustment of a lifetime.

I felt enormous relief. He had definitively demonstrated the benefit of sitting with an incarnate being "with skin on," as they say of Jesus.

Dr. F. told me months later that I looked so bad, he almost called 911.

If I'd stuck to "do-it-yourself," toughed it out myself, and not gone to him? I'd probably be dead.

Don't try this alone.

"Ribbett, ribbett... I overloaded the washer," I emailed Steve and Sherry. "Please don't let me do three grief sessions in a row again."

Notes

1. The photo is real (this tigress was raised by a pig). But the email has been exposed as a fraud by BigCatRescue.org. The photo is in fact from a zoo in Thailand that fattens tigers on pigs' milk, then sells the tigers' body parts illegally, they report.
2. Burke Harris (2014). Years later this was described by pediatrician Nadine Burke Harris. "Imagine you're walking and you see a bear," she said. "Your hypothalamus signals, 'Release stress hormones!' and you're ready to fight or run. That is wonderful in a forest with a bear. But the problem is when the bear comes home every night."
3. Cloud (2003).
4. Cloud (2000).
5. Demme (1991). "Well, Clarice, have the lambs stopped screaming?"
6. Muktananda (1981).
7. Muktananda (1981).

Attachment Disorder

12.1 Dropped at school. (Kathy Brous)

Only support from God, Steve, Sherry, and the yogis got me through what came next. There are no accidents, only more anomalies. At my CoDA meeting January 19, I was struck to hear Vicki sharing about her childhood. She sounded just like me.

"What does your therapist call it, when we're missing all this software from infancy?" I asked.

"Attachment disorder!" she whispered, as though the words were an explosive to be handled with gloves.

I'd read about the sick baby monkey with no attachment, but this was the first I'd heard of a diagnosis that a sick baby human could maybe take to a doctor.

In early 2011, all Google had on "attachment disorder" were a few adoption websites. On January 21, I dove into online adoption case studies and got another "motherless" shock. I look like a xerox of my parents, yet the scary feelings described by adopted kids were feelings I'd had all my life.

Attachment disorder is "damage by being abused or physically or emotionally separated from the primary caregiver during the first three years of life," said one website. Horrible, but that sure felt like me. Such people "have difficulty forming lasting relationships." Me again, 3,000 miles from nowhere with no relationships.

The list of what causes attachment disorder hit me hard. Seven of ten items described me:

- Unwanted pregnancy. (Sure, but Whu Nu it mattered?)
- Pre-birth exposure to trauma, drugs or alcohol. (All that cortisol in the womb.)
- Abuse (physical, emotional, sexual). (Emotional what?)
- Neglect (not answering baby's cries for help). (Isn't that how parents are?)
- Illness/death of mother, illness/hospitalization of baby. (Mom's & my infection, my incubation.)
- Moms with chronic depression. (What about chronic anxiety/anger?)
- Caring for baby on a timed schedule. (Isn't that how parents are?) (1)

I couldn't tell attachment disorder from a take out-order, but again I felt it: I'm sicker than I ever imagined.

On January 24, I sat up at 3 a.m. with chest pains. "This is a condemnation nightmare," I told my tape. I dreamed a flight attendant on a space ship was about to give me an injection to knock me out, because something was wrong and they wanted to shut me up. I recalled *Invaders from Mars*, a TV movie which gave me nightmares for years as a kid, in which a boy sees a spaceship land, but the adults won't believe him. They go investigate and return with dead eyes, repeating mechanically that everything's fine, it's just his imagination—because they got an injection in that spaceship and they're Martian robots now.

"I've been getting these condemnation eyeballs, hard-hearted stares, all my life," I said. "People acting like Martians, saying 'we're fine; what's the matter with *you?*' But they weren't fine; the Martians were lying. They looked at me as though I were some piece of equipment that didn't work. Like the Martians stared right past the kid as though he were furniture."

Where the Lambs Scream

Nightmares began waking me every night. "The younger back you go, the more it hurts," I journaled. "The damage occurred before I ever had a mind. Plus it was really painful, so it's been shoved down forever. This will make for nightmares, because that's all we had back then."

"Gosh, my kids didn't have so many horrifying or repeating nightmares," said Steve. "*Peter and the Wolf*, *Invaders from Mars*, Hole in Your Heart, Cookie Monster! That's not normal. This is too much for you!

"I got a real startle last week," he added. "Looking at you, I saw the eyes of a frightened little girl."

I was shocked, too, at the lambs screaming in my basement. A psychological whack-a-mole was underway within, odd events popping up everywhere. On January 25, I decided to write a "Mom Attachment Letter" about my very earliest memories. I was not, however, going back to that incubator.

My earliest actual memory was being left alone in a back room to cry, after I was sent home. There I was raised by a stuffed black cat Dad got at Macy's New York, whom I dubbed "Pinky." Asked why later as a kid, I said, "What else would you call a black cat?" (OK, her nose was pink.) In my 30s, I got a live tiger-striped tomcat, named him Tom (what else), and found a black female so I could name her Pinky.

Next I remembered the day my infant sister was brought home from the hospital when I was four and a half. I've always had a vivid image of running from a friend's home up the street to the front door of our house, to find Mom inside the screen holding a baby. I put out my arms and said, "Gimme."

They gave me the baby and I never put her down, for about eight years. It was a lot better than holding a stuffed cat. My sister actually saw me; I was important to her! Whu Nu people could look at me with such love? I still dream about it.

Oh, look: this huge milestone revolved around attachment.

"I want to be important to someone," I told my tape. "I was important to Linda. She couldn't wait to be with me. 'Hooray, you're here–let's hug!' It was spontaneous, like kittens and puppies just curl up together."

On February 8, a book arrived from Amazon, listing procedures to heal attachment damage in adopted babies:

- Carry the baby in a snugli or fabric carrier on the front, facing mom, four to six hours daily.
- Hold and rock infant with loving eye contact, smiles, singing or reading in joyful baby talk each day.
- Baby sleeps with/near parents at night.
- No baby carrier. Baby is carried in loving arms.
- Baby must not be left to cry alone for longer than three minutes.
- Respond to baby's attempts to get your love and attention with joy! (2)

Facing Mom? Loving eye contact? Sleep with parents? Not left to cry? What planet is this?

I'd never heard of any of that and never dared enter my parents' room at night. "I never had that!" my emotional brain yowled loudly, "I've always wanted that!"

"It's too late," my thinking brain moaned back. "This had to be dealt with in infancy. I'm toast."

Human Contact

Now what?

I was too grief-crazed for real research in 2011; I was just trying to avoid suicide.

"Hold with loving eye contact" said the instructions, so starting February 11, I read up on the use of hugs for attachment disorder and found case studies that said it works. One mom wrote that her adopted son cried for hours as she hugged him daily. "I continued to tell him that I was his forever mommy and I would never leave," she said. "Afterward our son was a completely different child. He was at peace." (3)

I was dying to hear someone say, "I'm your Forever Mommy," Forever Daddy, Forever Whomever, I didn't care.

"I've got a letter," I thought desperately.

On February 13, Steve and I debated whether to add hugs, plain old human contact, to our grief letter tool kit. Eye contact is "limbic resonance" and we'd experienced healing when people watched us read. Touch, however, is forbidden by most groups and therapists.

"If you recall Newport," said Engineer Steve suddenly, "you had to use it with me."

In spring 2010, near the second anniversary of his wife's death in 2008, Steve and I went sailing in Newport. He wanted to strew flowers into the ocean where her ashes were interred. We arrived early and sat by the dock so Steve could read his grief letter. Then he rose and dropped a few blossoms into the water.

Steve sat down, and suddenly began to weep, all six feet geek of him in glasses. He was mortified. "This is terrible," he said, "I've never cried in front of anyone in my life, not to mention a woman."

"Tears are a gift from God," I repeated reflexively after Sherry. Then another reflex kicked in and with no thought whatsoever I put my arms around him and hugged.

Steve's tears grew and so did his distress. "I can't cry in front of a woman," he repeated. I didn't think; I was on autopilot. I just hugged until he could feel that I was committed to hold on, because tears are good. He resisted, then finally relaxed and wept quite awhile. I let go. He rested and felt much better. We were both amazed at the healing it brought him.

Two months later, at my July 2010 Larry Funeral, my friends held me up—physically.

"We've got a track record," said Steve. "Didn't your parents ever hug you?"

"No," I said, "or I wouldn't feel such a huge need now." Then I remembered my sister. "But Linda hugged me!" I said. "That's why I tear up at the mention of her name. I started hugging her the day she was born and never stopped. Then she had kids and I didn't."

I emailed friends, proposing to read letters with two new additions: eye contact and hugging. "The partner maintains eye contact until the griever is able to achieve eye contact," I wrote. "This may take time. I never got that; it's hard."

People: the Magic Band-aid

Intrepid Nurse Sherry gave it a whirl; we started out hugging while I read my Mom Attachment Letter. Then we dissolved in giggles as we realized one can't hug, make eye contact, and hold a letter, unless you're a three-armed Martian.

Eye contact is key, we knew, so we settled on a "Roman handshake," clasping each other at the wrist, allowing eye contact and leaving the other hand free to hold a letter. On February 16, I attempted to hold her arm and her gaze as I read:

> Mom, I feel terrified to feel what it was like to be an infant crying and screaming for hours, days, months, years, but nobody ever came... I'm scared because my vulnerable layers are really damaged down here.
>
> Mom, I hate going home alone; that's why I fall asleep in my car. Because there's a lot of pain, the all-consuming pain of being enmeshed in barbed wire in the Tiger's Cave.
>
> Mom, I'm frightened of all the hard-hearted Martian eyeballs in the world. I feel like I was up against a stone wall of people who refused to respond to me no matter what, from birth.
>
> Mom, I'm so frightened of the lambs screaming in my emotional basement.

Reading like this was very difficult—in just the way it needed to be. At first I was too terrified to maintain eye contact with Sherry holding my wrist. I'd glance at her, then look down repeating, "I'm mortified! I'm so embarrassed, I could die."

Yet the real gut-wrench came from the new experience: to have someone hear me confess such horrors, and hold on to me so I know they care anyway.

You're not fleeing in disgust? You're still holding on?

Now I have to actually feel what I've written.

On February 20, I read it to Sherry at my place. It was really intimate.

Holding Sherry's wrist and looking at her while I read those awful words, my torso went into involuntary full-body sobbing spasms centered in the gut.

I hung on for dear life, shaking my chair like a great fish thrashing at the end of a line.

"This is the 'I Hate This Part' part," I wailed. "*I hate this part!*"

The pain went through the roof until I was gasping for air, then it subsided.

"Your Mom was finite," she said after I finished, "but the One who created you is Infinite. *He* wants you here, and He will hold you up until you heal from this. We're here for you now; your tears are finite."

"You see me, you see my soul, and you don't hate me?" I exclaimed.

"No!" she smiled, "I love you!" It was beyond intense.

I couldn't speak awhile, then gradually felt a deep sense of relief. Human contact was a game-changer.

"I feel so much better. How can this be?

"People, the magic band-aid!" I exclaimed involuntarily.

That Scream Again

On March 4, an adoption website about the "primal wound" pushed my worst button; I'd already been floored by primal screams.

"A child separated from its mother at the beginning of life… experiences what I call the primal wound," writes Dr. Nancy Verrier, "not only as a loss of the mother, but as a loss of the Self, that core-being of oneself which is the center of goodness and wholeness… a physical sense of bodily incompleteness, a hurt from something missing." (4)

Bingo: I'd had that hole in my heart, that "hurt from something missing," all my life. I could feel my terror at age five watching the TV film of the hole in the baby's heart.

Trauma occurs when "action is of no avail," so "the human system of self-defense becomes overwhelmed and disorganized," she notes (5). "The baby who cannot get his mother back, despite his cries…. goes into shock" in 45 minutes. (6)

"*Babies in incubators experience the same helplessness,* where neither resistance nor escape is possible… At the basis of this is a profound, fully-justified fear an infant instinctively feels, that if left alone, it will die." (5, 6) "Babies scream at this denial of the basic human need to be held," and were often drugged with phenobarbital to quiet them, she adds. (7)

"What guilt or shame; I go straight to panic!" as I told Dr. Rita. Now we learn why. Was I drugged? Oh, no...

Then came the science to prove that "parts of my brain are dark."

Recent studies show that attachment experiences create the way our brain neurons connect, or don't, writes Verrier, citing a Dr. Dan Siegel. "Repeated experiences of terror... can be ingrained within the circuits of the brain," he reports. (8) "Your brain synapses connected according to your perception of your environment which seemed unsafe, unfamiliar, and in need of constant vigilance," which "filled you with anxiety," says Verrier. (9)

This causes emotional pain so deep, it feels "cellular," she adds. (10)

"I've got trauma at the cellular level," I told my tape, "cortisol poisoning since the sperm hit the egg. My earliest cell divisions were fried. It was baked into my Reptile survival brain stem to fire off endless anxiety."

Vicki confirmed it. She'd seen a video in which doctors said that a happy pregnant mother produces a sea of the "cuddle chemical" oxytocin in the womb to nurture the fetus. Then they showed a film of a fetus carried by a mother who smoked. "You could see the baby recoil from the nicotine," Vicki said. "It was contracting inside the uterus against attack. If the mother is stressed or it's an unwanted pregnancy, the fetus is flooded with cortisol toxins just as damaging, they said." So, Dan's oxytocin was addictive.

Next came something dreadful:

When no adult provides limbic regulation, the child's unregulated emotional turmoil doesn't just stop. These emotions may still be operating in the adult decades later, "as formatively today as they were when he was an infant," Verrier quotes a Dr. Allan Schore to say. The infant's un-comforted emotions are literally pushed down, where they continue to "build and seethe" as Kevin McCauley put it, deep in the pre-memory circuits of the brain. (11)

The newborn screaming on the plane... *That was still down inside of me.*

"As much as 80% of the emotional juice" of most adult conflicts is actually "leakage... of stored feelings from childhood" that we later transfer onto other adults, she adds. With childhood trauma, we project our traumatic baby feelings onto adult partners. This "transference" creates relationship disasters. (12)

Tsunami

I felt a stab of fear at such an unimaginable wound.

I *am* a freak. I *don't* belong to be.

My cure was based on stumbling blind through trial and error in a way that almost killed me.

I was playing with explosives blindfolded.

Human contact is a powerful delivery system for emotional impact. "Touch plus eye contact creates earthquakes in my soul," I wrote. Indeed it does.

But today my jaw drops at how I misused it, experimenting on myself like Froggy the lab frog. I was propelling myself deeper and deeper into the infant hole in my heart.

Then I added the "cellular pain" bombshell to my Mom Letter and read it to Sherry March 9. It was too much.

Next day I was physically ill with a blinding migraine.

That night March 10, I had nightmares of being drowned in a tsunami of cortisol, huge waves the size of a house mowing me down.

Since the sperm hit the egg I'd been crap, I dreamed, so how could I "get under" pain at the cellular level? We were debriding down into my psyche like doctors debride dead skin off a burn, to get below my damaged mental tissue to healthy tissue that could heal. But my tissues were damaged *from the first cell divisions*! No matter how far back I go, I'll only find more damage. Panic struck.

"How do I get out of something with no start?" I woke up repeating at 1 a.m. No matter how far back I go, there's always more pain.

As I drove to work at 7 a.m. on March 11, Steve called to talk about the disastrous tsunami in Japan.

The night of March 10 in California was March 11 in Japan.

I was asleep in Dana Point dreaming that I was drowning in a tsunami, just as the 2011 Tohoku Tsunami hit Japan around 11 p.m. California time on March 10. I lived in Japan for years, traveled there many times, and I love the Japanese people. Did I somehow feel their pain?

Even I couldn't imagine anything this crazy.

At work, I couldn't take my eyes off the news.

In a world where God allows over 15,000 innocent hard-working people to die for no reason, why shouldn't He allow my pain to go back infinitely to where healing is impossible?

To say I had a crisis of faith is a massive understatement. I thought I was finished.

Dropped at School

On March 15, I read past midnight, then had to face bed. I put on a Henry Cloud CD just to hear his voice. He was describing a client whose wife got upset when the client went bowling once a month. "She's not old enough to be dropped at school," Cloud joked. (13)

Suddenly it wasn't funny. "She's not old enough to be dropped at school," I repeated.

Around and around it began to spin in my head: "Not old enough to be dropped off at school..."

In the middle of washing my face, I crumpled to the bedroom floor in spasms. There was nothing cognitive about it—my body reacted to Cloud's statement and my legs went out from under me.

"Actually not," I thought.

"She's not old enough to be dropped off at school. I didn't have the confidence to be dropped off. I was told to perform and bring in the grades, so I did. I had to; I was afraid they wouldn't let me come home otherwise. And I wasn't dropped off; I had to walk there myself."

I sat on the bedroom carpet bawling. I *hate* not having enough EOC inside to be dropped off at school. How will I get to work?

Fifteen minutes later I rose to brush my teeth, then dove instead for the two-foot plush stuffed dog pillow on my bed. I was terrified. I couldn't even be alone long enough to brush; I had to hold onto the stuffed animal for dear life.

Dog under arm, I dragged myself from bed to sink, grabbed my toothbrush, wet it—and slid to the floor again.

I lay in a heap sobbing in a fetal position for a long time, clutching the stuffed dog and my soggy toothbrush. I stared at the toothbrush as though it were an alien object, remotely dangerous. (Figure 12.1)

Rising an hour later, I still couldn't brush without clutching the dog. "Not old enough to be dropped off? She can't even brush her teeth alone," I muttered. "I hate not having enough EOC to brush without a stuffed animal."

"Broke through a layer of rocks on my heart to a qualitatively different place," I told my tape. "I'm not drilling through hard rock layers of the Grand Canyon anymore. I've fallen through the Grand Canyon into rushing water; down here it's like a river torrent. Now we're going down the Colorado River through the rapids without a paddle.

"It's a qualitative break into an extremely vulnerable layer, a really hard place to reach very far back in time. I'm really frightened because this is where I don't know whether there is any floor, any point at which the hole under my feet ends.

"Down here is where my Reptile brain stem got flooded with cortisol acid from scratch. This is where my vulnerable layers are really damaged, so when I broke through into this space, I felt 100% un-safe."

On March 18, I fell asleep in my car and had a nightmare so vivid that I made a tape titled "The dream that was not a dream."

"Want to confirm with a specialist, but this must be an actual preconscious memory," I said. "I was very little and had no words, everything was pre-verbal, and it just hurt. I was crying and crying but no one came, and holding the stuffed animal to my chest, but it couldn't relieve the chest pain. Oh; it's the same pain I get when I think about an arsonist like Bob: 'I don't belong. I need to be held, but they don't notice I exist. No matter what I do, it's futile; I'm helpless and there is no love or anything else coming in.'

"Then it starts to feel as if there's no oxygen coming in, and I feel like I'll die if I just keep lying here crying alone, but I'm helpless to do anything else.

"Wanted to vomit; wanted to crawl out of my skin. I can't run or crawl away from it anymore; it's in my gut.

" 'Frightened little girl,' he says. This is what I actually lived for years as an infant."

Somewhere I had read about regression, the devolution of the mind back through childhood developmental stages.

Surrender

By March 21 the pain was so bad, I finally realized that "do-it-yourself" psychology can kill.

Don't try this alone.

So I did the unimaginable: I went back to therapy.

Instantly came my third therapy failure. I had Kaiser Permanente insurance so I went to their mental health office. I told the doctor that I had infant attachment trauma causing mental and physical pain. "I've never heard of that," she said. "Infant stress before the onset of thought can't create trauma. I only need to know: are you having a behavioral health crisis, or are you performing at work?"

"I perform spectacularly at work," I replied, "but I'm in even more spectacular emotional pain."

"If you're OK at work it can't be that bad," she said. "I'll refer you to a Cognitive Behavioral Therapy (CBT) group." She was reading from a script and not in the room with me emotionally. She gave me a document on CBT and left. I was to be re-trained in a behavioral lab like a rat, to ensure the widget performs at work. Who considers a widget's emotional well-being?

Her document followed another "one size fits all" approach. "If you stop negative thoughts, you may be more able to handle life's challenges," it said. "Think positive." Been there, done that in 2009; it shoved me into the Marianas Trench.

I'll always be grateful to my friend Lucy from CoDA, who spent 25 years healing her own childhood trauma. From experience, Lucy urged me to find a therapist who'd *personally suffered* childhood trauma, and had done serious therapy themselves to feel it, walk through it and heal it.

"This is the only way to be sure a therapist can really understand us," she said. "With trauma it *is* different and we *do* need an expert." Now I could see what I did wrong in 2008, and how to go forward:

1. Don't choose a therapist without researching what ails you.
2. Only accept an expert in your type of damage.
3. Don't skimp on cost. "Your money or your life!"
4. Interview as though you planned to marry them; it's a serious long-term relationship.

On March 22, I began emails and calls to two dozen experts, including the offices of John Townsend, Henry Cloud, Thomas Lewis, Nancy Verrier, and more, asking for referrals with expertise in infant trauma. I spoke to three mental health institutes and counselors at four local churches. I interviewed all over Orange County. I interviewed with Vicki's therapist, Vicki's therapist's husband (also a therapist) and therapists referred by other friends' therapists.

Frontal, my Big Thinking Brain, was in a race for time against the collapse of Limbus, my Little Emotional Brain.

I had to warn friends so on March 25, I filed a sort of accident report by email:

Dear Marla,

I'm not sure we should meet for a few weeks.

I started out trying to heal my family "'root issues," so I wrote letters to my Mom, Dad, and ex, the letters I've read to you for two years. It now seems that this "regressed" me back to before I met my ex at age 19.

But oddly there was still a lot of pain left. I researched and found that I never had bonding to Mom or Dad. I discovered that I had no "emotional object constancy," no ability to be "dropped off at school" and feel OK alone. So I did another round of letters, reading quotes about bonding.

I was breaking the denial, and allowing the pain of all this to come up into consciousness. That's what regression is, I think. Now I was regressing myself back to between ages five to ten.

Then I stumbled on books which took me even further back, books about kids whose parent dies. They explained why I've always felt a "hole under my feet" with no grounding.

It was all an accident. I didn't mean to do any of this. But some people would call it a "God thing."

Next I got books on attachment disorder: what happens to a baby taken from the mother at birth and put in an incubator or orphanage so it never receives parenting software? This unfortunately was pay dirt. The case studies hit me like a ton of bricks. These were the feelings I had all my life which never were explained.

I was more or less regressing myself back to infancy. The further back I went, the more pain turned up. The more layers of denial I removed, the more I found. It was very weird. The pain now can be pretty severe and I don't want to impose it on anyone who's not equipped.

The Bus Driver

On March 28, I crawled up the steps to the office of yet a fourth therapist, grasping that summary and a half-dozen grief letters.

Dr. R. had 25 years' hands-on experience, featuring decades of collaboration with Cloud and Townsend, plus work on his own childhood trauma. He's a Christian therapist, but by now I'd have hired Moses, Buddha or a Kashmiri guru if he were a trauma expert and could relate to me.

I presented the goods in my email to Marla. Then I told him I'd been hearing "little voices" since July 2008 when I heard myself in grade school cowering in the back seat, and read him parts of my Mom and Dad letters.

"Do you think I've just accidentally regressed myself back to infancy?" I asked.

"Yes," Dr. R. nodding solemnly, leaning forward, eyes wide.

"Aren't you scared?"

You said it, brother, but not nearly as scared as I was gonna be.

"I can't do this anymore," I replied. "I've been driving this process too long. I want to give up the wheel and let someone else drive."

"It's too scary in there, you can't go there alone," he replied confidently.

"I'm an experienced cross country bus driver. I'll drive."

Thus I hired my current therapist. You could hear Carrie Underwood singing about the wheel.

God loves me after all. Dr. R. was definitely the man for the job.

On April 11, at our first session, I read him my Mom Attachment Letter and told him about my "dream that was not a dream" in which I was very little, crying to where it seemed there were no oxygen coming in.

"Probably right," he said. "It was really horrible as an infant to be left alone, and that probably is *an actual memory you're feeling, not a dream*. This is really good!"

"No, this is awful!" I almost yelled, it hurt so bad.

"It hurts a lot," he said gently, "but it's a good development if you can *just let the feelings come up*. Feelings can't kill you. It only *feels* like they're going to kill you.

"Some feelings are OK to feel with friends. You got great healing by reading to friends about those," he said. "Bigger feelings may be too much to feel, except in here with me, under supervision."

"Some stuff I've felt, I simply can't tolerate. I get physically ill," I objected.

"Sure," he said. "You got sick after your last letter because it artificially brought up feelings which are too horrible to feel right now, period. Not even with me. The pain was too big, so your circuit breaker went off.

"When our circuit breaker trips, the pain goes into the body. So when you feel physically ill, we back off.

"Stop the letters, stop trying to provoke these scary feelings. You're rubbing your nose in your losses, which are truly huge. Stop trying to control this. Stop!" he said. Where have we heard that before?

"What am I supposed to take to people if I don't have a letter?" I objected.

"Just live life, and whatever emotions come up, take those to people," he said. "You're so far back down into childhood that plenty of childhood emotions will come up if you let them. You don't need to provoke it."

"No one wants to hear my raw emotions; they're terrifying," I wailed. "That's why I write letters."

"No letters; just bring the raw emotions to me," he insisted.

"Actually your situation is good. You've done all this work to crack your denial. We almost never see anyone come to therapy having done that. Most of our tool kit is methods to help people crack their denial, over five or ten years. You did it in two. That's much too fast; it's dangerous.

"But now you're with me, so it's OK. As long as you can stay feeling vulnerable, it's good.

"Your next challenge is to live 'in the now,' and see what feelings come up. Then try to deal with the feelings in the now. We devote careers to finding ways for clients to strip away enough denial to where this can happen.

"But we can't allow distractions that push feelings away," he warned. "Unsafe men are a distraction. Books are a distraction; you've had more than enough head talk.

"Your work now is emotional. Just feel your feelings.

"First, you need people time. Lots of time making real human contact with safe people like girl friends. Then you and I build a real relationship, so you can learn to attach to a safe person. You need this to feel safe enough to let feelings come up.

"Second, you need a lot of emotional content in each contact. Go see a girly movie with the girls and cry. You need time feeling deep feelings you can share with others. Time where you get to be real and vulnerable like you're being now, sharing your deepest parts and fears.

"Third, you need to receive a deeply compassionate response; choose safe people who can give you that. They probably will admire you for what you're doing."

Clear, yes. Simple, no.

"This shrink's crazy!" I left muttering.

I walked in feeling that two years of grief letters and funerals had completely exhausted both me and my elephant support network.

Now he says I need more people support? "Nobody wants to keep doing all this with me!" I thought for the nth time. Even I was shocked at the hairballs my inner cat Tom was bringing up.

Me? Ow!

Notes

1. In 2011, I simply read this website and felt it in my chest: "I need this!" Not until 2015 did I read that this author's work had been cited to justify using force with patients. That's awful, but I don't know if it's true, so no citation. See Appendix.
2. Book by same author, so no citation. See Appendix.
3. For children, see AttachmentTraumaNetwork.org. My book is about me as an adult. In 2011, all I wanted was a friendly hug. I'm against so-called "attachment therapy" using force. See Appendix.
4. NancyVerrier.com/position-statement, 3rd para, retrieved 9-30-17.
5. Herman (1992, in Verrier 2003, p.8).
6. Verrier (2003, p.7-8).
7. Verrier (1993, p.8, p.15)
8. Siegel DJ (1999, in Verrier 2003, p.13-15).
9. NancyVerrier.com/information-for-adoptees, 4th para, 9-30-17.
10. Verrier (1993, p.xvi).
11. Schore (1994, in Verrier 2003 p.436).
12. Taylor & McGee (2000, in Verrier 2003, p.318).
13. Cloud (12-6-10).

13

Tidal Wave Within

I thought my brain was fried for life. Then on March 30, 2011, I clicked the wrong link in an email from Lucy and stumbled onto the latest brain science. Now I had a therapist, so I dove into it.

"The brain is amazingly plastic," said one MD; new brain scans show that contrary to prior belief, the brain is the most plastic body part, able to regenerate itself.

13.1 The Great Wave. (Hokusai, 1832)

They call it "neuroplasticity." He reported on two doctors who rehabilitated their father from a stroke, teaching him to walk again by crawling first. When the father died mountain climbing years later, an autopsy showed he had grown new brain circuits after the stroke.

It was a whole video series by UCLA Med School's Dan Siegel, Allan Schore and others I'd just read about. Literally an answer to prayer. (1)

Clicked the wrong link? Got the scientists in Verrier's 2003 book? What are the odds? "You keep getting what you need, when you need it! Who loves ya, baby?" said Steve (referring to God, not Telly Savalas.) I bought a dozen of these science mp3s and listened daily for months.

There are a lot of wounded folks like me, they said, whom neither medicine nor psychology are helping. It's the professions that need to wake up.

What a relief! Science Sez: I'm not alone, and I'm not the only one having trouble with the pros.

And look: there's the prevalence of the problem, again.

Psychologists don't even have a definition of the mind or of mental health, said Siegel. His med school professors taught students to ignore the mind and focus on the body part to be fixed. Siegel didn't like it, so he switched to psychiatry to study the mind, but those professors taught that the mind is mere brain activity. Siegel didn't like that, either. He insisted that the mind has to do with relationships, but his peers said, "you're going to kill science" talking that way. (2)

In fact, however, it is relationships, specifically loving attachment interaction, which develop the brain and the mind in infants, said Schore, a neuropsychologist. He wrote three books on this in 1994. (3)

Today's brain scans prove Schore right. The brain more than doubles in size from the end of pregnancy to 24 months, he wrote, during which "attachment communications which are emotional are forging the connections within the early developing right brain... impacting the brain circuits of the developing child which are also being created."

Relationships can also heal adults who took attachment damage as kids, Schore adds. That's how therapy works. (4)

The scientists also confirmed that the yogis are right: meditation heals. "Neurons that fire together, wire together," they say. By repeatedly being present with our own minds, brain scans show, we fire up new neural pathways which increase feelings of well-being. (5)

Next I learned what PTSD is, and that I have a fat case.

Conscious thought begins at 24-36 months, said Siegel, when neurons in Frontal the thinking brain finally grow enough myelin coating to fire. There's no thinking, and no "explicit" memory until then. That's why we can't remember much before age two or three. Before that, all we have is pre-conscious aka "implicit" memory, raw data from outside that gets stuck in Limbus, Reptile, and mostly in our body.

"Say I'm six months old and I'm bitten by a dog on the hand, then at two again I'm bitten by a dog in my hand," said Siegel. "I'll have many fragmented, dis-integrated memories: a feeling of pain in my hand, a visual impression of a dog, a barking sound, a feeling of fear in my chest, a feeling that I'm ready to run" in my legs. These "implicit" memories are stored scattered around the body.

Only near 36 months does the brain's hippocampus come on line to integrate these fragments into a concept: "dog." What is a "dog," as opposed to merely a pain in my hand? We also need "hippo" to understand *when* this occurred; was I two, or ten? Without "hippo," we can't "put a time tag" on events, he explained.

"Now today I hear a dog barking," said Siegel, but I don't remember the past, because my hippo wasn't working so I never got the concept "dog." Plus my memory fragments have no time tag. Instead, "I see the teeth of a little puppy and I think it's a dangerous wolf. Fear hijacks my perceptual apparatus. It does not feel like it's from the past. I just get ready to run." (6)

Not the Disney wolf again...

Adults can also suffer enough stress cortisol to turn off the hippocampus. A soldier in an explosion is hyper-stressed, so his hippo shuts down. His memory is only "dog bytes," incoherent fragments with no time tag.

That's the definition of PTSD. Fifteen years later in LA he hears a car backfire, but to him it's not a car. It's an explosion with no time tag, so he feels like he's IN Iraq—and now.

I recalled dropping my keys in the dark recently and feeling that same panic. It hit me that making a mistake terrified me as a kid, so the stress cortisol turned off my hippocampus, and still does today.

"Every trauma they describe, I've got it," I told my tape. "Naturally, babies are fearful; they're helpless. They say babies need loving touch to develop the neurons that handle stress. I can't even put the key in my door without feeling stressed! My neurons never learned how."

"They say we need the hippocampus to regulate emotions, but humiliation destroys it. I had a lifetime of humiliation. Siegel says humiliation is 'a profound assault on a person's integrity,' causing a cortisol release which 'can actually be neurotoxic... kill synaptic connections... and destroy neurons.' I can feel it. (2)

"We're built to go to other humans to regulate our fear, they say. But what if the person you go to is a saber-toothed tiger and you get more fear?

"In constant fear, a kid's amygdala (the brain's security alarm) can get stuck in 'on,' they say, so it fires at the slightest notice for life. 'What guilt or shame?' as I told Dr. Rita; 'I go right to panic!' "

Hard-Wired to Heal

Plasticity? My brain's a knot of fried plastic. Can neuroplasticity fix that?

"Yes," insisted Dr. R. May 2. "We're hard-wired to heal—*if* we go to safe people with our fears and feelings, people who have compassion and accept us. That's why you're with me; that's why we have support groups.

"When you feel agitated, your body's telling you: you need comfort!"

"Comfort? What's that?" I asked. "Chicken soup? A hot tub?"

"People to share your pain with who will listen. You've had thousands and thousands of bad emotional experiences with people for decades," he said. "Repeatedly, people refused to hear your emotions when you needed that. *We can't think our way out of experiences.* Now you need thousands and thousands of good experiences with safe people who will hear your raw emotions and love you anyway."

"I need holding, not talk!" I moaned. "I read that Bob's part of my bad pattern, so I cut the physical contact. Hugging friends has limits and therapists have a rule against it. Now what?"

"Now I do the adult version: emotional holding," he said quietly. "You feel all your emotions with me, which no one ever let you do. Using words, I get my arms around your feelings. I understand them, I validate them, then you feel accepted. Did Bob feel like that?"

"Bob felt like intense attraction, then he'd disappear for two weeks," I said. "That went on for a year. He says his heart got nuked by divorce."

"Take you home with him, then not call for two weeks?" said Dr. R. "A decent man calls. No divorce causes such behavior. He's been that way all his life. Just because someone else put up with it for 25 years, doesn't mean you have to."

"But being alone hurts too much," I cried.

"Of course," said Dr. R. "Limits without love is hell. The crazy ones were the ones who didn't give you the love you needed as a kid. What you need now is a lot of safe, platonic love and comfort. You can't set limits with Bob unless you have others who will love you emotionally, not sexually.

"But you can't heal if you let Bob keep dissing you, as he does every time. That's like letting tigers dig up your lawn.

"You're hard-wired to heal. Get the tigers off the grass and it will grow."

Tsunami Again

But I still wanted hugs. On May 16, I showed Dr. R. a photo of a mother holding her daughter and gazing into her eyes.

"If you hold on despite entreaties to let go, the child's full range of emotions will emerge, starting with anger but also eventually fear and sadness," I read aloud. "You can ask, 'Why can't you look at me?'... If, while holding fast, you have told your child how his actions make you feel, you have forcefully and truthfully conveyed the full message: 'Nothing, nothing can come between us. Not your anger—and not even my anger.' " (7)

"I am very moved by this!" exclaimed Dr. R. "I want this, too. We all need this, to be pursued beyond our resistance. Then we know we are truly loved."

"I've never experienced that," I said, agitated. "That eye-gazing looks like there's about to be sexual abuse."

"Oh, you sexualized it?" said Dr. R.

Whoa, Mr. Nice Christian Therapist. My NCT, I later called him.

"Sexualized what?" I retorted.

"I never knew people looked at each other like this—until a boy looked into my eyes at 16 to kiss me the first time. There *was* no 'it' before that!"

"No, ever since birth you were urgently seeking that eye contact," he insisted. "When we don't get it as a kid, and our first experience is in romance? You were so unprepared that when you got a whiff of what you were made for, *it hit you like a tidal wave.* Any connection at all just carried you away, so you accepted people who were bad for you."

There it was again: the tidal wave, not in Japan, but inside me.

It was that tsunami feeling of overwhelm I'd talked of for months. I found the paper fan I got at the 2000 Okinawa summit. On it was the Hokusai tidal wave print in Figure 13.1. That was the feeling.

Ye gods, I've missed 16 years of software that normal children get but I never knew existed. Now any little bit of it drowns my ability to function.

How do you know you're missing something like eye contact, when everyone takes it so for granted that no one talks about it?

Back to *General Theory* I ran. An infant "needs continual feedback from the mother's face to learn how to run basic physical functions," it says. "By looking into his eyes and becoming attuned to his inner state, a mother can reliably intuit her baby's feelings and needs... Attachment penetrates to the neural core of what it means to be a human being." (8)

But a lab monkey whose limbic emotional brain is removed, no longer recognizes other monkeys, they add. It stares blankly and walks on them as though they were rocks or tree roots.

Evidently I'd been raised as a tree root by Martians.

I hadn't seen Bob in months, but that hadn't stopped him from calling every few weeks. I knew it was nuts, but I still longed for him. That's why one pays a shrink, so on May 31, I laid it on Dr. R.

Then we discovered another missing software input.

"I've been moving the tale from Bob to Dad for six months," I said, "but I'm still crazy for Bob. I read that 80% of the juice in adult conflicts is childhood pain that we transfer onto adult partners. It's some nutty sexual urge for my Dad and I want out.

"I remember taking a whiff of Dan's hair one night in 2008, and I couldn't stop drinking him in. 'I'm guy-crazy like a teenager,' I thought even then; 'I go nuts just for the smell of a man.'

"I'm sick of it! I want it gone, like an alcoholic never wants to hear about booze again. I want to flush it like Drano; it burns holes in my gut."

"There's nothing wrong with you," said Dr. R. "You never got to rest in the strength of a man who loves you. You needed that!"

"Is this shrink nuts?" I muttered again. Again it sounded like child sexual abuse.

But again it wasn't. It was more missing software.

"It's your female instinct to need maleness," said Dr. R. "Little girls feel so much like Mom that their need to be around males is huge. When we don't get that as kids, we feel overwhelmed by Mom.

"Later the urge for male protection builds up into another tidal wave. Yes, Bob longings are really Dad longings, but it's not true that you should be done with Dad.

"You didn't get what you needed from Dad, and you still don't have it. Of course you still crave it, so just keep moving the tale and feel your real cravings—for Dad. That's how you grieve a loss this huge. As you feel through it and share those feelings with safe people, you'll heal.

"Bob, you avoid. Men like that only use women to sooth themselves, then they blow you off and disappear. Anyway what really hurts is your baby feelings and Bob can't heal those. Send him no emails, take no calls.

"Do nothing. Nothing is the hardest thing to do. Action cuts off feelings. It robs us of the opportunity to feel our feelings and release them.

"Bring your feelings in here and feel them with me. Try to find more safe men at church, pastors, group members, men who give you air time, not romance."

I couldn't follow a word. Separating feeling from action in particular seemed bizarre.

Emotions had meant the need to act all my life. Doesn't "acting out" refer to kids throwing tantrums? Aren't adults required to take action?

Weeks later I read about an entire discipline for non-action. It's called **AAAA**, a mnemonic for "Just feel; don't act out; don't even act:"

A1. *Acknowledge* what I'm feeling. Get beneath thought and identify an actual feeling, but do nothing.

A2. *Allow* the feeling. Just sit with it. Let it be be huge. "I want to punch this guy; I want to slam the door and leave!" But do nothing. Simply sit and feel my anger, without punching the arsonist.

A3. *Ask*, "To what principles am I committed?" I don't believe in punching. Focus on my principles.

A4. *Act* on my principles, not my raw feelings. I gave my feelings airtime, so now I don't feel compelled by them. I can take measured action that respects my principles and my feelings, such as leaving quietly in self-protection. (9)

Dad Funeral

But Bob kept calling, and the loss of love kept hurting. I decided to hold one last funeral to move the tale to Dad, and feel all my Dad losses. For simplicity, I invited just Steve. "I can't tell if I'm your Dad or friend anyway," he said. "You remind me of my kids."

On June 3, I found a 2' x 1.5' x 8" carton at the office. After work I stood it in my back car seat and taped up a large display montage with 8 x 11 color photos of Dad, Mom, my sister, Sherry, my best friend Cynthia back East, Lucy, Steve and my furry cats.

In the center was Dad,

13.2 Accept the loss. (Kathy Brous) with the 10-inch sign "Accept the Loss." I've had those words taped to my wallet since Dad passed in June, 2008 (and still do), so I blew them up to ten times original size on a copier.

We found a park in Laguna Beach with a barbecue to burn documents and an ocean view. I stood the carton on a picnic table. The ocean always reminded me of Dad, I realized. I sat down staring at the photo display and the sea beyond. (Figure 13.2)

"It's like they're all here," I whispered. Without thinking I touched Dad's face with the words "Accept the Loss" as if it were a tombstone. I knew they could hear me, Dad and Mom.

"All the trees in the forest are going to fall," I said, handing Steve my lighter stick.

I had a "Burn List" taped to my Dad Letter, to remind me which papers to burn as I read aloud:

- The words to Handel's "O Sleep."
- The map to Bob's home which he drew for me the night we met.
- Three years of Bob's valentines and poems.
- A print of Bob's favorite, "Yes Virginia, There is a Santa Claus."
- The "Compensations of Calamity" bookmark Bob gave me.

I also had a copy of Dad's death certificate and a 10-inch copy of the "Accept the Loss" sign to burn.

I got out the bookmark. It was so lovely that holiday night when Bob put it in my hand and kissed me.

"Burn the bookmark?" gasped Steve. Apparently I'd been talking about it for years.

Banks assign trainee tellers to handle a lot of good money, says John Townsend, so if they're handed counterfeit bills, they instinctively *feel* something wrong. It hits them without thinking: "Oh, that's counterfeit." We need to experience "rivers" of safe platonic love, he says, to learn how real love feels. Only then can we distinguish love from a come-on.

"I've had counterfeit all my life," I said. "Nobody ever made a real commitment to me. My parents divorced me. My ex was in it for himself; so were the rebound guys. I've never felt anything but counterfeit. How would I know what's real?

"I'll start here. Bob's stuff is counterfeit, so burn the shit," I said.

"Whatever feelings I have for him, I've got to pin them on Dad and mourn my Dad. I've got to tell my emotions, 'We can't have Bob, but it only feels so bad because what we really want is to have Dad back. But we can't have Dad back. We've got to Accept the Loss.' "

I walked to the barbecue and read my five-page letter, which described every document. I burned each one in turn.

Dad Funeral Letter - Excerpts

Dad, I feel so sad that when you died in June 2008, I couldn't cry.

Dad, I feel so terrified to realize that children are programmed to feel safe in the cave with Mom, protected by Dad from the tigers outside. But I was made to sleep in the Tiger's Cave, to be clawed at random, with no one to protect me.

Dad, I feel so angry that you didn't say "stop torturing the child" when I was attacked. I feel so scared that I wake up screaming, "I don't want to sleep in the Tiger's Cave anymore!" That's why I can't sleep, so I'm burning this copy of Handel's aria "O Sleep."

Dad, I feel so sad for how hard it hit me last December: "Bob, I just wanted to fly in the plane with you." Dad, the truth is, I needed you to show up, to pull me up out of being enmeshed in barbed wire in the Tiger's Cave. So I'm burning the map to Bob's house.

Dad, I feel devastated to hear that "girls need maleness." They need know from Dad, "Am I attractive?" and "Do you respect me?" Dad, I feel so sad that I can't imagine such an exchange with you.

Dad, I feel so sad about my little voice crying in the El Toro parking lot, "Daddy I'll never be bad again, Daddy please don't tell me I'm bad because I'm crying, Daddy my chest hurts so bad..."

Dad, I feel devastated because now I see why I couldn't cry when you died. It's because you always told me, "Stop crying!"

Dad, I need to Accept the Loss of not being held when I cried, so I'm burning this sign "Accept the Loss."

This went on for two hours until my folder was empty. "I really feel done," I said.

Shark Attack

Two days later I woke in a cold sweat from the most terrifying dream I'd ever had, after a lifetime of nightmares.

I was on a sailing catamaran far out to sea when the crew landed an enormous heaving shark, alive, glaring and furious with a harpoon in its side spilling blood. Then the boat lurched, throwing me and the bleeding shark into the ocean together. I couldn't climb back up the pontoon, the boat bore off at speed, then the shark came at me and I woke up screaming.

"Wanted to die" say my notes. "This horror is still inside me. I want OUT! It doesn't matter what I do! I have no software inside to go on with and I'm too exhausted to start over from zero."

I tried to put the fearful image of the huge killing machine beast out of my mind but it was impossible.

Walking around in the morning light didn't help; I was deep in panic. I left Dr. R. a frantic voicemail; he called back, on a Sunday, no less.

"Go for comfort," he urged again. "Stop provoking this with letters; it's too much to handle. Go for comfort!"

"What do you mean comfort?" I asked for the tenth time. "I'm walking around in broad daylight terrified out of my wits! Chicken soup won't help!"

"What would comfort you?" he insisted, "and I don't mean Bob. Can you call Sherry or another friend?"

"My thinking brain knows there's no fish here, there isn't any water in my condo, but my emotional and survival brains are terrified and they're not listening," I said. "Ideas and logic mean nothing to two brains of three!"

"Your survival brain has lived in unsafe situations so long, of course it can't believe it's safe," Dr. R. said. "You didn't feel safe as a kid, in marriage, or dating. So now you've got to do something completely different.

"*Get into a safe situation*. Go for comfort. You've told me how scared you are; that's a start.

"Now go physically sit with a safe person, to convince your survival brain that you're safe. Use music. Sit together and listen to comforting music until you feel better. Get your emotions feeling safe first. Only *after* that, try the thinking exercise of telling yourself there's no actual threat."

I called Sherry, Lucy, and Marla; they were tied up with family. Everyone else has family on Sundays... It hurt so bad I hit the floor. "I can't handle this; I want out!" I wailed. But then there was Steve... Damn. I'm stuck alive.

Well, he'll have to pay... so I called poor Steve. When he heard what Dr. R. said, God bless him, Steve drove down to sit with me. I put on "Narayana," the yogi prayer to the Protector that always felt so calming. We listened for 40 minutes. Gradually I did feel better.

Next day June 6, I met Dr. R. "Of course nightmares like this happen, after feeling all that horribly deep grief," he said. "That's why I prefer no letters and going more slowly."

"It feels like I just shoveled out the Augean Stables and sprayed 'em with Lysol," I said, "but now I'm left sleeping alone on the bare floor. My gut is killing me."

"Exactly," he said. "You feel like you're sleeping on the bare floor alone because you are. You got nothing as a kid; you had to sleep on that floor alone for years. So now you dig back down to what it felt like, and it feels hideous. You don't have any experiences how to get out of it, because you never *did* get out; you were stuck in that for years."

"I did that letter to get rid of this because I can't take it anymore," I said, "but now it feels like I've fallen through the Grand Canyon into the river again, down the rapids without a boat."

"The letters re-wound the wound," he said. "That's what you're feeling now: re-traumatization."

"I want to *die*, like, *now*," I cried. "But I can't do that to my sister. So down I go. I **hate** this!"

"It's OK to want to die, that's natural," said my NCT, "as long as you don't act." Really, he said that. (Christian and all).

"When a baby's hit with a feeling too big to handle, it goes into shock," he said. "That's a protective mechanism. Our circuits aren't made to feel something as big as you just felt. I said before that the letters bring up too much and your natural circuit breaker shuts you down. 'I want to die' is how that feels."

Yes, but back then it just enraged me.

"The way I feel is this," I almost shouted, showing him the baby monkey huddled on the cage floor. "Tell it to the monkey, 'that's natural!' My reaction to sharks and fish is beyond abnormal. When I saw the *Jaws* poster in Manhattan in the 1970s, I wanted to run to New Jersey. If most people were like me, Hollywood would be bankrupt.

"Look, I'm sick; I need serious help!"

"The monkey couldn't make the call," replied Dr. R., gently but firmly. "You made calls to me, others, and then Steve.

"You have really *deep parts inside* you that never got loved. You need to talk about them, be heard, and feel loved through the hurt.

"Every part of you that you were told to hide or get rid of, that got treated poorly, misunderstood, or never got noticed, needs you to describe it to safe people who will accept you."

"No one wants to hear to what's inside me, it's insane," I wailed.

"What's inside you is precious," said Dr. R. "When you get that honest and vulnerable and share real emotions, that goes directly to a listener's heart. Safe people will be touched by that and value that."

"I did Golem and Precious last year," I sobbed. "I've been told my whole life that 'what's inside me' is a mess to be gotten rid of."

"That's not true, and it never was," he said. "What's inside you is incredibly valuable! And you're not jumping into traffic; you're in here, telling me your pain. If you keep talking to me and others about it, without acting, you'll be fine."

Notes

1. Doidge (3-30-11).
2. Siegel DJ (4-6-11).
3. Schore (1994).
4. Schore (6-15-11).
5. Siegel DJ (2011); Hanson (2011).
6. Siegel DJ (6-27-10).

7. Years later I read that this author, too, was referenced to justify use of force; no citation. See Appendix.
8. Lewis et. al. (2000, p.63, 76).
9. Verrier (2003, p.65, citing Britten R. (2001). Fearless Living).

14

Adrenaline No Mas

14.1 *The Lord is my shepherd.*
(Barbara Hughston)

Then I read about a woman whose support group held her while she cried all night.

People, the magic band-aid!

"Can I find people support like that in my neighborhood for these emergencies?" I wondered. On June 17, after over a year in Dana Point, I switched to a church near my condo.

The service in a large room featured a rock band with serious amps. "God loves me," the band sang with utter conviction, and the amps delivered it right to my solar plexus. I walked in, sat down, and fell apart for no apparent reason whatsoever. My whole body went into sobbing spasms, banging against the pew as with my car seat.

"You will be safe in His arms," the band sang, and here was a whole room of people resonating to that feeling of safety. Wham, it hit me that finally I could maybe feel safe. That would be a huge relief after a lifetime of never feeling safe.

"Savior, He can move the mountains," they sang. I thought of the mountains of rocks that God had removed from my heart, and rose to my feet singing. By late June, I was in three church small groups.

At church July 3, we saw a children's video of kids hugging themselves, singing "God loves me this much." You could see that they felt really loved to the core.

"We need to know that Someone Bigger than us loves us," I thought. "First that's parents. They make a baby feel loved, so it gets 'love inside.' Later they tell the child 'God loves you.' Then they all go to Disneyland and it's wall-to-wall love. It's instinctive to them: 'Someone Bigger loves us.' That's why I never liked Disneyland: I didn't get it.

"That's what I want: to feel God's love inside." I bought that kids' video and watched it three times a week while working out, for months.

I listened to so many church songs about how God loves us that I was making CDs. It helped. I listened to Cloud-Townsend CD talks for hours on end. It helped. At bedtime I read *Jesus Calling* and Bible studies.

Mornings I chanted the epic yogi poem in Sanskrit. It helped. Tuesday nights I chanted with the yogis as usual. I kept chanting *Om Namah Shivaya*, I honor God's love within me. It helped. I kept singing Mozart and Beethoven's songs about how much God loves us. It all helped.

I recited the 23rd Psalm when I was scared, which was most nights. I told everyone that the Valley of the Shadow of Death can't be so bad, because I live there and I can still walk.

I talked about it so much that one lady at church gave me a football jersey numbered "Psalm 23" and another gave me a teddy bear. (Figure 14.1) I chanted "Be still and know that I am God" endlessly.

God loves me, I sang over and over in English, Sanskrit, Latin, German, and Italian. (Luckily people have been talking about this forever.) It all helped.

But I was still terrified to be living alone.

September 11

I tried hard, but by late August I wanted to take Bob's calls again.

"There's bad pain, and good pain," said Dr. R. August 29. (Just as I thought.)

"Bad pain is when you act out and take his call. That relieves your pain now, but later when he disappears, the pain comes back with redoubled force and keeps getting worse. Good pain comes when we do the right thing. It's agony now, but later we feel better and better.

"I've got to fold the phone on Bob?" I whispered.

"Why wouldn't you?" he said. "No one who *ever* related to a woman would treat you this way.

"You don't have to like it—you just have to do it."

I didn't like it.

On September 11, 2011, while I was not liking it and not doing it, the phone rang.

It was Bob from JFK Airport in New York, again.

"Kathy, you've got to help me," he moaned. "Ah'm having an anxiety attack so back mah chest is pounding fit to kill me and Ah feel like Ah'm goin' to die. Ah'm afraid Ah can't fly the plane. But Ah've taken too many sick days due to this damn divorce, and if they find out I get panic attacks, Ah'll lose mah job. Mah kids will be on the street.

"Kathy, please say you'll come to mah house if I make it to LAX. Please, Kathy, Ah need your help."

This actually happened. I have enough problems; I don't need to make them up.

It was 9-11-11. It was the tenth anniversary of the most horrible experience any American has had since Pearl Harbor, and all over the media. I'm born and raised in New York, and worked blocks from the World Trade Center for years. I've been too terrified by the TV images of the attack to set foot in lower Manhattan since it happened.

Plus I'm so deep in my own PTSD that I see sharks in my bed and wake up screaming.

Now I've got an airplane pilot on the phone who's about to fly a jumbo jet from JFK to LAX, utterly out of his gourd? Carrying the same amount of fuel as those flights ten years ago? He's asking me to help him maintain sanity long enough to land and not kill more people?

"You're unfit to fly," a reasonable gal might say. "Hang up and go to the ER."

But I was from New York and seeing sharks, not reason. I didn't think he'd listen, either.

I promised to help and took Bob's call when he landed at LAX. That evening I went to his house where I hadn't set foot since December, 2009. I talked to Bob half the night trying to calm him down, slept a few hours, and left for work next day. Nothing else happened.

After work I returned, certain that Bob's call was a breakthrough. No one was home. I thought we had an appointment so I sat in my car, fell asleep, and awoke past 9 p.m. No Bob. I called but got only voicemail. Finally I drove home.

Next day Bob returned my call. "Last night Ah got tired of sitting at home, so Ah went to Walmart," he said.

"It's a life and death emergency, I'm in your driveway, but you're wandering around Walmart?" I thought. Un-bunny-lievable.

"It's urgent you see a doctor and a therapist," I said.

"Ah'm hungry," he said. "Ah'm going to have lunch and deal with my cleaning service. Call you later." Just like that. As though nothing had happened.

"That's it; I'm done. S T O P!" I told Dr. R. on October 3.

"Bob really got to you with his death cry," he said. "Now you have to let go of him all over again. He's never given you anything and he never will. He's a disconnecter. They unload on you to sooth themselves, then they blow you off.

"It's imperative that you block Bob's phone and email, that you not read his mail.

"Next time he'll say he has a gun to his head and he's about to pull the trigger. Are you going to discuss that, too?

"*If a tiger is coming at you, you don't discuss things; you pull the trigger and shoot.* It's going to hurt but that's reality.

"And I will love you through this."

War on Arsonists

On Friday, October 28, I prepped my phone and email to block Bob.

Adrenaline addiction to romance? It's gonna kill you, says Norwood. I stared at my computer. Out came something titled "Adrenaline No Mas."

We who grew up in the Tiger's Cave,
Are on constant alert to expect attack,
Accept being hurt as the daily norm,
Chase arsonists who don't see our souls.

Neurons that fire together, wire together,
Burn adrenaline grooves deep in my brain,
They demand repetition, and scream if I don't,
These, my internal structures of sin. (1)

God has kicked over my entire life. Now all I've got is "No's." No family, no home, no husband, no boyfriend, no safety.

No, no, no, no. No! Worried about X? "Fine," says God, "I'll remove it."

Now I have nothing to look at but myself.

So I looked, and saw that I've never been without an arsonist to chase, since birth. With Mom, I had to focus on her wants, not on myself.

Since high school it was boys, then men. When Jim left me as a college freshman, I hid in the dorm for a year. I was so totaled no one could understand it, least of all me. Now we know. After parental rejection, one more rejection felt like the world had collapsed under my feet. I had nothing inside to fall back on and no way to recover.

Next I met Larry, then I married Larry, and went without connection for 30 years, trying make him love me, chasing my live-in arsonist. Then he got violent and I looked in the mirror and said, "I'm done."

Suddenly I had no arsonist.

Within weeks Dan appeared, because when I have no arsonist, my body screams for an arsonist and men come running—bad men. So I went from one to another, and there was never a time I didn't have an arsonist to chase.

I've been holding Open House in the Tiger's Cave for predators all my life.

Now I've hardened my heart to Bob, and that is why I must go through the physical exercise of blocking the phone and email: for closure.

Only then comes the first time in my life that I am without an arsonist.

And that, is the point of all the "No's" flooding over me. God has kicked over the chess board and wiped out my hard drive.

"Pain is the thing that gets us to drop what we're holding, so that we can receive the love of God," says C. S. Lewis.

I can't convince my sick emotional brain, like a cat that's been kicked all its life, to come out from under the bed, while I put it near people who kick it. I held on to those donkeys until it hurt too much. If I say "No" and drop them, it's the first time in my life that I can actually feel God's love.

Total war. Look for every arsonist in my life and Clean. Them. Out.

I pushed the button and blocked Bob's phone and email.

Next morning I crashed.

"Oh, no: it's autumn, and here comes Yorba Linda again," I told my tape. Rehearsals were starting for the annual *Messiah* at the Nixon Library in Yorba Linda where I first met Bob in 2008.

"*What am I so disappointed about?*" I yowled. "I keep seeing Bob's house with the fireplace and the kitchen window overlooking the pool, like Dan's house with the kitchen window overlooking the lake.

"I needed to be taken care of when I was little, to feel safe. Instead, I was overcome by Mom's fear of the Depression, as if we could be on the street any time; how she didn't trust Dad to protect us; that there was no God. It all deeply terrified me.

"So when I saw those two homes, my gut screamed 'Oh, would you take care of me?' And when they said, 'No, we won't!' it was incredibly painful."

"Why is it so excruciating to say 'No' to all this?" I asked Dr R. October 31.

"You've never done it before," he said, "plus now you're the one shutting the door; that's harder. Then you see the vast panorama of all the people you've lost. This is *good pain*; the hurt is big up front, then gradually we feel better."

I read him "Adrenaline No Mas."

"This is the best thing you've written," he said. "Yes, God's many 'No's' were to unsafe people. He did that to prevent you from going back in the cave with the tigers.

"Your parents should have said 'No' for you. They should have protected you from hurt, to show you how to protect yourself, but they didn't, so you lack safety inside. Starting to say 'No' now builds up safety inside you, which starts to feel good.

"This is your exit pass from the Tiger's Cave. It's your declaration of independence."

The Right Diagnosis

On Sunday November 6, I sang "Rejoice" from Handel's *Messiah* at church. Then I drove an hour to the *Messiah* rehearsal in Yorba Linda, singing all the way to the CD. Once there I thoroughly enjoyed it.

Then someone made a minor joke at me; I felt my mood drop and had that same old Yorba Linda meltdown. I watched it happen, I was aware that it was stupid, but I couldn't control the feeling.

"I can't regulate my emotions!" I thought. "It's like being crippled from birth." It got worse as I drove home and collapsed in my car until midnight. I crawled upstairs and Here It Comes Again... That's why God made word processors, lady; it's the same crap you felt last week.

"Oh, no: Yorba Freaking Bobs-ville Linda. Here Come The Holidays again." I cried my throat raw.

This time, however, even during the "I Hate This Part" part, I could tell that if I just tolerated the pain, I'd feel better when it was done. I imagined that Dr. R. was there with me. Finally the pain resolved. I did feel better.

So goes "good pain." I hurt; I get relief. I cry until I choke, then I'm perfectly reasonable in ten minutes.

Crazy. Or is it?

Is this how I learn to regulate baby emotions? By walking back and forth through emotional extremes and learning how, as a baby does? Learning to crawl to learn to walk?

On Sunday November 13, I had another Yorba Linda rehearsal. Again I had a meltdown.

Now I got mad. Hey, I pushed the button on Bob! I didn't like it, but I did it, and it's cost me a boatload of pain. I've faced my issues with Dad and men. Why do I still feel so bad?

"Oh God, I've been in the pain incubator with Mom dying in the hospice and now I'm back in Yorba Linda," cried a little voice in my chest as I drove home.

Suddenly it **was** 2008, and I **had** just flown from Mom's Miami hospice to her New York funeral, then I **was** just off the plane at LAX, driving to Yorba Linda to meet Bob. I saw myself driving the 57 Freeway as if from a helicopter, from out-of-body.

"Yorba Linda was the hospice was the pain incubator," said the voice. "Yorba Linda hurts because when you got here the first time, you'd just been mauled in the Tiger's Cave and you were bleeding bad. Then Bob rejected you again."

Wait. I still feel bad because I have an issue deeper than Dad, which facing my Dad pain can't fix.

Mom.

There's still more Mom pain inside that needs work.

Oh, no; Flatten Me XXIII?

"It helps to have the right diagnosis," I told Dr. R. next day.

" 'Pain incubator?' In 2008, the hospice, Mom's funeral, then Bob's absences, triggered what the infant felt in the incubator. Sitting in that hospice room under Mom's attacks felt exactly like being locked in a box.

"Most people don't leave a hospice except in a box and I couldn't leave, either. Just like the incubator: I had to sit in that box and feel like death."

"Exactly," said Dr. R. "That hospice was living Hell; it did bring up the terror as an infant, the feeling you were going to die.

"Then you went from the hospice to Mom's funeral to Yorba Linda and Bob? Ouch. Yorba Linda's a perfect PTSD storm. You were so traumatized the first time you were there, that going there now will flash you right back to the hospice and the incubator, like a vet flashes back to Iraq.

"Mom showed up. It's the holidays, when Mom died attacking you. Now she's clawing you again.

"Here is what you must do: mobilize your anger against Mom."

"I thought the whole point was to eliminate my Mom anger!" I protested.

"We can't remove anger without giving it air time," he said. "You've felt through such terror and pain, but you still feel awful.

"Time to feel anger."

"You can't forgive a feeling you haven't felt," says the *Grief Handbook*.

"This year, find your anger. Say 'No' to this tiger clawing, and walk out of the hospice," said Dr. R.

"Say 'No' to every critical, negative voice in your head. Those voices aren't yours. *Those are Mom's voices* and what she's saying isn't true.

"Any voice that attacks you is like a tiger coming; it turns on your panic reflex. Shoot it! Shoot the negative voices *now*, ask questions later. You don't debate with a tiger; you shoot. Practice just shooting the negative voices, again and again.

"Any voice which isn't comforting? That's Mom. Voices asking why you still have painful emotions? You've had a lifetime of hurt! Any accusing voice? That's Mom. Shoot it!

"Do not ignore Mom's voices or attempt to repress or annihilate them; it can't be done. Confront her and say 'No.'

" 'No, Mom, I shouldn't be remarried by now. No, I shouldn't have a boyfriend. No, I shouldn't anything. I should be respected for being exactly where I am.'

"Don't judge or try to fix yourself. With yourself, be gentle and accept your feelings. Think, 'I've suffered a devastating loss; of course I feel scared.'

"But with Mom's voices, you mobilize the anger, say 'No,' and shoot.

"Because you couldn't fight Mom while she was alive, *you must fight her now*."

Don't Tread On Me

I posted his warning and the Revolutionary War flag "Don't Tread on Me" as a large sign on my microwave:

Because you couldn't fight Mom then,
You must fight her *now*.
It's survival: Protect your *Self!*
Get Angry now—or Die.

I tried it, and told everyone about shooting tigers. By early December I'd been shooting them for weeks.

"Amazing, but it starts to feel good," I told Dr. R.

" 'No' creates a zone of safety inside you," he smiled. "The more times you shoot the tiger first and ask questions later, the safer you feel. 'No' is like a loving Dad protecting you. It makes you feel loved."

Steve had hit a plateau reading his grief letters and was very interested. He wasn't getting relief—or even connecting with what he wrote. "Maybe I have the wrong diagnosis?" he asked.

It did feel wrong to me when Steve read his letters, because he dumped on himself so much.

"You know," I said, "many of your Apologies to Lena for your failures, might actually be Forgiveness items. You say your failures to stop Lena's actions were the problem. Maybe that's the wrong diagnosis.

"What if Lena's hurtful actions were the problem? Maybe that's the right diagnosis. Her actions hurt you, but you're not forgiving her; you're busy apologizing. But if we don't forgive hurts, we keep hurting! Try to feel what hurts, then try forgiving her."

Later Steve told me that this was an "Aha" moment for him. "I did have the wrong diagnosis," he said. "My condemnation voices from 'way back kept repeating that everything was my fault. So I didn't see the truth: *I* was the one being hurt. So I never grieved a lot of the hurt. No wonder I didn't get relief! We need grief letters that actually find the grief."

For me, shooting tigers began to stop the adrenaline flow until suddenly, for no reason, I felt better.

I found myself out celebrating Christmas for the first time in a decade. I sat for hours in a church garden at the Laguna Beach Christmas Walk, singing with the carolers. I had tears hearing "Silver Bells" ("it's Christmas time in the city"), which triggered sadness about New York. I felt the sadness, so it passed. Then I felt better.

The next Saturday, I went to the San Juan Capistrano Mission, sang along with more carolers, then crossed the street and two-stepped the night away at the Swallows Inn honky-tonk.

I bought the first Christmas tree I ever had in California, took it home and decorated it.

Then on December 12, 2011, I came home, opened my postbox, and the bottom fell out. Again.

There was a Christmas card from Bob. Just like Christmas 2010.

I didn't toss it unopened. Then I couldn't put it down, like the former alcoholic who "just found a drink in her hand." For days I wrote and deleted emails, the "bad old grooves" in my brain engaging again.

On December 15, at 2 a.m., I sat up in bed, took a pad and wrote with my hand shaking:

I can't stop the Male.

It's him, or me. Choose.
It's life or death survival.
Focus on the arsonist and I won't live.
Shoot the arsonist. Dead.

The Cookie Monster comes with its knife.
What's it doing in my room when I'm so little?
It demands that I cease to exist.
It demands I perform for food.

It demands, it demands—*and it's got a knife.*
It demands my total focus, or else.
Focus on the arsonist means *I don't exist.*
Christmas card? Counterfeit! Burn the shit.

In the morning I posted this on my microwave:

No! Burn the mail until it stops.
Just let your bad grooves scream.

That night I met my friend Ellen at church and got a hug. We burned Bob's card and dumped it in the trash.

On December 18, Steve wanted to show me San Diego's Coronado Silver Strand and the Hotel del Coronado at Christmas. Walking the long shoreline, for no reason I came down with back pain, neck pain, and a migraine bad enough to deck me. By the time we found a bench with a great ocean view and opened our lunch, I couldn't eat.

"Here I am on the beach voted the most beautiful in America and I'm miserable," I said. "But you know, it feels like I've had this before. Is it Bob's card?"

"Wait: the first time I "moved the tale" off Bob last December and felt all that childhood pain about Dad, I had a nightmare and body pain so bad that I ran to the chiropractor howling.

"This June after the Dad Funeral, I had that shark attack. This October after canceling Bob, I had meltdowns in Yorba Linda. Now I've ripped up Bob's card—and I'm toast.

"Maybe we can do the right thing and get slammed by body pain?" I asked. "Maybe it's my bad old neural grooves screaming because they feel like doing my bad old patterns?"

"Could be," said Steve. "I bet our feelings run down the same grooves automatically, like water stays in a furrow. Maybe when we have to break them up, it hurts."

"I did it right!" I thought. "My bad grooves don't like it?

"Mobilize the anger against Bob! Shoot the bad grooves! No, no, and no!" I repeated to myself. I was too embarrassed to do it aloud, but I did it.

Ten minutes later I began to feel the iron grip release from my lower back, then from my neck, then from my jaw and forehead.

"I feel better!" I said. "It's going away. Suddenly I'm hungry."

"Shine a light on bad grooves and they run like roaches," laughed Steve.

"Break, break, break and it feels like hell, but two months later I feel *so* much better!" I said.

On December 23, Ellen and I were still celebrating Christmas, visiting the fancy Roger's Gardens decorations in Newport Beach. Santa was waiting for kids in the gazebo but he was alone.

"Let's sit on his lap and make a wish," said Ellen, herself reeling from divorce. She insisted and so after her turn, I carefully perched on the poor gent's knee.

"Well, well," said Santa, "and what do *you* want for Christmas?"

"What I really want is peace of mind," I sighed, looking at him.

"Well, ahem, I'll see what I can do," he said softly, tearing up.

"Isn't that what we all want?"

We sat there weeping together for some time.

Notes

1. Breen. (2008).

Reassociation

15.1 *Polar bear frozen by biologist's sedative. (Budd Christman/NOAA)*

On New Years Day, Steve and I went to IHOP. "I'm still queasy," I said. "Could I get a hug?" I moved around the table from my bench to his. Then we noticed the little girl in the booth behind me. She saw me, so she moved around her table to snuggle with her Dad.

"Soon the whole place will be moving around to snuggle!" I joked. "People come to IHOP thinking they need comfort food, but it's really to fill some emotional hole. Hugs are what they need. Fun sight gag if this story is ever a movie."

January 2012, however, was not fun. I kept saying "No" to my urge to call Bob, and my brain's bad grooves kept putting me in hell.

"I've blocked Bob and burned his card," I told Dr. R. January 9. "Why can't I ignore the card?

"Well, since the sperm hit the egg, I've been crap. That pain was embedded in my cells as they divided and it hurts too much to feel what's down there. But if I ignore Bob, there's no distraction to drown out my cells.

"Now I feel what's in my cells and they're screaming. *My cells are the issue, not some guy.* But the pain is huge."

"Yes," said Dr. R. "Cellular-level pain drummed into your body before you had thought. Plus, the baby was stuck in that for years, screaming for rescue. That's why you want Bob's airplane: rescue. Saying 'No' now and killing the 'rescue wish' is huge. Most people can't do it.

"This was rape and betrayal!" added my NCT (unquote). "Where's the anger? 'Bob, you used me like a drug, then ignored me!' Give your anger its airtime, until you have no desire to read his stuff."

Days later a link to a book on "brain music" landed in my email. As an embryo's first cells divide, it said, the mother's emotions and heartbeat are "encoded" into the baby's cells as vibrating memories. Cell division is a rhythmic process, so the child's cells are "entrained" to the mother's rhythms on a deep, cellular level.

It's not just my imagination, says neurophysiologist Galina Mindlin, MD. Another accident.

"Newborns almost immediately show memory of sounds in the womb," she writes. "Lyrical and comforting 'motherese,' the singsong way in which parents speak to children, instills feelings of calm, safety, and love... By only their 14th week, children can distinguish their mother's footsteps." (1)

"Motherese?" Anxiety broke loose in my chest. What "lyrical and comforting?" What "calm, safety?"

My cells had to recoil from stress acid and Mom's anxious heartbeat, and now I could feel it again. At "their mother's footsteps," I felt terror. *"Oh, no, the wolf at the door!"* screamed a little voice. "The sound of *my* mother's footsteps was the sound of a predator." The terror ambushed me so fast I was shocked.

"Those rhythms from the womb feel like Mom: anxious and angry," Dr. R. confirmed January 16. "When you heard footsteps, something bad was gonna happen, so reading that touched your infant terror.

"Sure you felt overwhelmed on a cellular level. It was that deep; it went on a long time; and your body *organized early life* around it. You had to escape the terror of Mom, terror of alone, and terror of your own anger. It all felt threatening to your existence."

The Red Berries

On January 28, Steve came by to read a letter; later we took a walk. "Every cell in my body is screaming, 'We're not supposed to *be!*'" I said, "yet by survival instinct, they're also screaming, 'We *want* to be!'"

"That's what made me do all the crazy things I've done," I said. "I'm not supposed to be? Well then, I'll do this and this, and then I won't be. I did crazy stuff in college, hitchhiked cross- country at 20, crazier stuff in Asia at 22. I just wanted to *get it over with.*

" 'Most people take this to the grave,' a psychologist at church once told me. They have no way to deal with it; it's too thorough-going:

"Should I exist, or not?"

We reached a bridge over a ravine. I leaned on the rail, spent.

We looked up and before us were large bushes of berries. Despite thick winter fog, suddenly the sun came out from behind my church blocks away across the ravine and poured rays of glory onto the berries, lighting them a rich, beautiful red and revealing the blue ocean beyond.

See the photo on the back cover. Cross that bridge two minutes earlier or later and we'd have seen nothing but fog. But I saw it, and it hit me:

"Most people take this to the grave; that's why my Mom died shaking her fist at the sky," I said, dazed.

"She had the same thing! She must have felt unwanted to exist; that's the only way she could have transmitted this feeling so strongly. It was horrible watching someone die who felt unwanted to exist.

"But now, that's not going to happen to me," I blurted out, tearing up and waving an arm toward the red berries and the sun. "And anything else–family, friends, romance–is icing on the cake.

"Because now God is here, and **He's** saying, 'Mom wasn't in charge; Kathy's not in charge–**I'm** in charge, and yeah, you are supposed to exist.

" 'Look: I made all this Beauty for *you!*'

"Now I won't have to die like that, because I'll know: Someone Bigger loves me. I **am** supposed to exist. This starts to get at the cause of my anxiety. And as the anxiety cracks, it moves every tectonic plate in my soul."

" 'You shouldn't exist...' What a horrible message," said Dr. R. February 6. "It's great you mobilized your anger. You changed it from 'I shouldn't' to 'No! I *do* have the right.' "

"The change feels physical; it feels like God's love is rushing into the empty hole in my chest," I whispered. "Am I growing emotional object constancy, what they call 'love inside'?"

"Yep," he said. "When you feel God loves you, it feels like the earth's plates are moving because of the intensity of the shift in your emotional viewpoint. You're developing a standing point! Try to take it in more and more:

"*You were made on purpose.*"

Being hit so hard by those red berries was a breakthrough, but in anger, not joy.

The nightmares returned, with hard-hearted Martian eyeballs who didn't respond. I'd wake up and make tapes. "They never had a commitment to me," I yelled at my tape. "My mother didn't want me; she told me so herself. My husband had no commitment."

In one dream Larry took me somewhere for Christmas and he looked like Pinocchio with Martian eyes. "I'm leaving now," he said and left me there. I was on stage at a Handel's *Messiah* rehearsal (I've sung it almost every Christmas) and suddenly I'm weeping.

From nowhere my best friend Cynthia appears at the foot of the stage and says, "Come down here, you need a hug!"

It's Cynthia! Cynthia!

So I jump off the stage and she wraps her arms around me. Suddenly she's there for me saying, "You need a hug." And hugging her tightly, I break down and cry uncontrollably in the middle of the rehearsal with everyone staring, and say, "I don't know what it is about my mother and Christmas, but it makes me fall apart."

Days later, just as I was transcribing the tape of this dream, my cell phone rang. It was Cynthia. I'm 3,000 miles away but *she* heard me. This was no dream; this actually happened.

"Maybe the whole time I was growing up, I was alone at Christmas," I told her, "while everyone else talked about family, exchanging presents, and eating at table. What table? At my house it was Martian eyeballs. It was 'How do we push her *under* the table and get rid of her? She doesn't belong!' I never belonged anywhere."

"You belong to me," Cynthia announced. I could hear her grin.

The Body Knows

But by mid-February, the nightmares and anxiety were back. I came to the end of my rope with talk therapy. Again.

I'd wondered for years why my body spasms so violently when I sob. "Emotional pain is physical," I journaled back in 2009. "Do we need to re-spasm muscles which got into spasm during the trauma decades ago, for them to release? Is it like vomiting: the body can only eliminate poisons with violent contractions? Is this the instinctive reflex to release emotional pain?"

"Full-body sobbing is common in child trauma," said Dr. R. "As a baby, you cried but nobody came. That felt like a life threat, so your whole body still repeats its survival reaction. Just let the reaction come up. Then verbalize it. Tell someone it hurts! That worked in Coronado."

"Just let it come up? It feels like a daily trip to the electric chair," I journaled now.

"It's physically too much. I've got the same nausea that decked me in 2009. The frequency and severity of the nightmares is unacceptable."

Back to last year's brain science tapes I ran.

Dr. Dan Siegel speaks of a "window of tolerance" for emotional pain. If we're in such denial that we can't feel it, we're under the window. That was me for decades: I had a Grand Canyon of rocks on my heart, and felt nothing. (2)

Then I nuked the Grand Canyon, and now I feel torrents coming up. But when the pain is so enormous, emotional arousal goes through the roof and we're over the window of what we can tolerate now, and still think. Our hippocampus shuts down and we re-experience the original trauma *as if it were happening now*. That's re-traumatization.

Infant trauma occurs before we have thought. It's stored in the body and lower brains, not in Frontal the thinking brain. When talk therapy fails and bodily pain increases, trauma needs "body work," aka somatic psychotherapy, I read. (3)

"Of course it's physical," I exploded. "I've had backaches, migraines, and jaw pain all my life. You could hear Mom grinding her teeth to bits in her sleep. That's me, all night every night. I wake up with jaw pain, headaches and crowns breaking off my teeth."

I recalled a study comparing an incubated baby to her un-incubated twin sister. "Her 'baby mind' would react *bodily* to *emotional* pain," it said. We have no thoughts or thinking memory before 24-36 months, only "dog bytes," raw data stored in fragments in the body and nervous system. (4)

How can talk help that? That baby had no thoughts to discuss.

"Most therapists are not trained to notice the body, or to intervene at the level of body signals that indicate fight-flight," said Dr. Pat Ogden. Somatic psychotherapy, she said, trains therapists to notice the body when it gets over-aroused, then pause talking, and work with the body. We need both talk and body work.

"Incest survivors often can't talk about the trauma; their emotions go through the window," Ogden said. "So we pause talk therapy and have them do physical exercises." She had one girl stand up and push away with her entire body, to complete that motion, which was forbidden as a child. "Just sit and pay attention to the body," she said. "Then just stay with the body and let the body process what it has to process. *The body knows how to do it.*"

"If in talk therapy, the nervous system experiences the same level of over-whelm as it did in the original trauma, it can't distinguish the difference, so the person is re-traumatized," warned Dr. Peter A. Levine. Somatic psychotherapy instead watches for physical symptoms of fight-flight or shut down. "Then we help them become aware of their body," he said. (5)

Check out both Ogden and Levine to see what resonates. I ordered Levine's book "Healing Trauma" for two personal reasons.

Levine's study of wild animals hit me hard. I already had a zoo popping up inside me, the voices of my traumatized emotions. I had a baby monkey, my inner cat Tom, Froggy, reptiles, fish, elephants, unicorns, tigers, piglets, lambs, alpacas, hobbits, and whatnot.

"Healing Trauma" also has an audio CD with Levine reading exercises. Hearing a human voice was priceless to me. (6)

The evening of February 21, I developed back pain for no reason. By February 22, it was crippling. I sat down at one point and nearly couldn't get up. I was bent over double, afraid to walk, and terrified.

How could I do the gym? Then I recalled the brain science tapes saying, "Pain x Resistance = Suffering." Try to accept physical pain, they say. Fighting it and worry roil up stress and just worsen the pain. Also exercise normally; it may resolve [see Siegel RD. (4-15-11)].

I took several ibuprofen and crawled to the gym. I dragged myself through most of my usual workout and sat in the hot tub for an hour. Going home I was walking funny but felt better. Amazing. The pain cleared up.

Yes, this was psychological, and on February 23, I finally asked, "Why now?"

Then I ran to my email. The first thing I'd seen on February 21 was an email from Dan. Just back from a tropical vacation, he was reminiscing suggestively about our last trip to Mexico—four years ago.

"When people don't see or respect you, it will trigger the way Mom didn't see you as a kid, and you'll have a dream or a nightmare to work it out," said my NCT back in January. "You went to them (Dan or Bob) for care and comfort, but you got rape and betrayal. *Where's the anger?*"

"You'll have a dream or a nightmare," I muttered now, "or a really bad back ache."

Dan casually sticks his finger in my eye by email and my reptile brain flares up. If I don't feel that fight-flight cortisol, it gets frozen in my body. "Mobilize the anger," says Dr. R., but I didn't. I blocked the email from consciousness, so my body had to pay.

Time and again I'd fall into this "anger trap." When people upset me, I'd blank it out completely. Mostly I didn't express anger and mostly I got a migraine.

On May 3, night before my birthday, Bob called. On May 4 came more calls from people only pretending to relate. I was nice—and got a terrible migraine which almost ruined my birthday dinner. On May 20, I sat politely through an entire concert with people who were unfriendly and got another migraine.

On June 8, a gal unloaded on me via email; I wrote a conciliatory reply, and got a migraine. In August, I heard a talk at church which really upset me. I kept smiling, and got a migraine.

I realized that I had to "mobilize the anger" whenever people upset me. I learned not to express anger to them; that's chasing the arsonist. They're not safe to hear my feelings and they'll only hurt me again.

Instead I move the tale from the person today, to childhood, to see what it triggers; then I express that pain. That's what's really bothering me. I learned to express it to a safe person or God—and don't stuff it.

Re-Traumatization No Mas

"Re-traumatization no mas," I told Dr. R. February 27, "I want to do body work." In 25 years' practice, he'd never used it. A lesser man would have blown me off, but not Mr. Compassion.

"Great! You're standing up to protect yourself!" he replied. "You couldn't speak up as a kid; now it's really important you do. That's how you learn to run from people who won't listen to you.

"Too much of your trauma is pre-cognitive. Sick to your stomach? We can't have that. That's your body warning us: we're off track. I should have focused more on body language and physical symptoms. This somatic approach really resonates with you."

We agreed that I'd find some somatic work we could do together.

Then he sighed, "I don't think you get much comfort in here."

"I hate that word," I repeated. "How can chicken soup help?"

"You have so much emotional pain that it's going into your body," he said. "If we do body work, we'll uncover worse pain.

"The only way through such pain is to be *connected with another person* as you experience it. Connection lets you feel emotions, so pain doesn't get stuck in your body. That's comfort. As you feel me comfort you, you learn to regulate emotions.

"But you take notes the whole time, so you're not present with me. You can't feel me comforting you."

"I can't remember a thing without notes," I protested. "My hippocampus is toast from all that cortisol as a kid."

"Could you make tapes?" he asked.

Hallelujah! I began taping sessions on March 12, 2012. Now I could actually hear what Dr. R. was saying. Hearing myself revealed even more.

Dr. R. would ask what I was feeling, and I'd tell him what I was thinking. He'd repeat, "But what's the feeling? Sadness?" and I'd give him more head talk or interrogate him.

"I'm questioning him like a researcher in a lab coat interviewing an engineer for data," I realized. "That's nuts. I'm here to let my unregulated emotions loose with him, so he can show me how to regulate."

Who is this labcoat gal? I dubbed my thinking brain "Susie Labcoat" and made running jokes. I came to see Dr. R. with a yellow pad, wearing horn-rimmed glasses and a disposable white coat that I got at a blood test.

Once Frontal had a name, I got a sense of my other two brains.

Aha! My limbic emotional brain didn't feel like an infant anymore. "Haven't seen Tom (my inner cat) lately," I told Dr. R. "After saying 'No' so much, my emotional brain feels like it's eight or ten." I named her Chrissie Limbus; she's all over the map like Christopher Columbus.

Then I read that God put a survival brain stem in us to help us. "Help me, Rhonda!" became my battle cry and Rhonda Reptile was born, thwacking her tail. If I ever get a cartoon, she'll look like Juliet in "The Flintstones."

I had to separate out what my three brains were doing. I had to get Susie Frontal to stand aside, then ask what Chrissie Limbus is feeling, and what Rhonda Reptile needs. Just then I heard therapist Rick Hanson say that he likes to check in with each of his three brains on waking. He reviews each of their feelings and asks if their needs are being met. I tried it and it feels great. (7)

I wake up and notice Rhonda first; she wants to know if we're cold, thirsty, hungry, etc. (I doubt she sleeps or we'd stop breathing). Then Chrissie asks whether we're loved and safe, or must we to rush around to perform? Next Susie produces endless thoughts about everything we need to do today, this week, this year. I try to stop her and relax everyone by taking deep breaths.

It's a zoo, but all three are really there and the more attention I pay to each one, the better I feel.

I still ask "The Girls" to find out what I'm feeling. I'll enter the gym, whip out my mp3 and ask, "OK, Ladies, what'll it be?" trying to let deep places speak. "We want Matchbox 20!" they may yell; OK, someone's angry. Or they may want upbeat Bach and there's joy. The music they pick lets me discover what I feel. Add an hour banging the machines and I always feel better.

Steve likes the system, too. "Want to eat at Ruby's?" he'll say. "Let's ask all six of us," I'll reply. Some tables get pretty crowded.

Return of the Tiger

On March 19, I brought Peter Levine's book to Dr. R. "Trauma is a fact of life," Levine writes, "but it need not be a life sentence."

"Life sentence is how I feel," I said. "I'm stuck in fight-flight with No Exit.

"But Levine says that while humans get stuck in trauma, wild animals don't. They have an instinct to shake it off. He says humans can learn this."

In the 1970s Levine saw a client for psychosomatic illnesses: migraines, chronic pain, fatigue. Talking with him she relaxed, then for no reason had a panic attack. Watching her react as if under attack, Levine reports that he imagined an attacker. Suddenly he saw in his mind a tiger about to pounce. "A tiger's coming," he exclaimed. "Run for your life!" (8)

At that, his client experienced physiological motions which shocked them both: head-to-toe shaking and trembling, sharply elevated body temperature, then spontaneous deep gasping. This went on for almost an hour.

"I don't want to sleep in the Tiger's Cave!" I woke up screaming two years ago. I've talked about tigers and fight-flight panic for years. There must be something in human genes about caves and tigers attacking.

Levine's client reported that she had just flashed back to age four when she was held down for ether in surgery, overwhelmed by terror that the mask would suffocate her.

Suddenly I was back at age four myself after swallowing that penny, held down by my angry mother on the hulking black X-ray table at midnight. It wasn't the past; it was happening NOW. Suddenly I too was sobbing and shaking uncontrollably, moaning about the Tiger's Cave. I felt a flash of heat through my body. My sobs became spontaneous gasping for air.

Only since Sherry told me it was OK to cry, I realized, has my body felt safe enough to do what it needs to do: full-body sobbing, thrashing, and gasping.

The same physiological motions.

After Levine's patient physically shook off some of her fear, her physical illnesses began to disappear.

Levine was astonished. He knew that the reptilian survival brains of people and animals are similar, so he began to study the instincts of wildlife under attack. Wild animals, "though routinely threatened, are rarely traumatized," he found, observing them live and on film. (9)

Animals go into fight-flight if threatened, but can't stay there indefinitely. They escape, are killed, or go into shock like a mouse passing out in the jaws of a cat. Levine calls that freeze. This instinct either saves an animal from the pain of death, or lets it "play possum." Freeze is useful since many predators won't eat a dead thing; they drop it and leave.

Animals also routinely come out of freeze, Levine found. Films showed dozens of animals undergoing the same physiological motions as his patient: trembling, elevated temperature, and gasping. Levine cites the 1982 National Geographic video *Polar Bear Alert,* in which biologists in a helicopter chase a polar bear to hit it with a tranquilizer dart (like Figure 15.1). Coming to, it trembles as if having a seizure and heaves deep gasps. Its body spasms from the gut, like many animals Levine observed. Just like my body. (10)

Animals which do this, Levine found, shake it off and go about their day as if nothing happened. Animals that don't shake it off, an African game warden told him, "will die." (11)

Animals also complete the actions their bodies were attempting before they froze. One biologist in the film notes the polar bear's gyrating legs. "He's running and biting," he says; the bear was fleeing and making biting motions when it froze. On waking it completes these actions, to discharge the fight-flight chemicals from its body.

Humans, however, usually don't do this "polar bear dance," as I call it. We stay in freeze and that's trauma.

Now we're "dis-associated" from our bodies: dissociated. We grow a Grand Canyon of crust over our feelings, so we can't feel anything.

But the fight-flight cortisol surge we had at the time of the original trauma is still inside. Our nervous system, muscles and other parts are still ramped up. The rage and terror are still down in our mental sub-basement, and all over our body parts, strewn around in "dog bytes."

"Recognize the symptoms the body puts out as messages," says Levine. He's got check lists to read to see if we resonate with this or that symptom. I checked off every one. (12)

"Describing this, often you have stomach pain," said Dr. R. "What was that like as a kid?" "Constant tension," I said, "but to mention it meant trouble. I had to suck it up. In family photos I had a grimace or a frozen grin."

Enter the Impala

"Visualize a cheetah," writes Levine next, "as it prepares to attack a swift impala. Track your own responses as you watch the cheetah overtake its prey in a seventy-mile-an-hour surge. The impala falls to the ground an instant before the cheetah sinks its claws in." (13)

"An instant before the cheetah claws it? An instant *before?*"

That repeated in my head until it nearly exploded. Doesn't the impala keep running until the cheetah drags it down? No. Something *inside the impala* knocks it over—not the cheetah.

The impala isn't dead, Levine says; it's passed out.

15.2 Freezing like an impala. (Steve McWhan)

When fight-flight is of no avail, mammals instinctively go into freeze, like that mouse. The impala doesn't think, "Oh, I should play dead." It doesn't have much thinking brain.

It's involuntary.

Past a certain point, an animal's survival brain stem has a deep, over-riding instinct to knock it out. Nothing outside the animal knocks it out. The animal's own reptilian brain hijacks it into freeze.

Reptile also does that to us humans, and it's not pretty.

Levine's colleague Stephen Porges calls this "neuroception, detection without awareness." He recalls a reporter interviewing passengers on a plane which nearly crashed. One woman was asked how it felt. "Feel?" she said; "I passed out." Porges says it's a primitive reflex deep in our brain stem. (14)

This is serious, Levine warns; "people even describe it as living death." Freeze shuts down digestion, the immune system, anything not for fight-flight. "You don't need to eat lunch if you're about to be lunch," they say. If the cheetah leaves, the impala does the "polar bear dance" asap.

Why don't humans do the polar bear dance?

We are frightened by the intensity of our own energy and latent aggression, says Levine, so we *brace* ourselves against the power of the discharge, before it ever starts. We fear the full blast of our own instinctive terror, rage, and our urge to kill in self-defense for survival. (15)

Gentle ways to help humans discharge trauma and "re-associate" now exist, Levine says, to help us feel what's happening in our bodies.

He warns, however, that exercises like his should be done with another person present. Human beings don't feel safe alone. When alone, often our bodies and brain stem do not feel safe enough to come out of freeze. We stay frozen even if our intellect wants to unfreeze. Doing such exercises all alone can even re-traumatize us.

Notes

1. Mindlin et. al. (2012).
2. Siegel DJ (6-27-10).

3. GoodTherapy.Org (full web link in References).
4. Verrier (1993, p. 36).
5. Levine (6-1-11); Ogden (6-22-11).
6. Levine (2005).
7. Hanson (1-23-13).
8. Levine (2005, p.2).
9. Levine (2005, p.27).
10. Levine (10-15-14; see video minute 10).
11. Levine (2005, p.29-31).
12. Levine (2005, p.15-23).
13. Levine (2005, p.29).
14. Porges (7-6-11).
15. Levine (2005, p.31-32).

This is My Hand

16.1 Living to see Easter. (Steve McWhan)

On March 24, Steve came by to read a letter, so while he was around, I decided to try Levine's CD. In Track 1 we're told to tap our hand. Pretty innocuous. "The body is our boundary; this boundary gets ruptured in trauma," Levine says. (1)

We sat down and I played Track 1.

"Start by gently tapping the palm of your left hand, with the fingers of your right," says Levine. "Do this as many times as you need to get a sense of that part of your body.

"What do you feel? Notice whatever you feel. Then look at your hand and say, 'This is my hand. My hand belongs to me; my hand is a part of me.' "

I tapped my hand. Nothing.

"Now turn your hand over and tap the back," said Levine. "Again notice the sensation... Say something like 'This is the back of my hand. I *feel* the back of my hand. The back of my hand belongs to me.' "

"This is my hand; my hand belongs to me," I said, tapping my hand —and suddenly I was yelling: "*But I'd like to put it through my mother's nose!*

"What's this 'My hand belongs to me' nonsense?" I shouted out of nowhere. "I don't believe it! Nothing ever belonged to me; it all belonged to Mom and I want to punch her out!"

Steve's jaw dropped. I was only half conscious. On went the CD.

"Continue through every part of your body," said Levine, "lower and upper arms, feet, calves," etc. "You may be tapping the outer part of your arms, saying 'These are my arms; I can feel my arms; my arm belongs to me.' "

"These are my arms; my arms belong to me," I tapped, and again I was almost screaming:

"*Bullshit!* My arms were violated, early and often. Mom must have pulled me around by the arms a lot."

I had one shocking outburst, then another, then began sobbing violently and choking for air.

Two minutes into the CD, I had to turn it off. "I hate this part!" I groaned.

When my body spasms subsided, I tried again. Still a lot of sobbing and gasping. "I want to punch Larry!" I shouted. "He made you work; your arms didn't belong to you!" Steve shouted back.

"I'm feeling a snowball effect, thinking about the cheetah chasing the impala, then the bear kicking its legs," I said. "Something in me is getting in touch with 'what does it feel like if I *didn't* get to do that?'

"What does it feel like if all that energy is still *stuck* in my body?"

After decades of trauma, my body was exploding in delayed fury.

"I want to run around the block or slam a punching bag," I said, but it was dark outside and my limbs felt so out of control that I was afraid to trip and break a bone. I put on the church rock song "Blessed Be Your Name" and hit my living room elliptical machine.

Whoosh! My whole body exploded to the beat, slamming the machine hard with all four limbs, choking and sobbing and raising my fist. The machine was shaking off the floor as I banged like a berserker, shouting with the music, "When the darkness closes in, Lord/ Still I will say/ 'Blessed be the name of the Lord!'"

Steve was in shock. Where did this come from?

Fifteen minutes later I collapsed over the machine like a corpse, gasping, then glanced at Steve, who looked like he'd seen a ghost. Later he said that I was the one who looked "dazed and haunted."

"Also, rather than scared, you looked amazed," he said, "and there was such *aggression.*"

"I wasn't ever allowed to do aggression," I whispered.

"First it was your hand," Steve said. "You made a gesture 'No, that's not my hand!' Like you had to give your hand away."

"Mom always said that I could never do what I wanted, including going to the bathroom," I blurted. Good grief.

"Then Larry," Steve went on; "he made you work." And arms are closer to home, I thought, meaning my torso, which had all those violations... but not for Steve's innocent ears.

"I must have been terrified, at the rate I was running away," I said, but there he objected.

"You looked more like you were running *toward* someone to fight," he said. "There was a lot of flailing of arms. Or if anyone did catch you, they were going to get hell."

Next day March 25, I felt unbelieveably terrific.

On March 26, I walked into Dr. R.'s office beaming. "You look like a school girl who's just been given the greatest present ever," he said.

"Levine says the body is our boundary," I said, "and it gets ruptured in trauma. He had me tap my hand and wham, I got violent. Then he had me say 'my arms belong to me' and I screamed, 'No they don't!' "

"They never did," said Dr. R. "You had to dissociate your mind from your emotions and your body."

"But afterward I felt fantastic," I said, shaking my head. "Not just relaxed; I felt–yikes–powerful?"

"God created you with power; it's always been there," he said. "But it felt too dangerous to feel it until now.

"If you as a kid had felt power with Mom, emotions of protest and anger? She'd have been furious. If you felt the natural urge to push Mom away? Or even the urge to hit her? You couldn't have handled it. Mom couldn't have handled it.

"Your power felt dangerous to you, because you weren't big enough to survive alone. You felt completely overwhelmed.

"So your circuit breaker went off, to stop you from feeling. That's freeze; it's a survival instinct. It saves us from emotional drowning. But we lose all connection with ourselves, so it's hard to reconnect."

"Why does 'this body part is mine' make me so angry?" I demanded.

"It never felt like it was," he said. " 'Hell, it's always been mine but I didn't know? Why did they lie to me?' you ask.

"And let's add something. I want you to add 'to nobody else'," he said. "I want you to say, 'This is my hand, my hand belongs to me—*and nobody else.*' And bring that CD in here from now on.

"New body parts in here from now on, so I'm here to help if your reaction overwhelms you."

Touch My Arm?

On April 2, I brought Levine's CD to Dr. R.

"My body's still reverberating just from tapping my hand, like the animals thrashing," I said. "I wake up and my torso wants to convulse, and I think, 'Oh: polar bear!' I lie on my back and my body shakes. There's so much inside to come out. How many chases by a tiger, by a cheetah? Hundreds, thousands of terrifying incidents, all stuffed down."

He waited until I settled down. "Let's hear the CD," he said. "Try to let your body do whatever it wants." He played minute two.

"This is my shoulder," said Levine. "My shoulder and my arm are connected. My shoulder and my arm are part of me."

"Wait," I said. Dr. R. hit pause.

"If someone touches my upper arm, they're liable to touch my shoulder too, and then my torso," I said. "There's fear that I was violated there. Maybe my mother pulled me around by the arms a lot?"

"Levine talked about feeling the connection of your arm to your shoulder," said Dr. R. "Could you stroke from your hand up your arm to your shoulder and feel what that's like?"

"Stroke my arm?" Suddenly I was very nervous. "I'm scared," I said.

"But this is comforting," he said. "Afraid something bad will happen?"

"It feels bad," I said.

"This is how parents comfort kids," he said. "That's how I comfort my grandkids. I want them to know I'm right here, my hand on yours, so whatever happens, you'll be OK."

"I never heard of such a thing," I whispered. "It feels bad."

"No," he said, "This is about helping you connect to your body. So you know what comfort feels like on your shoulder. That loving stroke that says 'I'm here with you.' You know loving touch, versus other touches?"

"No!" I said.

"Maybe when Mom touched me it was mostly hostile. Later I found men who violated me. I was so frozen, I had no idea anything was wrong. Now it all feels terrifying!" I was growing visibly furious with him.

"Let's back off," said Dr. R. "Better stick to the CD."

Next, says Levine, try to find a place in the body where it's non-threatening to feel a connection between body parts. For example, touch the top of our head, then try to feel that it's connected to our forehead.

I closed my eyes and touched my crown, forehead, and face. "I feel like crying," I said. "Nobody responded to what was on my face. They looked past me like I was a rock or a tree root."

"Right!" exclaimed Dr. R. "But you had a lot to say on your face, a lot of emotion."

Therapy hour was done and we were only three minutes into Track 1.

Rhonda Reptile, however, came home with me. I mobilized to handle traffic, but as soon as I pulled into my space and turned off the car, she knocked me out again. Just like the impala's survival brain knocks it out before it's caught. "It's protective," they say; it keeps me alive.

But it's sure no fun. "Click! You're out," says Rhonda, like Spock giving me a Vulcan neck pinch. Suddenly my bad emotions disappear like a clam under the sand. I just feel nauseous. Probably developing a migraine.

Yeah, *somaticization*. Presto, the emotional pain is totally unavailable to consciousness, but it ain't gone. Nope, it goes into my body.

Who'd suspect it of a singer/dancer, but I lived my whole life dissociated from my emotions. I lived alone devoid of human touch, a situation lethal to mammals. To feel that aloneness would have blown my circuits—so my survival brain froze all emotions below consciousness. I couldn't feel my feelings, so I couldn't bond to people. I had textbook attachment disorder.

Shark Tank

"Reptile's a scary place!" I told my tape April 6, jarred awake at 2 a.m. The following raw blurt that I taped doesn't make sense and doesn't need to. Logic means nothing to two brains of three:

"Punch my mother's nose?" I growled. "The more I feel what's down in my survival brain, the more I want to *kill* her!

"Reptile says 'Get me out of here before I kill something!' So I ran to Japan, ran to California, then got yanked back to that hospice in Florida. And I want to kill her! That's what reptiles do.

"The survival brain doesn't care if it's your mother.

"I said that in my grief letters. I talked it through with my chiropractor and Dr. R. They say we all get enraged, it's no crime, provided we don't act. Why is it still eating me?

"Well, er, I can't stroke my arm.

"As I un-freeze and begin to feel what's actually down inside me, I'm shaking. 'What's Inside Me' is scaring the *crap* out of me.

"Stroking my arm feels like my body boundary is being slashed. It's beyond yanking my arms. I'm terrified by that cold fisheye Mom had, that didn't care what I felt.

"What's eating me?

"A shark. This is why the shark attack.

"Mom violated my boundaries like a shark: she ripped into me. 'What's Inside Me' is a terror of being overpowered so big, it feels like a huge shark is about to eat me alive. It can come at me from any angle; I can't run, defend or breathe. The stress chemicals are drowning me and I'm gasping for air.

"There's a place deep in my survival brain even worse than the Tiger's Cave. Most mammals treat a child better; the apes cared for Mogley. The tigress was nice to Piglet.

"Mom was no mammalian tiger. She was a shark.

"It wasn't a tiger's cave, where at least I could breathe. I was born in a shark tank.

"I see that shark and every sensory organ screams 'Here's Death.' It's not 'thinks'—my whole body perceives it *physically*. Reptile knocks me out before the news ever reaches Frontal.

"My survival brain has said for decades, 'It's too much!' Not just 'I don't want to do this anymore.' It's 'I can't *experience* this anymore!' That's not a thought; it's an instinct, like the mouse blacks out.

"That's why I talk about the 'dating shark pool.' " End tape. (See Chapter 1 page 1, plus "shark," pages 19, 56, etc.) I rang Dr. R.

"It feels like my body's being ripped apart," I said when he called back. "I saw a DivorceCare graphic of a heart being ripped apart and blurted out, 'my parents divorced me.' It made no sense until now."

"Exactly," he said, "An infant has no thoughts to say 'this hurts.' The flood of frightening emotions feels like its body is being physically torn apart."

"I'm terrified of my own reptilian instinct to kill or be killed," I cried. "Levine says we're afraid to unfreeze due to the enormous amounts of energy of our own aggression coming up. It's terrifying! I remember at 25, after leaving home, becoming obsessed with Mozart's *Requiem*. What's a young girl doing with a mass for the dead? I was so horrified at wanting to kill, I probably convicted myself of murder by age four!

"I feel like a reptile and reptiles are disgusting. Oh shit, I'm one of them! I'm a killer like the other Martians!"

"It's OK to want to kill," said my NCT (sic). "The difference with murderers is that they do it. You are experiencing what we call 'murderous rage.' Everyone can. It's normal."

"How much rage is stored up in my body from millions of hostile experiences?" I sobbed.

"Talk about it, hear it normalized," said Dr. R. "Realize it happens a lot. As you talk about the terror and rage, get angry about your body being violated. Next time you'll speak up to protect yourself before it happens."

I needed a Christian scholar to tell me it's OK to want to kill my mother.

"No wonder I have a fish phobia," I said. "I hate aquariums. That's how Mom looked at me. She left a dead goldfish in my bed when I was 12. Later she chased me around the house with a two-foot frozen game fish someone caught. Why? 'To hear you scream,' she laughed. It all flat-out terrified me.

"Mom attacked me at a dinner in 2006. 'I looked into her eyes but there was no way to make a connection with what I saw,' I wrote back then. 'It looked like a very cold fish or something more dangerous.'

"I've felt this all my life! I probably condemned myself as a killer by age four. Now you say I'm not bad for having a brain stem? We can't control its reflex to kill in self-defense, any more than we can control our body temperature?

"Think of the burden over decades that I've just put down. Think of the burden! I had back pain all my life? I was holding all that rage in my back."

"Exactly," he said.

I felt so relieved that I had a good cry right on the phone. Monkey made the call and it worked.

By Easter Sunday April 8, my body was relaxing at an incredible rate.

I woke at sunrise, went out on my patio singing Haydn's *Creation* and broke down sobbing, "Thank You God for resurrecting me to see Easter." I leaned on the railing and sang half the oratorio, crying and laughing.

I went to church with a grin, still wearing face paint from the day before when we painted kids at the Easter festival. (Figure 16.1)

"You look so happy. Did you find a guy?" a friend asked. What a thing to say in church. "Oh, no" I said, "Much better. I found God inside."

Later Steve and I trekked around an enormous flower farm to match my colorful face paint. I could hardly walk for my wobbly legs. I kept collapsing on benches in tears of joy for the sheer physical release I was feeling.

"The relief is incredible," I told Dr. R. next day. " 'Feel the support of the floor,' they say in yoga; 'feel the support of the chair.'

"But I never felt it before. I always had a hole under my feet. My body was dissociated from physical reality.

"Then sitting in church yesterday, suddenly I felt the support of the pew underneath. I was crying to the music and it felt so fantastic just to be held by that pew that I didn't want to leave.

"I can't believe how much better I feel than last week," I said.

Shower Exercise

Next on Levine Track 1 was the "shower exercise." In the shower, we let the water fall on various body areas, so it does the tapping and we can just feel. I had told Dr. R. that I'd do it the night before our next meeting.

On April 11, I got an Easter card from Bob. He kept violating my postbox like that every few months for two years. So did Dan back East, who sent me birthday greetings until 2013. It all felt like a poke in the eye.

On April 15, I had a friend wait in my living room. I went to my room, closed the door, and played Levine's CD.

"Put your hand up to the shower," said Levine, "and again say 'This is the palm of my hand. The palm of my hand belongs to me.' Do that with as many parts of your body as you want."

I was crying before I even touched the faucet. I felt so sad and lonely about Bob and life. What kind of a weekend is this, experimenting on my body because I'm sick? I put my hand to the stream. "This is my hand, my hand belongs to me, and nobody else," I recited.

Suddenly I was bawling, "which means I have to be alone–because if I say 'this is mine,' then *everyone's going to leave!*" Huh? That's what I reported to my tape 15 minutes later.

I let the water fall on as many parts of me as I could, then dressed and returned to the living room.

"If I ever said anything was mine, I'd have been locked out in the cold," I told my friend and my tape.

"In the shower, when I said 'This is my arm, this is my shoulder,' my body went into spasms. 'I don't believe it,' I was yelling, 'I was told this belonged to someone else. Now if I say it's mine, it feels horrible because I'll be left alone!'

"Then I put the water on my face. 'This is my face, the part that nobody ever saw,' I blurted. 'You didn't even notice I exist,' as I wrote to my ex, Dad, and Bob. I flew into such a rage about all the people who never noticed my face that I couldn't tolerate the water there anymore.

"So I turned around in disgust. At random the water fell on my butt and suddenly I was screaming, 'This is my butt, and *I hate you guys!* Bob's card? I can't stop the Male! *I hate you guys!*' I was shouting loudly enough to alarm the neighbors. Then just as suddenly, I was too scared to stay in there alone. I had to dress and come sit with another human being."

Next day I told Dr. R. how I exploded in the shower screaming.

"It's your psyche coming alive!" he said. "Unfreezing releases physical body pain, so our feelings are freed up.

"It's fine to hate them!" he smiled.

I remembered pumping Dan's tin can full of bullets in May 2008, then 19 months later finally feeling my anger and shouting "I hate *all* of you!" to the planet at large.

Now, the angrier I got, the more the crust on my heart broke up and began to move. The more I repeated "I hate all of you," the more strongly I felt heavy tectonic plates moving in my chest.

Go Out and Feel!

Every Monday for 12 weeks until the end of June, Dr. R. and I worked to complete Levine's CD. Each track had more explosive healing than the last. Each one hurt like hell, then I felt terrific.

"Six months ago I said 'No' to Bob and it felt hideous. If I hadn't been paying a shrink $130 an hour to tell me to do it, I never would have," I wrote April 28. "But slowly, 'No' did make me feel safe.

"Break, break, break and it feels like hell, but six months later I feel *so* much better!"

More and more I'd be out walking or traveling and say, "I can't believe how much better I feel than the last time I was here!" It got to be a standing joke.

In Levine Track 2, we worked on grounding, feeling the floor and the earth beneath, and finding the body's physical center of gravity. In Track 3, we checked my resources for handling emotions. In Track 4, I had to find areas inside my body which felt safe and strengthen them by feeling my feelings about a safe object; I used my faithful stuffed dog. I wish I had a photo of myself in business garb, entering Dr. R.'s imposing marble office building

16.2 Mood swings. (Steve McWhan)

with that large furry toy hidden in an oversized tote.

"We can have very bad feelings, but then we can walk through them and come out feeling very good," said Dr. R. "Now you're moving from painful feelings to relaxed feelings, and seeing they go hand in hand.

"And the freedom is: "I can just *go out and feel!* Because if things go bad, I know what to do to get relief. I don't have to avoid feeling anymore!"

"All my life," I said, "I'd have a bad emotion and it would stay for days and weeks."

"In trauma bad emotions do stay forever, because we're constantly pushed back into the baby's experience when there was nothing we could do," he said. "Now you experience that you can do something: go to people and get comfort. It's like a miracle."

"People, the magic band-aid!" I smiled.

Progress wasn't smooth; things got perfectly hair-raising before they got better. I'd leave Dr. R. furious voicemails when I couldn't understand.

Yet overall Dr. R. was a Miracle Worker to my emotional Helen Keller.

First and foremost he was safe to hear all my feelings. "Mobilize your anger!" he'd say—even, especially, against him. "Is this shrink crazy?" I'd mutter. The only anger I felt was rage when I couldn't follow him.

"You have friends who don't care if you're angry?" I retorted once.

"A few, actually," he replied, "I hand-pick them. They're keepers."

The man had confronted his own childhood trauma until he healed it, so he was able to tolerate mine. He knew that the child's rage must be shared to be tamed, and graciously allowed me to have that experience with him.

Kick out the Moon

As I began to feel my feelings they would swing wildly, and my limbs would spontaneously thrash. My feet kicked and my hands pushed involuntarily as if they had a life of their own.

After a workout May 13, I had so much energy left that I was dancing around the gym parking lot. I met Sherry to picnic in the garden of a hotel and almost danced in their lot, too. Walking through the lobby I couldn't contain my energy. When we reached a cliff high above the ocean, I was walking double-time.

Suddenly I looked up wild-eyed as if to say "I can't control this," and handed Sherry my bag as though about to dive off the cliff. My body propelled me running down the long, steep hill to the ocean as if pulled by wild horses, then back up, running all the way in an explosion of energy. Then I was gasping as if to drink in the sea.

"Don't ask me," I said, "I'm just renting. My real masters are downstairs in my sub-brain. Rhonda Reptile is releasing stress I didn't even know I had. She bypassed my thinking brain and hijacked my body."

Later I could hardly eat, I felt so good. "I just want to sit and 'feel the fantastic' in my gut," I said. "It's like drinking Love Potion #9: 'I didn't know if it was day or night/ I started kissing everything in sight...' "

Then on May 27, I was alone and miserable for Memorial Day weekend when the country song "One-Way Ticket" came up on my mp3.

My right foot exploded banging on the floor, unstoppable. "I have walked through the fire/And crawled on my knees/Through the valley of the shadow of doubt," I sang along, "Then the truth came shining like a light on me/And now I can see my way out!"

"Say '*No!*' " I yelled at my mp3. (I'd begun using its record function since it was always on me). "*No* to bad treatment, like I said '*No*' to Larry and bought a one-way ticket West! *No* to people who leave me alone now!

"If I re-associate, I'm going to feel, and it's huge.

"Alone feels bad, but I'm gonna feel bad when I should feel bad—and that's good."

My body was still bursting with decades of stress energy being discharged, so I ran to the beach and jogged for two hours. Then I beat up the gym. Returning home the physical explosion was still on, so I danced around my condo again. "Let the horrible emotions come up and *out*," I told Dr. R. by voicemail.

Next day May 28, Steve arrived for a grief barbecue. We sat on my patio swing having coffee while I listened to Dr. R's return message.

"Being alone this weekend triggered feelings from childhood of being alone," he said. "First is the loss at being dropped by friends; that brings up terror from when your parents dropped you. Second is the rage of 'I hate them!' That rage is too much to feel. So your survival brain freezes you, and then you feel lousy. To unfreeze, mobilize your anger! Journal about how enraging it is to be dropped. Express the rage to people who can handle it."

Suddenly my feet were kicking into the air over the swing, as involuntary as a loud sneeze. Coffee flew everywhere.

"My feet went off like rockets. I wanted to kick out the moon," I told my mp3. "It was whole-body kicking from the groin. My ankles shook like grass in a hurricane. I couldn't stop it."

It felt as if an oil drill ramming around in a mile of rock layers had hit a gusher. I felt a sudden, massive force, and then the ancient anger under pressure exploded like a load of liquified prehistoric dinosaur flesh, spewing gunk.

"Yeah there's rage—I'm kicking like an infant," I realized. There was so much energy in my hips and legs, I was afraid to break something. I had to use the elliptical machine again to discharge the bodily fury.

"Don't ask me," I told Steve, bewildered, "I'm just renting."

We set off for the barbecue.

At San Clemente, walking on sand my legs were as wobbly as jello; it was evident that my back and hips were unfreezing. "Let me take a video," a bystander laughed. "Your walk will go viral on YouTube!"

We reached a stretch covered in rocks. Suddenly for no reason, I began picking up large rocks which usually would be too heavy for me to throw. I checked for a spot with no swimmers and began furiously hurling rock after rock into the ocean. I kept throwing until my arm was sore. "Rhonda has the urge to smash her way out today," I said.

Then we saw swings. After all that energy washed through me, I felt like a million bucks and wanted nothing so much as to swing, soaring to the sky as my sister and I did together. Notice my goofy grin in 16.2.

My body's outbursts tapered off over the next few years, but have never completely stopped. It can still be wild. Each time I discharge some long-repressed stress, I feel better.

In late June, I visited the Meditation Garden overlooking the Pacific in Encinitas. I'd been here once in 2007, on a very bad date. I recalled being so crazed with grief and adrenaline back then that I could barely see. I longed for a place of my own like this, where the sun shines on the ocean, but I felt too awful to belong then.

Now I saw that this lovely spot represented the ideal safe place for which I'd longed all my life. The sun on the ocean again; the message in a bottle.

"I can't believe how much better I feel than the last time I was here!" I thought. "Now I *do belong* here.

"In fact, I live here. I live a 12-minute walk from the ocean where I can see the sun dance on it every day. I feel like I belong because God wants me here."

By closing time I was one safe impala. Looking out over the sun setting on the water, my body began to shake spontaneously, then I was sobbing over absolutely nothing, just for the feeling of sheer safety.

Notes

1. Levine (2005, p.39).

17

Butt End of Evolution

17.1 Feeling "Love Inside." (Kathy Brous)

When we do the polar bear discharge we start to feel fully, often for the first time. That's a huge experience; suddenly I felt such murderous emotions. Yet if I un-braced and let the rage and terror rip through me, it did discharge.

Then I would feel God's love flood in and a joy for life that I'd never imagined before.

This is how a baby with an attuning mom feels from birth, Dr. R. kept saying; many people just grow up that way. "Huh?" I'd say.

I saw it with my neighbor and her infant son (above). She smiles and carries him face-to-face a lot and he's always beaming. You can see the joy grow as it resonates back and forth between them. Living limbic resonance.

I also recognized that feeling of resonating later, hearing neuroanatomist Jill Bolte Taylor describe living in her right emotional brain, after a blood clot silenced her left logical brain.

"Energy streams in through all of our sensory systems," she says, "then explodes into this enormous collage of what this present moment looks like, smells like, tastes like... My spirit soared free." (1)

By mid-July, however, my mood swings had become alarming. Agonizing pain and tears of joy kept alternating for no reason. "This is insane!" Susie my thinking brain would tell Dr. R.

But he was pleased.

"Pain comes with the package," he said July 23. "Unfreezing old painful feelings feels like healing frostbite. We have to suffer the agony of it coming back to life. If we can walk through it with others and they comfort us, the pain discharges. Then we feel new well-being and a lot more joy 'in the now.' "

"How do you spell relief? A-G-O-N-Y? " I said. "Yep," he replied.

"I experience God washing over me, but then I lose it," I sighed.

"You've gotten a glimpse of love with Someone so Big that He washes over your whole body," he said. "It must be like what an infant feels when it's born. Suddenly there's a flood of terror—but then we're wrapped in those arms of love..."

"Or not," I said.

His eyes grew wide.

"Not me," I said. "What happened was: nothing. I was just left to scream in stress chemicals. The loving arms and feel-good oxytocin never came."

"You were dropped splat on the floor," said Dr. R. solemnly.

"Or locked in a box," I said. "What really freaks me out is that after 45 minutes of protest, the baby goes into clinical shock. The end. All that cortisol just sits in the muscles and nerves around the heart and viscera.

"That baby learns there is no comfort, 'emotions are terrifying, and the world is a scary place,' says Allan Schore." (2)

"That's why this has been so hard on you," said Dr. R. "When you experience intense emotions, the association has been: 'and next will come: nothing.' You're stuck with that horrible emotion for days or weeks. Now it's different; you make calls, and I and others respond. But you'll still have times when that fear is triggered, and that's what makes it *so* horrible."

Exactly.

Now I began to feel a terror from infancy deeper than my brain stem had ever let me feel before.

"Something Bigger than me is trying to kill me," I woke up bawling to my mp3 August 12. "Here comes the wolf at the door again.

"Oh no, not the Disney wolf! Make it go away!" Again the six-foot beast stood in my bedroom door with red eyes and teeth to rip. It glared at me, then came in and bit me in the back of the neck, and I woke screaming. This lifelong nightmare had stopped when I talked about it for the first time ever, in my 2009 grief letters. Now it was back.

"Someone Bigger than us loves us? When I was little, Someone Bigger was coming to get me, so I had to wake up kicking and screaming," I told Dr. R. August 20. "People are scary. They're *bigger* than me. They're gonna take chunks out of me."

"You didn't have words for that as an infant, but you knew that sickening fear well," said Dr. R. "Later when you got words, the next thing you saw which looked like that feeling, you said, 'That's it!' You pinned that old terror onto that wolf image."

"How could I feel so loved before, but now feel so awful again?" I asked.

"Don't be alarmed that it comes back," he said. "As a kid you had thousands and thousands of terrifying experiences. Now you need thousands and thousands of good experiences to overwrite bad patterns.

"This will take more than a few months."

The Shark Within

Then the shark attacks returned.

"Sharks in My Cellar," I told the tape about one nightmare. "The shark feels a lot deeper inside me than the wolf, in layers even younger than age two."

Later I dreamed that the beach where we went as kids was shark-infested. The waves grew to 30 feet, then into a horseshoe like Niagara Falls around me. Suddenly the wind blew me up a high cliff to a house on top where I found a baby. As I scrambled to find warm clothes for it, the waves rose up the cliff and engulfed the house.

I woke with chest pains, heart pounding.

"Why am I still in this?" I asked Dr. R. August 27.

"The terror of that shark is wordless and it's so big because it did happen before age two, when your whole nervous system was under development," he said.

"The waves were your infant experience of helplessness. You were helpless facing those waves. Then you found the baby, which was you, but you couldn't help it. You felt helpless again, so the waves returned and overwhelmed you."

"Those were real waves!" I retorted. "Any reasonable person would be terrified."

"No, that wasn't the ocean," he said. "Those waves were actually a feeling from infancy *inside* you.

"Try to feel that it's not happening now. Try to feel that you were re-experiencing infant terror, and the infant was terrified for good reason, but now you're safe."

"That's what my parents always said," I snarled. " 'It's just a dream, grow up.' I can lie there forever repeating that, but the terror is real at night because I'm really alone. It's like the claustrophobic scientist who needs an MRI. He knows it's harmless, but he panics, can't think, and has to be removed from the machine. Trying to 'think it away' is like trying to think my digestion into running backwards. (3)

"I can't handle this anymore! It's like driving an icebreaker through a volcano. It feels like a bone marrow transplant every day for the last four years."

On September 10, entering Dr. R.'s lobby, a photo of Golem from *Lord of the Rings* on a magazine cover turned my stomach. "Fight-flight or freeze were the only options I had as a kid," I said, waving it at him. "There was no third option for mammalian attachment. The anxiety I feel now is from a lifetime of waking up to hostile fisheyes like this."

Then came the physical reaction; I began waking in serious jaw pain.

"Levine says we brace ourselves to avoid the polar bear discharge," I told Dr. R. "My jaw had to clench and brace up as a kid in that aversive environment. All my life my survival brain contracted my jaw so I grind my teeth at night. I've lost two molars that way."

"Your survival brain might be clenching out of anger," said Dr. R.

"A clenched jaw is known in the literature as the seat of anger," retorted Susie Labcoat. "But they say we get angry to hide fear."

"For you, *fear hides anger*," he said, "As a kid it was too dangerous to be angry. You had to freeze before you ever felt your anger. You had to clench up and shut up.

"Time to mobilize the anger again."

Tapping My Anger

" 'No' is survival," I journaled. "Mom's anxiety was so overwhelming, I had to focus on her or else. I couldn't feel anger, just panic. But Levine says that if we don't feel our natural aggression, we don't survive."

I stared at the "Don't Tread on Me" flag on my microwave. No anger. All I felt was nausea and a really bad pain in my jaw.

That's when I began to practice "tapping," aka Emotional Freedom Technique (EFT), for releasing feelings.

When I clicked on the wrong link in Lucy's email and got the brain seminars, Lucy actually meant to send me to a tapping website.

Dr. Roger Callahan, a psychotherapist who studied acupuncture, treated a patient for water phobia in 1980. He had her verbalize her fear of water while using her fingers to tap her head, cheekbones, chin and a total of nine acupressure points, without needles. To their amazement, she felt relief and ran to his pool to splash her face. (4)

I've got a Big Thing phobia. Someone Bigger was hostile to me as a kid. Now my emotional brain is sure there's a big something in my room and all I feel is fear. But my real problem may be anger frozen so deep I can't feel it.

Tapping creates a structured time to verbalize feelings while we connect to our body, as Levine advises. First I tapped a round on each of the nine acupressure points, saying how terrified I felt at the Big Thing. Nothing.

Next I tapped the same nine spots, saying how angry I felt at the Big Thing. Nothing in this second round.

Then, tapping the nine spots again and voicing anger, *wham* came the reaction in the third round. "I'm so angry they're always attacking me! I'm so angry they treated me like crap!" I yelled at my family and the world (infants can't tell the difference). My torso convulsed with rage.

The oil drill in my rock layers had hit another gusher, another purely physical release. Again the baby emotion under pressure exploded like a load of liquified dinosaur gunk.

For 15 minutes, the more I yelled and tapped, the more rage I felt, until the volcano "spiked" to a roar. The white-hot rage ran through me and just as suddenly disappeared.

I added "I'm so angry they treated me like crap" to my Revolutionary flag.

Afterward I felt like a million bucks, bursting with life. I walked around my condo feeling the floor grounding me, gazing at the avocados in my kitchen in awe, and weeping for the beauty of the trees by my patio.

"It's crazy how I'll be hit by a wall of pain, but if I can process it, 20 minutes later I'm laughing," I told Dr. R.

"Once we discharge old feelings, we can enjoy life 'in the now'," he replied. "Levine said it with those wild animals. Once the threat's gone and they shake it off? *Boom*! Off they trot. After we release bad emotions, we lose interest and think 'What's for breakfast?' "

Discharging infant attachment trauma is no one shot-deal.

It's an ongoing commitment the size of owning horses. One must clean the stable regularly. Work on feeling and discharging trauma regularly and it's agony for ten minutes to two hours, then I feel fantastic. Don't do it and I feel stinking lousy for weeks.

Mabel Hated Babies

Then the doubts returned. Maybe what I feel is the terror of being locked in the incubator for weeks, which my baby mind projected onto Mom? Only a jerk blames their mother for everything!

On September 23, I called an uncle about a family reunion. "By the way," I said in closing, "I'm in therapy and my doctor would like some data.

"Do you recall how my Mom behaved when I was a baby?" His reply was such a shock that I hit "record" on my mp3 player.

"Mabel was a strange lady," he said. "Before you were born, we bought our house and were delighted when your parents Ralph and Mabel moved in next door. But we couldn't get close.

"Mabel wouldn't show any affection towards my daughter Bonnie in her baby carriage," he said. "She would pass by without looking at the carriage. That bothered us... it wasn't right." My cousin was born three years before me. (The same Bonnie interviewed earlier.)

"Gosh," I said, "Bonnie was the first born of all us cousins; wouldn't everyone be thrilled to see her?"

"Not Mabel," he repeated. "I don't know about her babies, but she didn't like my babies. We just couldn't get close."

I recalled again that whenever the subject "boys" arose, Mom would repeat, "Don't get stuck pushing a baby carriage," as if having a baby were a death sentence. Now we know:

Mabel hated babies.

Nothing personal, baby.

Or, more likely, *she was terrified of having babies.* As a baby, I didn't have a PhD, so I didn't know that. I just felt hated. Now an eye witness reports that this was obvious three years before I was born.

Later my uncle's son called about the reunion. I told him the story, but he began to laugh.

"That's not news," he said. "Dad's been repeating all that about Mabel refusing to look at my sister's carriage for years!"

Months later at the reunion dinner, my uncle repeated the story to everyone again, unprompted. Evidently I was not the only one traumatized by Mabel's reaction to babies.

Now the sign on my microwave read:

Mabel hated babies.
I didn't break it—
I *don't* have to fix it;
It's Not My Coat.

Then a light went on.

Why did Mom grind her teeth all night, just like me? What was she braced up against?

What in blazes happened to my poor Mom that she was so terrified of babies, years before she had any?

Butt End of Evolution

I thought it through and phoned Steve.

"Good evening," I said. "Thank you for flying Re-Association Air. This is your Captain speaking from the Butt End of Evolution. It hits me that my trauma is a cosmic joke. I'm the logical consequence of evolution.

"Fear has been bred into our neurons since the cave days; it's called the 'negativity bias' of the brain. Brains that feared more were the ones that survived to pass on genes. (5)

"Finally my great-grand parents faced so much fear in Europe that they traveled from England to South Africa to Australia to California in the bellies of steamers, having 13 children in 13 different cities. My Mom's mom was the twelfth.

17.2 Luggage, LAX.
(Steve McWhan)

"Babies need a mom's attention to grow brain structure. How much attention could #12 have gotten? Do the math.

"Poor immigrants went in steerage; #12 of 13 born in hellholes?

"Grandma couldn't have gotten much more parenting than the luggage! She had no parenting software to give Mom. 'Mothering well doesn't come naturally,' says Allan Schore. 'What comes naturally is mothering *as you were mothered.*' (6)

"Great-grandma treated Grandma like luggage, so Grandma only knew to treat Mom like luggage. Mom didn't even want the luggage. I'm third-generation luggage. I have so much emotional baggage, I couldn't even procreate. Shrinks call it 'refusal to repeat.'

"Folks: if you have emotional baggage, maybe it's because you were treated like luggage."

I finished my rant. "Good grief," said Steve, "that actually hangs together." Research confirmed it in spades.

My maternal great-grandparents were English, Grandma always said, and there they were on Ancestry.com. Great-grandpa Maurice, a traveling salesman, was born in London in 1860; his wife Esther in 1872. I found the 1910 U.S. Census showing Maurice in Denver in 1906. Grandma said she was born in Denver in 1906.

I found the 1920 Census showing the household of Maurice (60) and Esther (48) in New York. All the names of their children correspond to Grandma's siblings, people I've met or heard about. They included Rose, 34; Clara, 21; Gertrude, 16; my Grandma Jean, 14; and Simon, 11.

I felt shock seeing such a large family in official records; it brought flesh to life. How could poor Esther take care of them all on the boats? Did she ever sleep? Did they have enough food?

Plus, if Rose were 34 in 1920, then she was born in 1886—when Esther was 14. Apparently Maurice knocked up Esther at 13 and took her abroad. Worse, I can count only six children of 13 births. Did half the children die in terrible voyages or epidemics?

They lived in fight-flight 24x7. That ramped up cortisol gets frozen into our back muscles. That's why Mom had back pain all her life and so did Grandma; we all had the same trauma as infants.

"Many mothers have trouble handling their own emotions," says Schore. If she's too preoccupied, "she just can't read the baby's tone... facial expressions and gestures. You see inter-generational transmission of these deficits."

If you were Mabel, you wouldn't want to look into a baby carriage, either.

Bottom line?

About half of us get the loving attention we need as infants. We begin life as a sea of emotions and stress chemicals, then an attuning adult comforts our emotions again and again. This turns off the stress and turns on reward chemicals like oxytocin. We have thousands of good experiences, so we learn the neural patterns to "do comfort," and we stop crying. We "internalize" the

Big Person's comfort; now we have their "love inside" us. It's constant. That's emotional object constancy. (7)

We learn to handle emotions, to enjoy good emotions, and also—very important—to tolerate and fully feel negative emotions, to release them. Our "Self" begins when we start to regulate our own emotions this way, without screaming for someone else. That's when we realize we are not merely part of mom. We've got an independent "Self."

Then once we have words, it makes sense to hear God loves us. The existence of loving moms explains why we recognize God's love: we got a big dose of it while our brains were developing.

We feel safe and strong to have God's love inside. We attract friends and spouses who treat us lovingly, since we're used to that from birth. Folks who don't treat us well feel weird, so we shy away. (8)

Or not.

The other half of us don't get enough attunement as infants. We're born in that sea of emotions and stress chemicals, but they just keep coming. "It's impossible for a baby to regulate its own emotions," says Allan Schore, "*the mother is the regulator of that baby.*" If she can't or won't, we have no model for managing emotions. We have thousands and thousands of bad experiences while our brain is developing, so we don't grow "love inside." That hurts so much, it's terrifying. This stress doesn't stop; it's shoved down into the subconscious and body. It's still down there decades later. (9)

These are new findings. Until the 1960s, scientists expected most kids to run to mom. Then they studied over 6,000 toddlers and were shocked to find that 45% actually fear mom to a degree (see Appendix). And if Mommy was scary, everyone else is, too—including God.

So we spend our lives searching in adult romance for the love we didn't get as kids. Naturally this goes badly, because *a lover can't do* what parents are designed to do. That's why love songs have been mostly tragic for millennia. We keep finding people like our parents, who never received much love, so they don't have love to give us.

For half of us, Mommy is the root of all evil, so to speak.

But remember: it's not her fault. She *physiologically* couldn't help how her brain grew, after it happened to her mom, and her mom, and her mom.

Great-grandma Esther raised 13 kids in hellholes while being hungry, exhausted, and at risk for killer diseases. It's not biologically possible that she had much to give a child. I weep thinking of her.

"Stop blaming your Mom for your problems!" my internal voices retort. But in fact, stuffing it and denial are the culprits that have kept this cycle going for centuries.

It's not her fault, it's not her fault! My thinking brain knows Esther, Grandma, and Mom did their best. I weep for her, I weep for her! My emotional brain deeply feels their pain.

But I still hurt; that's *inside* me and it hurts a lot, those generations of pain propagating through my cells. The contradiction between "I weep for her" and "I hurt" feels like it's tearing my body apart.

Feel compassion for them, says *Grief Handbook* page 199, but *don't deny the pain inside us that resulted*. That's refusing to feel our pain; then we can't release it. Steve and I caught ourselves excusing others to avoid feeling our own pain so much, we began to say, "Oops, I did a page 199." (10)

If the pain is still inside us, it won't stop until we feel it. But if we do a page 199 and deny it, then we're stuck with it forever.

The only way to break the cycle is to mourn the effects on us and discharge the hurt. Feel our hurts in shared consciousness; don't try this alone! Plus, if we have damaged feelings inside us from the past, people in the present will trigger them. Yet it's the past that actually makes us feel bad.

Why yell at people in the present? Move the tale to childhood, and yell. I yell about the past, because past emotions are stuck in my body, needing discharge. I call a safe person and yell; yell to God; tap and yell; or hit the gym to angry music. Then I get relief. Damn the guilt torpedos, I feel my pain—then I'm done with it. If I don't, I'm stuck *in* it.

Hard Left, Hard Right

I didn't grasp all that instantly. Instead on October 1, after another letter from Bob, I threw up my hands.

"Mom's brain stem was fried since the sperm hit the egg, and her mother's was fried before her," I told Dr. R. "I'm the product of three generations of terminal sperm-egg fry. It's baked into my brain.

"I can't un-fry an egg, and I can't stop the male!" I howled. "A year after blocking Bob, I'm still alone.

"Pain comes with the package? I've walked through unbelievable pain. I'm like a fish that's had its scales removed, swimming around bleeding, and predators can smell it.

"I don't wanna do this anymore!"

"You're feeling incredibly deep pain with me," said Dr. R. "I feel honored.

"And that's what's new. Now you call me and others, in real time. You get heard. Then you put words to the feelings. You hang onto us as you walk through it, so you can release the pain. And you say 'No' to hurtful people like Bob.

"Next: mobilize your anger. Mom got hurt as a kid, but you still must feel *your* survival reaction to what hurt *you* (no page 199!).

"Keep mobilizing the anger," he repeated.

Driving home I didn't just get angry; I flew into a white-hot fury. "I want to kill them all," I thought.

"I can't stop the male, but I can move the tale. The excess of my upset about Bob must be projected anger at Mom.

"Mobilize the anger? Back to Mom music; I'll yowl my way through."

I put in the Mom funeral CD with the doom of Verdi's *Requiem*. At "Dies Irae," I went nuts on the freeway, banging the wheel and belting along loudly in Latin like some demon out of *Amadeus*.

"Day of wrath," I sang, "Day to dissolve the world in ashes. What trembling there will be when the Judge comes! I hate you, Mom! You want to kill me, shark? OK, I'm gonna kill you!"

This continued to "Tuba Mirum" with its horns blazing the call to the dead. "The trumpet sounds through the tombs of every land, calling all before the Throne," I yelled.

"Rot in Hell, you bitch! Screw you, Mom!" You want miracles? It was a miracle I didn't hit anyone.

Down the I-5 I went berserk until I reached my exit and turned onto the local parkway. On came the "Lacrymosa," an entirely different tone of voice, perhaps the saddest music ever written. "Tearful is that day on which we rise from ashes..."

Suddenly I was sobbing so hard I had to pull over.

"Lord, please spare my Mother's soul," I cried, utterly out of nowhere with no intention to say anything of the sort. Un-bunny-lievable.

"She had no idea what she was doing; she was completely unequipped.

"She was maybe one or two years old inside. That blind hysteria in her eye? That was the sheer terror of not knowing what's going on."

On and on I wept and pleaded for my mother's soul.

Once I could see to drive, I drove to the church parking lot and played songs about redemption from Verdi's *Don Carlos*. "Lord, please save us from this pain," I sobbed, "please free my mother's soul from all this pain."

I sat there another 40 minutes crying for the love of my Mom, felt much better, and went home.

"Don't ask me," I thought, dazed. "I'm just renting."

Next day it happened again. I was smashing up the gym to angry country songs on my mp3 when Whitney Houston came on. I looked out the window, saw the sun on the ocean, and saw Mom and Dad. "I——— will always love you, Mom and Dad," I sang along with Whitney. "Father, forgive them for they knew not what in blazes was up."

"Something remarkable has occurred," I told Steve by phone. " 'Mobilize the Anger' says Dr. R. and I sure was in a fury at Mom driving home the other night. Then suddenly for no reason, my body was flooded with love for her. It was like turning the steering wheel hard to the left—but the car makes a hard right turn. It feels impossible.

"Against my will, I felt love. In my body."

You could hear Steve's jaw drop 30 miles away.

I recalled Corrie ten Boom, the Dutch pacifist who after WWII forgave the SS guard that killed her sister. She tried to shake his hand, she writes, but physically could not. Then "suddenly from my shoulder along my arm and through my hand, a current seemed to pass from me to him," she reports, "while into my heart sprang a love for this stranger that almost overwhelmed me. When God tells us to love our enemies, *He gives along with the command, the Love itself.*"

"*Mirable dictu*," said Dr. R. "Tender feelings for... Mom."

"It was striking how it went from murderous rage to intense love," I said.

"It sounds like forgiveness from the gut," he said. "True forgiveness only comes from serious grieving.

"Loving feelings for Mom are always deep inside us, but if there is also hurt and rage, we must feel those first," he said. To come out of freeze we must first feel the fight-flight that prepares us to smash the predator, says Levine. "As a kid, though, having those feelings didn't feel safe," Dr. R. continued, "so your brain stem froze them to protect you.

"But now you're experiencing that you can feel through the rage and you don't die, so suddenly it feels safe. This time you didn't stop your anger by freezing. You could have your anger fully, until it was spent."

Once the anger is "caught and released," we start to feel the love at our core, because we're mammals. "She *was* your Mom," he concluded. "She did give life."

" 'Rot in Hell you bitch' flips to 'I love my Mommy?' You've seen this?" I asked.

"Occasionally," he said. "Home is supposed to be safe enough for a child feel anything, including to hate the one they love. Kids need to do that! And then they love their parents with all their hearts. Because both are true. You have found that your rage did not destroy your compassion."

It kept happening. Time and again I'd need to let my anger and rage pour out in release, then into its place would pour love and gratitude.

When I couldn't mobilize my anger, I felt nothing. Instead I developed a migraine or backache because the anger froze in my body. "Let's make a sign for your desk," I told Dr. R.

"Mobilize the Anger, Feel the Love"

Opening the Heart

I thought it was nuts, then heard scholars have long written about it.

I'd been listening to Buddhist therapist Tara Brach for a year. I couldn't understand a word but fell in love with her voice, playing her YouTubes over and over like a mule, trying to follow. At the gym, in the kitchen, some days were All Tara, All the Time. "It's the voice of love," said my NCT.

"Being present with what is" is the path to mental health, Tara says. "When we feel wonder at beauty, that's presence. When we are really there for another, that's presence... Even when it's unpleasant, we discover that by being with the unpleasantness, we have space for it." (11)

Space? That baffled me, but Tara mentioned it so often, I began taping quotes on post-its to my microwave. "If we investigate our feeling, then practice self-compassion," she'd say, "a space opens up." I'd post it: "Investigate and Say 'I Care'–A Space Opens Up." "If there's pain," she'd say, "be with ourselves and say 'This Being Hurts.'" I'd post it: "I hurt, Me-Ow!–A Space Opens Up." Post-its multiplied almost to "Burma Shave–A Space Opens Up."

Come home to ourselves, Tara says; sit quietly and try to feel what's in our heart. Then *be* with the feeling, no distractions. Huh? Ouch!

But weeks later I heard her teacher Jack Kornfield explain The Space. "The psyche has a deep healing capacity that's trustworthy," he said. Time and again he'd ask people to sit with him and be present with what is, including their worst emotions. Often they'd fear the feelings and be terrified to un-brace and allow the polar bear discharge.

"Let it rip," he urged, "sing it, dance it...let the tears wash through to the ends," until your "terror, rage and grief fills the room, the city, the whole planet."

Then something strange and wonderful happens, he said. If we feel enough of our horrible emotions, we somehow release them—and our hearts expand.

"I have learned this a hundred thousand times," said Jack. "When we turn toward what is difficult and *make space for it to open*, it will change and turn. It shifts from a contracted state, into... a larger space that can allow it. There comes a sense of well-being." In fact, he said, "it turns into its opposite." Just as my hate and rage turned to love. (12)

This was the meaning of the Buddha's call for "the sure heart's release," Kornfield wrote in 1993.

"As we heal through meditation, our hearts break open to feel fully," he said. "Powerful feelings, deep unspoken parts of ourselves arise... As we listen to the songs of our rage or fear, loneliness or longing, they do not stay forever. Rage turns into sorrow; sorrow turns into tears; tears may fall for a long time, but then the sun comes out. A memory of old loss sings to us; *our body shakes and relives the moment of loss... the pain of that loss finally finds release.*

"Both forgiveness and compassion arise spontaneously with the opening of the heart. Most often this healing work is so difficult that we need another person to hold our hand." (13)

A space opens up inside our hearts and there we find God's love.

"Hide the key *inside* them," said God in the yogic tale.

Notes

1. Taylor (2008).
2. Schore (6-15-11).
3. Porges (7-6-11).
4. Ortner (2014).
5. Hanson (9-28-11).
6. Schore (6-15-11).
7. Brous (4-12-17, 5-16-14).
8. Brous (7-26-17).
9. Schore (6-15-11); Brous (5-16-14).
10. James & Friedman (2009 Expanded Edition, p.199).
11. Brach (10-25-11).
12. Kornfield (11-7-12).
13. Kornfield (1993).

18

Emotional Object Constancy

18.1 *Crust, the restaurant.*
(Steve McWhan)

After that I often found myself crying for no reason. Less crust feels more vulnerable.

"Worry when I don't cry," I told friends; "crying shows I'm not frozen." When I first unfroze, fear, rage, joy, any emotion was so big that it swept through me like an electric shock.

I'd bet 30% or more folks in the OECD, where emotions are often discouraged, suffer traumatic freeze. If they unfroze, they'd have the same explosive experience. That's why we see people at concerts, sports events, anywhere emotions are OK, jumping up and down waving their arms. Their bodies are expressing a physical outburst of pent-up emotions. (1)

Gradually my nightmares decreased; dreams even became funny.

"Dreamed I was driving the Washington DC Beltway with a half-dead shark in my back seat," I told my tape one morning. "I was very much on dry land and so was the shark, so it was no threat. I left it in a bathtub at a rest stop and went on to my business meeting.

"Who should appear but Dan and his hunting pal Jake; they kill animals for fun.

" 'Hi guys,' I said, 'Can you handle this shark for me?' They left eagerly with a map I drew of the freeway exit."

"Caution: Shark in Bathtub," I scrawled on 8 x11 paper, posting it on my bathroom door. "I like that you got someone else to take care of it," laughed Dr. R.

My crust dissolved to where I could feel how painful it is to relate to people covered in it. "I like crust on my bread, not on my humans," I joked, clowning around at a local restaurant. (Figure 18.1).

One morning I woke up literally screaming at Bob, tapping about my anger on my acupressure points like a maniac. "Stop treating me like a slut!" I yelled, banging on all the points from head to chest. "Stop treating me like a slut!" I repeated in round two, over and over. Toward the end, my rage spiked to Mt. Everest.

"I'm so angry they treated me like a slut!" I shouted. Huh? "They?"

Move the tale, honey. "Don't get stuck pushing a baby carriage," said Mom. Who talks to a middle-school kid like that? No more "page 199" excuses! They did treat me like a slut and if I don't get angry, I'll get a migraine.

I did round three; took the recommended deep breaths—and dissolved into tears. My anger, having been felt, began to subside. In round four, I suddenly felt spontaneous gratitude. "God is taking me out of this," I found myself saying, "thank You for healing my pain."

Hard left: I meant to be screaming in rage. Instead I got hard right: suddenly I'm bawling in gratitude. "That's the curriculum," says Jack Kornfield. It's how our apparatus works.

Don't move the tale out of guilt or to plead mental illness, it hit me. Move it because that's where the real pain is, so that's where I get relief.

Afterward I felt terrific and hungry for breakfast. The impala does its shaking, then "Boom! Off you trot," says Dr. R.

And I didn't get a migraine. So there.

One Saturday in October, I finally said "No" to dating after the worst "match" yet. I met a gent who behaved so poorly that it felt like a memo from

God. Afterward I walked along Dana Point Harbor playing my mp3. I don't need a pacemaker; I already have one. In fact, I'd have forgotten half of what's in this book if I hadn't been recording events on my mp3 all the time.

"Call My name, say it now," a church song came up, "I want you to never doubt/ The love I have for you is so alive!" I saw the sun on the palms and the boats and my body reacted with sheer joy, bawling in gratitude. (2)

Flabbergasted, I left Dr. R. a voicemail.

"It's always 'No' and I'm left alone," I said. "But suddenly I don't care! Because I've got a love inside me now that is so enormous, these people will have to run to keep up! It's so big it makes me weep for joy. And yes, there's dancing going on in Dana Point; my feet are banging by themselves."

"Finding a mate is a disaster, but suddenly I feel fantastic?" I asked him next time. "Did I grow emotional object constancy?"

"Of course. Of course." he repeated, steel in his voice. "Your life no longer depends on someone else's whim. *You are free!* As you confront your trauma, you no longer feel helpless. As you say 'No' to unsafe people, you're free!

"As you unfreeze you can be present in the moment, which you never could before. When we're frozen, we're stuck in the past. As you experience God's love 'in the now,' it feels much bigger because it *is*."

Break, break, break and it feels like hell, but six months later I feel sooo much better.

Chocolate Doughnut

On October 21, every song at church made me bawl for joy, while my body shook the pew like a polar bear. "Don't ask me," I told Steve as we left, "I'm just renting.

"Apparently when God says 'No,' it teaches me to say 'No.' When I do it, I'm protecting myself, so I start to feel safe inside. Dr. R. says my EOC is kicking in, and it feels really good."

Then my senses kicked in, too.

We got a snack and found a bench behind the church overlooking the ocean. I sat staring at the sun on the water, my coffee, and half a chocolate doughnut Steve handed me, as if I'd never seen such things. Slowly eating the tiniest bits of frosting felt like an explosion. It must have taken 15 minutes. "Thank you for giving me the most delicious half a chocolate doughnut I've ever had in my life," I said, dazed.

Off we drove to the beach, playing the yogic hymns to Narayana the Protector, aka God. "Tvameva mata, cha pita Tvameva: You are my mother, You are my father," I sang along.

We parked at San Clemente and I got out singing. My brain needed mountains of retraining, so I'd been repeating those lines every day for two years. Now they wouldn't stop ringing in my head. Still in the parking lot I saw the wind in the palm trees and my heart exploded into "Jyota," the hymn of gratitude. "Thank You for removing the Me-Ow from my heart," I sang.

I walked toward the beach, saw the sun on the water, and suddenly I was bawling for the sheer beauty of it, my whole body going off again. "I have never seen the sun on the ocean like this before," I told Steve.

I walked down the steps and onto the sand, staring at the Pacific. I dropped my chair and everything else and marched into the water up to my knees. I stared at the light dancing on the waves and hit "record" on my mp3.

"This is it, there is *no* human power that could have made this, there is no human agency which can even remotely touch the power of this," I said. "You're attuning to Something over which these humans who have been torturing you have no authority. A Higher Authority is pouring on the incontrovertible, gigantic, in-your-face evidence: *you belong.*"

Just watching the waves break was overpowering, as I sobbed for the feeling *"you belong."* This time, I really felt it. That's big.

"Chocolate doughnut?" I told my tape.

"How about looking into the face of God?

"Talk about a message in a bottle. This was the demonstration that told me as a kid every day of every summer: 'No matter how bad they make you feel–you belong.' This sight resonated to my core but I didn't understand. Now I get it: God's been telling me all along that I belong."

I found Steve.

"I've never had senses like this before," I said. "It feels like seeing waves break for the first time. I couldn't taste or hear or see before compared to this.

It's like the *Wizard of Oz*. It opens in Kansas in black and white, then Dorothy lands in Oz and everything's in technicolor. I'm in a sensory assault."

"Sure," said Mr. Engineer. "If your brain is rewiring, now when it takes in the same sensory input, you'll experience it differently."

"Oh," I said, shaking, "Parts of my brain were dark, but *now they're lighting up?*"

"Yes," he said, "if neurons are developing and firing more, you'll feel sensations as you couldn't before.

"And the difference is visible now, between Susie Labcoat thinking that God loves you, and Chrissie Limbus and Rhonda Reptile really feeling it," he added. "It's obvious Rhonda feels it. For Rhonda to react this way, you've got to have God's love internalized. I saw it in church. When you say 'I don't know what's happening; I'm just renting,' that's got nothing to do with thinking. Suddenly you're shaking physically because you're feeling God's love *physically*."

Wham, I had another visceral reaction. I felt a fit of grief for all the decades in the dark, then a flood of joy at everything healing and growing inside me.

"Thank you for flying Reassociation Air," I announced. "We answer to a Higher Authority."

Trauma and Awakening

"Someone Bigger wants to kill me" was shifting to "Someone Bigger loves me, big time."

"I can't explain it," I told Sherry, "and it's so big I can't imagine feeling it without walking through the trauma. Do we have to go there, to get here?"

I recalled Peter Levine mentioning trauma and enlightenment.

Trauma can be "a doorway to awakening," he said. Healing trauma has a "transformative power" that can lead to "recovering a sense of wholeness." (3)

In fact, trauma and transformation were central to the Buddha. "I teach only the truth of suffering, and the transformation of suffering," he said 2,400 years ago. And no Calamity Jane, he. "Buddha did not teach 'Everything is suffering and there is nothing we can do,' " notes Thich Nhat Hanh. He taught that we can reach joy and happiness, otherwise known as Nirvana, by "refraining from doing the things that cause us to suffer. This is Good News!"

The key is being present with what is. Like the Christian, Jewish and yogic traditions, the Buddha taught that suffering, including trauma, simply "is." The key is how we handle it.

"We must recognize and acknowledge our suffering, and *touch it*," says Nhat Hanh. "We must look deeply into the origin and nature of our suffering, to identify how it came to be." Then we must find people to sit with eye-to-eye, so that we can actually feel our suffering all the way through. Pretty much what happened to me. (4)

Touch it? How fearful. "I hate this part;" it's so painful to actually feel. And then comes the polar bear reaction, another dreadful feeling.

Yet when we surrender to discharging trauma, Levine says, we go from frozen in the past, to being fully present "in the eternal now." Becoming present, "we gain access to the source of our own energy and enthusiasm... 'enthusiasm' is Greek for 'being with God'... drawing closer to God." (5)

Now we can feel our feelings, so we begin to feel more of the actual size of God's love.

"Our right hemisphere is all about this present moment," as Jill Bolte Taylor put it after her left brain was blocked by a stroke. With only her right brain working, she felt "right here, right now... I am an energy-being connected to the energy all around me. We are energy-beings connected to one another... And in this moment we are perfect, we are whole and we are beautiful...

"I found Nirvana," she says. "But if I'm still alive, and I have found Nirvana, then everyone who is alive can find Nirvana... So who are we? We are the life-force power of the universe, with manual dexterity and two cognitive minds." Other recent books also mention trauma and transformation. (6)

"I remember in fifth grade standing in the door enjoying the trees moving in the wind outside, and wondering how it could be that I was in here, and the trees were out there, yet I could feel their beauty," I told Dr. R. October 22. "It also happened summers as a kid, looking at the sun on the ocean. I'm on the jetty, it's out there, but what an impact on me.

"Taylor said she felt she was part of the life-force power of the universe. She felt she belonged, which gave her great joy.

"I felt that in nature. But with Mom it was often 'you don't belong,' and I didn't belong with the kids at school, either. So even at the ocean there was anxiety. It's hard when you're alone."

"But the point is: you *do* belong," he said. "You were made with just the right equipment to seek Creation's beauty. First we seek it as love from mom. If mom doesn't resonate with us, God's got a backup plan: the natural universe resonates. You can *feel* you belong to Creation.

"And what happened to you Sunday? That's 'love inside,' internalized love," he added. "Steve saw it. You didn't think; *you felt it.*"

"But it feels like love flooding in from the outside," I said.

"It comes from the outside originally," he smiled, "but now it doesn't leave."

"It won't?" I asked. "It really won't leave?"

"Once we internalize it, it becomes part of us," he said. "It's not only God doing it; now you're doing it: 'Oh—now I'm lovable. He's loved me so much, now I feel myself that I'm loveable!' "

"It's a deluge," I said. "He comes 'and my heart turns violently inside my chest,' as one song puts it."

"This is often described as the experience of falling in love," he said. "You felt overcome by the presence of God. No one could stop you from walking into that ocean. You've gotten a glimpse, and you're overwhelmed by just a glimpse. It invades the body, it invades the senses, and nothing's going to stop you from getting that.

"You're not frozen anymore, so now there's nothing in the way or muting it, it's just full on."

"When I heard Henry (Cloud) say parts of my brain were dark, I almost drove off that overpass," I said. "Now those dark parts are coming online, I feel the pain and the joy. Just talking about it, I have to hold onto your furniture."

"The important thing is: you're feeling," he replied. "You're feeling the pain that was locked up in that darkness. It's not natural for the brain to be dark; painful stuff happened. When all this comes alive, including the awareness that there were dark areas? It taps into a pain from before we had words.

"Now you've got enough love inside that you can handle the pain, so you don't have to freeze. You can move through it and get real relief."

Off the Velcro

Walking on the beach in late October, muscles all over my body begin to loosen and stretch from decades of clenching. "I feel really heavy," I told my mp3, "so solid on my feet it's like I weigh twice what I did yesterday."

Next day I woke feeling whole, good, and also powerful, energetic. Every muscle in my body felt somehow renovated. A deep muscular clenching all over my body, which I didn't even know existed, had begun to resolve.

Most amazing were my toes. Toes?

One morning in 2000 I had to throw out most of my shoes due to foot pain. Suddenly my big toes had tilted sideways over my second toes like wild tubers. The first podiatrist I saw wanted to operate. I went for a second opinion; this doctor prescribed expensive inserts instead. I avoided surgery and was able to wear custom-made office shoes and sneakers, but that's all.

In 2011, a friend had such a successful surgery for toe overlap that I saw her podiatrist. "Your left foot is inoperable," he said. "All we can do is cut off your second toe."

Now these toes were spontaneously stretching apart, as if an iron band clenching them together had been released.

For years I wore a night brace to pull the left toes apart, fastened with a Velcro strap. Now as the toes relaxed, I had to pull the strap tighter to engage the brace. Then they relaxed so much that the brace couldn't engage. I didn't need it anymore.

My toes were "off the Velcro." I could wear heels, the first time in years.

I recalled "Polyvagal Theory," Stephen Porges' study of the tenth cranial aka vagus nerve. Mammals have developed one side of the vagus to calm ourselves. But the other side, developed earlier in reptiles, slows heart rate, breathing and other core functions, Porges found. Great for reptiles, who hide under water, but it can kill mammals and does kill premature babies.

Trauma is when we're so innundated by fight-flight that our Reptile brain messages the vagus to freeze bodily functions—to stop us from feeling. Emotions are "somaticized," frozen in the body. How? The vagus triggers our nervous system to contract the muscles of the face, jaw, neck, back, viscera, legs, etc. Many digestive and back issue are caused this way, says Porges. (7)

Think of a spider when swatted: it clenches up into a ball to die. When I threw out my shoes, my toes were clenching up into claws like a dying spider. Now I realized that muscle pains all over my body were part of this "spider clench." My vagus nerve, traumatized since birth, had been contracting muscles all over me for years, until it pulled bones out of whack.

For example, knee pain had kept me up nights since the '80s. The best orthopedic surgeons in New York City were clueless as to cause, but did find that my right leg was half an inch shorter than my left. Finally my genius California chiropractor put a half-inch wedge in my right shoe.

Or digestion. One day in 2004, mine simply stopped working. My gut was frozen from years of fight-flight provoking freeze. (You don't need to eat lunch if you're about to be lunch.) Symptoms were resolved by months on the BRAT diet (bananas, applesauce, rice, white toast), but no one had a diagnosis. I also developed a nasty case of acid reflux.

Or jaw pain. My jaw pain, teeth grinding, and migraines all stemmed from vagus "spider clench." And jaw inflammation can propagate throughout the body, damaging entire systems. (8) When I got a tooth guard to ease the grinding, my toes unclenched even further next day.

Now I was addressing the cause, not just the symptoms, and I experienced a release of "vagal clench" everywhere, including in my gut.

My neck, arms, back, legs, everything literally from head to toe was releasing. No wonder so many foot and back surgeries fail! Surgeons break bones to realign them, but if the underlying trauma isn't addressed, "spirder clench" muscle cramps continue and pull the bones back out of whack.

Three months into Levine's CD, I slept on a friend's couch where I'd been comfortable a year before. Now my legs wouldn't fit. I had my chiropractor re-measure my legs. "Your legs are longer now," he exclaimed. "Your back and hip muscles have relaxed enough to allow your legs to drop into alignment, so now they're also the same length. Take the wedge out of your shoe!"

Muscle pain all over my body began to disappear, along with the migraines and acid reflux.

"I used to feel lousy 90% of the time, and good 10% of the time," I realized. "Now it's the reverse."

I Survived Yorba Linda

The holidays came and with them, Handel's *Messiah*. Thanksgiving loomed like a giant zombie vulture floating over the Macy's Parade, as I drove for weeks to Yorba Linda to rehearse. I barely survived this during 2008-2011 with major support from Steve and Sherry. Now in Thanksgiving 2012, they would be with their kids and I would be alone. Now what?

This year will be better, that's what.

This year if my infant pain is triggered, I won't need to feel like death. I can make the call and yowl to another mammal. I can tap on my acupressure points, rip up the gym, or run on the beach to discharge the fury locked in my body. I can ask my downstairs brain what music it wants to hear, and dance until I release the pain.

On Thanksgiving Sunday I dolled up in a gown, drove to the Nixon Library and sang *Messiah*. I felt great, enjoying the music, the people singing along, the glorious ballroom chandeliers and holiday lights. No sweetheart came to hear me, but friends make videos of my solo and took me to dinner.

I drove the hour home in the dark singing Handel at the top of my lungs. Then, "Home Alone for the Holidays" began to seep in. After all those rehearsals and effort, it didn't feel good to drive home alone.

Yet singing in the car, I was able to yowl to God.

"OK, Lord," I sobbed, "this is between me and You, nobody else. You were the only one around when the sperm hit the egg.

"Mommy didn't like me, so I've had a life sentence of people who didn't notice I exist and I have to go through life alone? I don't get it! Help me out here!" I threw myself metaphorically on my knees and half physically on the steering wheel, howling down the freeway again.

I got home and put on Mendelssohn's *Fourth Symphony* for no reason. I hadn't heard it since all this began in 2006. Sitting by the fire and listening as the third movement came on, it was so lyrical, so glorious, that I began to weep. I put my head down next to the speaker, just sobbing for the beauty of it.

"This is what Love should feel like!" I told my tape. "This is what Mom should have felt like.

"This is what God feels like! This is what 'people love' should feel like! *This* is what I like. What's up Lord, why is it always 'No'? "

I had a long sob with my body shaking the chair, the room, the condo. It almost kills me to let that course through me. It feels like someone's turning my guts inside out with a meat hook, but when it's done, boy, do I feel better.

I really felt that God had heard me. My external circumstances hadn't changed at all, but I felt so good and so spent that I grabbed the stuffed dog and collapsed into bed in my hose.

Just yowl to God and spill it; it brings enormous relief.

A trip to Hell can be OK, if you Move the Tale.

Recovery vs Romance

Next day I told Dr. R. the story and played him the Mendelssohn.

"Sometimes we are so much in God's presence that we start to feel it's OK, even if events suck," said my NCT. "It's OK that you're alone again and it hurts like hell, because there is a comfort here we can't put into words."

"How could an unseen Being make me feel better, when what I need is a flesh and blood husband?" I said.

"Still, I feel a whole lot better!"

"If we have EOC to rely on, we can feel that God's with us," he said. "If God's with us, or someone's with us, we can feel our worst emotions. Then a comfort comes, even if circumstances still stink.

"God spoke to you in that Mendelssohn. He knows you well enough to know that if He speaks to you in music, to say 'I'm Here and I'm holding you,' you're gonna hear it loud and clear. I think music has always been God's way of getting to you." (9)

"When I sang, it felt like finally somebody loved me," I said in tears. "I could do what the composers wanted me to do."

"This comfort is what a two-month old is supposed to learn when emotions flood in," he said. "He learns that if he feels all this and screams, people have a good response. 'Hey, I can feel this!' he realizes, 'because somebody comes and helps me, and then it goes away. I can handle this!' "

"I couldn't feel emotions and scream," I said. "They didn't like it. I had to stuff it quick."

"But now you do," he said. "You can feel your emotions with God, with me, with friends.

"Last night you felt what it's like to cry out and have your body explode, and get a good response. The way you describe it, you felt unconditional acceptance, a perfect parent's love. Today you feel it with me.

"This emotion has now been felt, and in all its rawness; it's been verbalized; it's been understood in a relationship; and the fear and the sting subside. It's the only way we can learn to regulate emotions."

"Just yowl and spill it," I thought again.

"One more point," he added.

"You've done all this *outside any kind of romance*. How cool is that?

"You had it backward, looking for this in romance. But romance can't do this. We're supposed to learn unconditional love as kids from parenting.

"Now you experience unconditional love and comfort from God and safe people, without romance. That feels better than expecting romance to do it. *Depending on a lover* to parent us feels scary, 'cos they can't."

A Car Can't Gas Itself

The Sunday before Christmas, I left church alone. Alone again for the holidays; not great.

I walked to the beach in impossibly sunny 72-degree weather.

My cell phone rang. It was Cynthia in Virginia. I hate it when people I haven't known long try to relate to me purely by phone, but Cynthia and I worked shoulder to shoulder for 20 years, seeing each other deeply. We logged so much actual limbic resonance (face time), that now I hear her voice and she's here with me, in person. She's also the only gal I know who translates Kepler from Latin for fun.

Guess I have Cynthia internalized, too.

I tell her about the chocolate doughnut and looking into the face of God. I tell her about my senses coming online and the dark parts of my brain lighting up. I tell her about Mendelssohn and what people love should feel like.

"Just like your red berries," she says. "You see the sun on the ocean and you know: God made all this for you!

"Remember Kepler writing that God made the harmony of the worlds and the harmony of music so we could know Him? He gave us a direct emotional experience of great beauty moving our souls. Kepler said we're created to belong to the universe, designed to see and be delighted by it.

"Logic alone can't prove we belong; first, we *feel* we belong.

"Yeah, you belong to this world," she concludes. "In particular, you belong to my world."

We share awhile more, then ring off. I emerge from the trees on the path to my favorite picnic bench at the edge of the sand.

I'm looking at a 180-degree view of the ocean about 90 feet away, tropical foliage with huge birds of paradise flowers, the sun on the water, the seagulls, the most gorgeous weather possible, and it hits me in the chest:

I'm in the middle of *all this.*

Do I have a question about whether I belong?

Nuts to reasoning why. Cynthia says I belong. Cynthia says I belong! Every cell in my body is suddenly singing at the top of their little cellular lungs, "We BeLO–NG" and yes, Virginia, they believe it.

Cyn sure has great phone timing. But I knew this weeks ago; why the impact of her call?

"A car can't gas itself," says Dr. R. I had to hear it from another mammal like Cynthia.

"Don't try this alone," I thought, or if an emotion is big, I just freeze.

We've got to have that furry mammalian presence, or we simply can't feel the really big, deep ones. The clam never even shows up.

I sat down, played Mendelssohn's third movement, and out poured the whole reaction again. "Oh my God, He's right here with me!"

Again I'm staring at the sun on the ocean, sobbing full-body heaves of joy and sorrow and who cares. "Whatever happens, let it be OK. Just watch," I remember a yogi saying. I sit for ten minutes letting it slam over my body and the fewer questions I ask, the deeper and wider the bodily reaction gets. Then suddenly it's done and I feel like a million bucks, just like Thanksgiving.

Do I have a new pattern?

"Thank you, Lord, I have never felt this wonderful in my life. I am safe," I said. "I can feel secure no matter what anybody does! I can feel safe no matter what happens, because *I can release my bad feelings.*

"Think of the freedom! Think of how loved I can feel, and no one can take this from me. I just want to sit here and cry and listen to Mendelssohn for about five years."

Steve had a lovely insight a few months back. "You've said that sometimes when you sing, you feel a spark inside, and suddenly it's not you singing. Beethoven and God are doing the singing; you just have to get out of the way. That's a pretty strong experience of God inside.

"Why couldn't you get to where you feel that way all the time?"

Suddenly it sank in and my body took off across that beach running for the ocean like there was no tomorrow. (Figure 18.2) Again I was almost not in control of my limbs.

I hit the water splashing, then my toes danced with the edge of the foam as it ran down the beach, at speed. I ran and danced the length of the one-mile strand for 45 minutes with the third movement on auto-repeat, over and over and over, skipping and jogging and singing at the top of my lungs. People stared, but I just smiled. I never felt so much flat-out joy in my life.

Finally I stopped, exhausted. I took a few long, deep breaths, and turned to wander back.

Then I clicked on Mendelssohn's first movement to hear the whole symphony from the top, and *wham*—the explosion started again. It didn't matter how tired I was; those opening bars just leap out and pull you in. I danced my way through the whole symphony for another 30 minutes, jumping and running like a madwoman.

The physical reaction was huge.

18.2 Salt Creek Beach, Dana Point, California. (Kathy Brous)

Notes

1. Felitti & Anda (1998).
2. Third Day (2008).
3. Levine (2005, p.4)
4. Thich Nhat Hahn (1998).
5. Levine (2005, p.79-81).
6. Taylor (2008); Epstein (2013); Rosenthal (2013).
7. Porges (7-6-11).
8. Jennings (12-12-14).
9. *Don't Try This Alone: The Music Edition*, forthcoming.

Licensed Psychologist #PSY ▓▓▓▓
EIN # ▓▓▓▓▓▓▓
29222 Rancho Viejo Rd. ▓▓▓
San Juan Capistrano, CA 92675
(949) 933-▓▓▓▓

Invoice for Service

Client Name: _Kathy Brous_

Date(s) of Service: _May 4, 11 2017_

DSM-IV Diagnosis: _F 43.12 - PTSD, chronic_

Service Rendered:	CPT Code:
Diagnostic Interview	90791
Individual Therapy (30 min)	90832
Individual Therapy (45 min)	90834

19.1 My official diagnosis: PTSD, chronic.
(Kathy Brous)

During events in this book 2008-2012, I was so worried about my own attachment disorder that I devoured the psychological literature. Now friends are after me to write another book on the brain science. Here's a start.

People say babies are resilient, but the myth is dangerous. Babies are malleable and all too easily damaged. They require a solid attachment bond from conception to age three for our brain itself to develop well, so damage can start when the sperm hits the egg.

I carried around severe damage like that for over 50 years, but no one knew it—starting with me. I never meant to do any of this. It was an accident.

I stumbled into discovering a major public health crisis by falling through the hole in my soul. I fell, and it hurt, so I researched it.

I found a solid scientific basis for why I was hurting. Research showed that some 50% of Americans have significant attachment wounds, it's painful, and it's biologically damaging.

I seem to be the first to write that it correlates to our 50% divorce rate.

In fact, *unaddressed childhood trauma takes 20 years off your life*. The DSM only recognizes trauma that is impersonal and based on incidents of finite number, such as war injuries or auto accidents.

But so much of trauma is *inter*-personal because it's attachment-related, so it's also continuous and ongoing, often starting before we develop thought. That's not academic or theoretical. Half of us have it, we're not taught to look for it, so we don't get healing. We just drop dead early.

Then I compared the psychological literature on the prevalence of childhood trauma to the medical literature on it. That seems to be another first; I was surprised to find no studies that had ever compared the two before.

I found that psychological data showing that about 50% of Americans suffer infant attachment pain, actually correlates with independent bio-medical data showing that about 50% suffer childhood trauma. The studies were so independent, neither set of researchers apparently knew the other's work existed. This confirms the accuracy and power of both sets of statistics. It's the theme of an article I'm drafting with Dr. Vincent Felitti, MD, Co-director of the Adverse Childhood Experience (ACE) Study.

"About 50%" Attachment Trauma

I began by checking the 45% vs 55% figures for insecure vs secure attachment with professionals at a UCLA therapists' conference. They confirmed that they commonly use these numbers.

Then I saw the documentation.

British psychiatrist John Bowlby developed attachment theory in the 1950s, writing that most infants seek to stay close to parents, since "attachment" promotes survival. To demonstrate this, Bowlby's associate Mary Ainsworth, her student Mary Main and their colleagues researched over 6,200 infant-parent pairs during 1977-1999. (1)

First, using the Strange Situation, they studied infant behavior. At Johns Hopkins, "Ainsworth structured the Strange Situation to include three of Bowlby's 'natural clues to danger'," writes Dr. Main. Researchers watch and video-tape through one-way glass as an infant with its mother reacts first to a strange room; next to two entrances of a strange person; and then to two different separations from the mother.

Babies were expected to seek their parent as Bowlby thought. Those "that Ainsworth termed 'secure,' play and explore happily prior to separation; show signs of missing the parent during separation, such as crying and calling; seek proximity immediately upon the parent's return; then return to play and exploration, 'secure' once again in the parent's presence," Main reports. (2)

But to researchers' amazement, 45% of infants did not show secure behavior. They avoided the mother, had no preference between the stranger and the mother, or could not be soothed or continue to play after the mother returned. Some even demonstrated "disorganized" behavior such as falling down or swiping at the mother's face on her return.

Researchers found that only 55% felt secure. "Infants with secure attachment greet and/or approach the caregiver and… are able to return to play… in 55% of the general population," writes Diane Benoit, MD, about a 1999 meta-study that confirmed the statistic. (3)

No one knew that infant attachment was even an issue, let alone that attachment damage was so prevalent, due to the taboo against looking into the private lives of families. It's often said that one needs a license to drive a car, but not to have a baby.

So the modest Strange Situation research packed a punch; it "put a camera into the bedroom." For the first time, science had devised a way to document the private relations of over 6,200 families via hidden camera in a benign way. Parent volunteers were fully briefed; infant distress past a reasonable point terminated the session. Yet the study's depth and large number of replications provided astonishingly consistent statistics about the states of mind that infants demonstrated—repeatedly—in response to their parents.

The infants were under 18 months and pre-verbal, so it was nearly impossible for anyone to influence their behavior in the lab. WYSIWYG. What the camera saw was what humanity was getting. It wasn't pretty.

Naturally, Dr. Main wanted to know why so many babies were so troubled.

Observing their parents, she realized as early as 1979 that "some mothers… could also be frightening." One mother even "treated her toddler as an animal," she reports. (4)

So as a second tool, Main created the Adult Attachment Interview (AAI) in 1982—to research the parents. In a longitudinal study at Berkeley, Main and her team followed the infant-parent pairs from their 1977 Strange Situation group for a generation. They studied the infants again when they reached age six in 1982, and at age 19 in 1995 as adults. They also gave the AAI to the parents each time. (5)

Results showed that about 45% of adults, too, lacked secure attachment.

Interviews revealed that when parents had been frightening to their infants, or merely unable to relate, those parents had been frightened or rebuffed by their own parents, the babies' grandparents. It was the insecure adults who raised the insecure infants.

In fact, the attachment level shown by each parent's 1982 AAI corresponded directly to the attachment level shown by their own infant in the 1977 Strange

Situation. "A marked relation between a parent's hour-long discussion of his/her own attachment history, and the offspring's Strange Situation behavior 5 years previously, had been uncovered," notes Dr. Erik Hesse. (6)

Dr. Main found that the attachment we have as children continues life-long, and we pass our insecurity to our children. *Nearly half the parents had been raised insecure by their insecure parents, who were raised insecure by their insecure parents,* and so on back in history. Like my family (see Chapter 17).

Worse, in 2009, a meta-study of over 10,500 Adult Attachment Interviews showed that secure attachment had *fallen by 17.1%,* since the 1999 secure estimate of 55% above. That would mean only 46% were secure in 2009, and the insecure rate was up to 54%—more than half the population.

"About 50%" Bio-Medical Trauma

Twenty years after these psychological studies began, medical doctors discovered that about half of adults experience childhood trauma. (They were unaware of the psychological studies.)

The Adverse Childhood Experience (ACE) Study of 17,337 adults was conducted 1995-1997 at Kaiser Permanente HMO in San Diego by Dr. Vincent Felitti, MD and Dr. Robert Anda, MD, with follow-up since. Middle-class medical clients were asked if they'd had any of ten types of inter-personal adverse childhood experiences, such as alcoholism or drug abuse at home, physical or sexual abuse, or emotional or physical neglect by parents. (7)

Results showed that 66% had one or more types of these childhood traumas, and 42% had two or more types. In inner city populations these numbers are over 70%. (8) A national average of US income groups would likely show that 50% or more suffer two or more types of ACE trauma.

The ACE Study further found that ACEs lead to impaired thinking, disease, disability, and *early death.* ACE trauma rates correlate to the likelihood of suffering the top ten causes of death in America, such as heart disease, cancer and stroke.

The fact that 42% had two or more *types* of childhood trauma means, for example, that 42% experienced both childhood physical and sexual abuse, or both childhood emotional abuse and emotional neglect.

The ACE Study lists ten such types, including traumas that happen to newborns like physical and emotional neglect. Such traumas put infants into chronic fight-flight, which shuts down the human organism's capacity for feelings of love and attachment.

The prevalence of trauma to children involving their parents was, and is, shocking. Whether the parents are perpetrators or victims, they're too overwhelmed by their own fight-flight to attune to the child.

By definition, that child can't possibly attach to them. Attuned parents feel their child's distress and act to protect the child. Parents who are too wounded or under too much stress can't do that.

Dr. Felitti also had no intention of confronting such issues.

Originally, his Kaiser obesity reduction program had developed a sharp dropout rate, and Felitti simply wanted to know why. He was shocked when 50% of those leaving reported childhood sexual abuse. They also often mentioned verbal and physical abuse, and traumatic experiences such as witnessing their mothers being beaten.

"This can't be true," he recalls thinking; "I would have been told these things in medical school."

No one expected the prevalence of childhood wounds or the lifelong medical damage.

"Prior to the ACE Study, there had been no basis for any opinion regarding the prevalence of child trauma, due to the taboo against looking into private lives of other people," Felitti notes.

Compare the ACE Study finding that about 50% experience childhood trauma to the Strange Situation/AAI finding of about 50% insecure attachment. Both show that child trauma is the cause of adult misery for a large percent of Americans. Both result in many of the same painful relationships and life-threatening illnesses.

Some psychoanalysts have long warned of this, but based on a few cases. The initial bio-medical ACE Study documented it in over 17,300 adults. As many as 400,000 people are now reported to have taken the ACE Survey worldwide with broadly similar results. Again, over 10,500 have tested similarly in the Adult Attachment Interview.

Silent Epidemic

The Impact of Early Life Trauma on Health and Disease: The Hidden Epidemic presents 27 psychological and biomedical studies by neurophysiologists and

MDs to document this. "Traumatic events of the earliest years of infancy and childhood are... often preserved lifelong," writes Dr. Felitti in the preface. "They are not lost; they are embodied. Only in recent decades has the magnitude of the problem of developmentally-damaged human beings begun to be recognized... The hidden epidemic is a problem not only for psychiatry, but also for medicine and society in general." (9)

And: what is the rate of insecure attachment *today*?

In 1999, around the time electronic devices began to replace human interaction, 55% of us were reported securely attached. In the almost 20 years since, we've become an "e-society" with email, texting, computers, and 24×7 work days further damaging our ability to relate in person.

"Well-developed human beings can self-regulate their emotional state with other humans. But what about people who regulate their emotions with objects?" warns neuroscientist Dr. Stephen Porges.

"We're in a world now being literally pushed on us, by people who are challenged in their own social and emotional regulation, and we're calling this 'social networking.' We're using computers, we're texting—we're stripping the human interaction from all interactions... We're allowing the world to be organized upon the principles of individuals who have difficulty regulating emotionally in the presence of other human beings." (10)

By 2009, studies of over 10,500 adults showed secure adult attachment had *fallen **an additional 17.1%*** since 1999. If so, only 46% were secure in 2009, and the insecure rate was up to 54%, *over half the population.* (11)

These number must be worse by now, considering Porges' point.

The first step to reverse this trend is to break the information vacuum about this silent epidemic.

UCLA neuropsychologist Dr. Allan Schore spoke up in 1994 for babies who suffer attachment damage during what he calls the "first thousand days," from conception to age two. Schore, America's top attachment scholar, wrote that the infant brain literally requires intense interaction with an adult's eyes and facial expressions to develop its own neurons. In a 2014 speech, Schore described the many theories he published in 1994 and since, which have now been confirmed by recent brain scans. (12)

Yet today, parents equipped to give attentive, attuned care are an endangered species, Schore warns.

"For decades, to protect the mother-infant bonding, there were families around it. There weren't single individuals raising babies; there wasn't early day care," he says. But now, "the early-day protections have been lost, so as a result... there is an increase in psychiatric disorders in this country, and the reason is that we have not protected this early phase of infant life, the early mother bonding..." (13)

When a mother doesn't respond to her baby positively, the infant's instincts read that as a survival threat. That baby learns that there is no comfort, emotions are terrifying, and the world is a scary place. (14)

Neuroscientists Daniel Siegel, MD, Bruce Perry, MD, and others have detailed how attachment trouble causes developmental trauma to the nervous system. (15)

Privileged families also suffer attachment disorder. Mothers working or living under stress pass it on. Moms who as kids had little deep contact with their mom are often tone deaf to attunement, and pass the damage to their infants. Dads too busy to relate create emotional disconnection at home.

America suffers from the large percent of our leaders who (like me) are middle- or upper-class, but took substantial attachment damage as children. I'm hoping this book will reach them.

Blind to our deep childhood trauma, the pain propels us to over-achieve. This achievement addiction drives many government and corporate officials. The pain of attachment trauma makes them fear human beings, creating a crust of numbness over the heart. That's why they're so callous to the population. Congress is "dissociated," specialists say, or they would have known that sending youth to war would bring back a flood of PTSD victims. (16)

Attachment What?

"Lots of kids feel insecure; that's no disorder," scoff experts who believe the APA's Diagnostic and Statistical Manual (DSM). (17) (See Preface.)

I disagree and this book demonstrates why.

Of course, I oppose using the terms "attachment disorder" and "attachment therapy" to excuse abuse. In 2006, the American Professional Society on the Abuse of Children (APSAC) exposed so-called "attachment therapy" based on "psychological, physical, or aggressive means to provoke the child to catharsis" using "coercive techniques." (18)

Instead, what's needed is "attachment-*based* therapists," trained psychotherapists who use Bowlby's attachment theory detailed above. (19)

Me? When I first heard of all this in 2011, I couldn't tell attachment disorder from a take-out order. I was just trying to avoid suicide. I read descriptions of it and felt it in my gut, like an army jackboot.

Yet the DSM says that only the tiny percent of the population with Reactive Attachment Disorder (RAD) has a "disorder." (20)

Again I disagree.

When I named my website AttachmentDisorderHealing.com, I certainly wasn't promoting child abuse.

There is a third category: legitimate attachment disorder. I believe it hurts 50% of Americans. I've never have RAD and I don't support abuse, but I did have a bad case of real attachment disorder.

Since the DSM disallows treatment for anything but RAD, I got no treatment until I collapsed after age 50. That can't be right.

"Attachment problems extending beyond RAD are a real and appropriate concern for professionals," agrees the 2006 APSAC report. (21)

The DSM minimizes the use of "disorder" because they define it as an illness requiring treatment. Insurance and drug companies go by the DSM, so if only a tiny percentile need treatment, they save money.

For example, neurofeedback has helped me enormously. It's covered by insurance, but my neurofeedback therapist had to find a diagnosis code for me in the DSM. Since I don't have RAD, he couldn't diagnose me for any attachment issue at all.

That's crazy, pardon the pun.

"Clinicians treating real people have this problem every day," he fumed. "The DSM is produced by statisticians who don't see patients. They only see what interests insurance companies."

He had to code me "F43.12," DSM code for "PTSD, chronic" (Figure 19.1). I sure have Post-Traumatic Stress Disorder (PTSD), but it's only a symptom of my root issue: attachment disorder. The DSM ignores causality.

Neurofeedback's purpose is to strengthen the brain's attachment circuits, so it's especially looney to put neurofeedback providers through this. (My blogs on neurofeedback are in References.) (22)

All most of us want to know is: "I hurt; can you help me?"

But because no one could diagnose a "disorder," I was turned away wherever I went for help.

That's what's happening now to most of us 50% who are hurting, and it stinks.

It leaves us alone, without recognition or a voice. We have no idea that we even need help, let alone any idea how to get healing.

I considered changing my website's name to Attachment**Trauma**Healing. Then I googled "attachment trauma" and saw that experts restrict it, too, to a tiny percent: those who as kids suffered the death of their mother.

Even if I rename my site Attachment Grief, Attachment Heartbreak, or Attachment**Ouch**Healing.com, the problem will remain. The DSM will still claim that only a few have a "real illness."

Words, however, can't magically remove the agony which so many of us feel, or lower the 50% divorce rate.

Many specialists disagree with the DSM on attachment and other issues, led by Dr. Bruce Perry, MD and Dr. Bessel van der Kolk, MD. Van der Kolk and associates submitted data on 200,000 children to the DSM staff to document Developmental Trauma Disorder as attachment failure. Yet afterward, DSM-5 was issued without mentioning it. "Clearly our field would like to ignore social realities," says van der Kolk, "and study genes." (23)

This book gets to the root causes of emotional pain, unlike many "solutions" that medicate the symptoms, but ignore the causes.

I asked the question: "Am I meeting so many emotionally-troubled adults in broken relationships because our healthcare system only treats symptoms—which is why so many of us are still so ill?"

"Yes. It helps to have a diagnosis!" say many of the over 900 comments on my website. "Thank you for telling your story so I can feel it's my story, too, and there's a scientific basis for the hurt. Hooray, I'm not a freak."

Self-help experts often prescribe shortcuts, but I don't believe in self-help anymore.

This book instead documents a long, painful road to recovery. The causes of infant trauma rot out our core, so healing is difficult and takes many years.

Doing it right, with deep psychotherapy and walking through the pain, actually works. It does heal, and the healing is profound. That means this book is realistic, so it's a message of hope.

Notes

1. Brous K. (4-12-17).
2. Main et. al. (2005).
3. Benoit (2004).
4. Main et. al. (2005).
5. Main (2005); Hesse (2008).
6. Hesse (2008, p.552).
7. Felitti & Anda (1998); Brous (10-2-13).
8. Family Center (2016).
9. Lanius & Vermetten (2010).
10. Porges (2012).
11. Bakermans-Kranenburg & van IJzendoorn (2009).
12. Schore (1994 & 9-28-14).
13. Schore (2012).
14. Tronick (2007); Schore (6-15-11).
15. Siegel, Perry et. al. (3-12-13).
16. van der Kolk (6-6-12).
17. APA (2003).
18. APSAC (2006).
19. Lewis et. al. (2000, p.189ff); Brous (7-20-17).
20. Wikipedia (7-27-17).
21. APSAC (2006).
22. Brous (11-21-14 & 8-10-16).
23. Brous (3-28-14); van der Kolk (2005 & 5-10-13).

References

American Psychiatric Association (APA) (2013). Diagnostic and Statistical Manual (DSM), 5th ed.

APSAC (2006). Task Force on Attachment Therapy. Chaffin M, et. al. Child Maltreatment. 2006 Feb;11 (1):76-89

Baer D. (2-7-13). Know If You're Working with Mammals or Reptiles.

Bakermans-Kranenburg MJ, van IJzendoorn MH. (2009). First 10,000 Adult Attachment Interviews. Attach Hum Dev. 2009 May; 11(3): 223-63.

Benoit D. (2004). Infant-parent Attachment. Paediatr Child Health, Oct 2004; 9(8) p.541–545.

Brach T. (10-25-11) Mindful Radical Acceptance. NICABM.com.

Breen JM. (2008). John Paul II, Structures of Sin and Limits of Law.

Brous K. (10-2-13). The ACE Study. AttachmentDisorderHealing.com/the-greatest-study-never-told

Brous K. (3-28-14). Developmental Trauma. AttachmentDisorderHealing.com/developmental-trauma

Brous K. (4-11-14). Perry: Rhythm Regulates the Brain. Attachment Disorder Healing.com/developmental-trauma-3

Brous K. (5-16-14). Allan Schore: What is the Self? AttachmentDisorderHealing.com/Allan-Schore

Brous K. (11-21-14). Neurofeedback Calms Fear. TinyUrl.com/y8uguf84

Brous K. (8-10-16). Neurofeedback Works. TinyUrl.com/y7622tna

Brous K. (4-12-17). Adult Attachment Interview (AAI). TinyUrl.com/yaxavdm9

Brous K. (7-20-17). Find an Attachment-based Psychotherapist. TinyUrl.com/ydy9o7pw

Brous K. (7-26-17). Romance, Dating and Trauma. TinyUrl.com/y78yhchy

Burke Harris N. (2014). How Childhood Trauma Affects Health. TEDMed.

Cloud H. (1993). Changes That Heal. Zondervan.

Cloud H. (2000). Do We Need A Father? MNS-57. Tape; CloudTownsend.com (CTC).

Cloud H. (2001). Is My Father Still Affecting Me? MNS-230. Tape; CTC.

Cloud H. (2002). Getting Love on the Inside. CD; CTC.

Cloud H. (2003). What About Dad? MNS-621. CD; CTC.

Cloud H. (2005). How to Get a Date Worth Keeping. Zondervan.

Cloud H. (12-6-10). Character Discernment for Dummies, Part 2. CD; CTC.

Cloud H, Townsend J. (1996). Safe People. Zondervan.

Cloud H, Townsend J. (2004). How People Grow. Zondervan.

Damon M, Affleck B, Williams, R. (1997). Good Will Hunting.

Demme J. (1991). Silence of the Lambs.

Doidge N. (3-30-11). Neuroplasticity Revolution. NICABM.com.

Edelman H. (1995). Motherless Daughters.

Epstein, M. (2013). Trauma of Everyday Life.

Family Center, Nashville TN (2016). FamilyCenterTN.org/our-impact

Felitti VJ, Anda RF et. al. (1998). Adverse Childhood Experiences (ACE) Study, Amer Journal Prev Med 14:245-258.

Felitti VJ. (2003). Relationship of Adverse Childhood Experiences to Adult Health, Child Trauma Treatment Network Conference, Sept. 2003.

Felitti VJ, Anda RF (10-17-11). Adverse Childhood Experiences. Retrieved 9-30-17: AlbertaFamilyWellness.org/assets/Resources/Vincent-Felitti-PPT-Presentation-RFA-2011-0.pdf

First 5 (8-2-13). Sean Casey, High Cost of Child Poverty. Retrieved 7-1-16: First5CoCo.org/blog/tag/child-poverty/

Fisher, H. (2004). Why We Love.

Gerson, J. (Undated). Understanding Secure and Insecure Attachment.

Glatt, M. (1958). Developmental Progress of Alcoholism. British Journal of Addiction, Vol 54, July 1958

Grant, R./California Endowment (6-14-16). Tribute to Vincent Felitti.

Grissom S, Grissom C. (1994). Session 1: What's happening to me? DivorceCare: 13 Video Sessions. DivorceCare.org/startagroup/sessions

Goodtherapy.org/learn-about-therapy/types/somatic-psychotherapy

Hanson R. (2011). Buddha's Brain. NICABM.com.

Hanson R. (9-28-11). Neurodharma: Train for Mindfulness. NICABM.com.

Hanson R. (1-23-13). Taking in the Good. NICABM.com.

Harlow HF, et. al. (1965). Social Isolation in Monkeys. Proc Natl Acad Sci.

Harris M. (1996). The Loss that is Forever.

Herman J. (1992). Trauma and Recovery.

Hesse E. (2008). The Adult Attachment Interview, Cassidy, Jude & Shaver, Eds., Handbook of Attachment, 2nd Ed., p. 552-598.

James J, Friedman R. (1994). Pay Me Now or Pay Me Later. GriefRecovery Method.com/blog/1994/05/pay-me-now-or-pay-me-later-high-cost-unresolved-grief

James J, Friedman R. (1998 & 2009). Grief Recovery Handbook. First Edition & Expanded Edition, paperback.

James J, Friedman R. (2006). Moving On.

Jennings D. (12-12-14). TMJ, Jaw Pain, & Substance P.

Kornfield J. (1993). A Path with Heart.

Kornfield J. (11-7-12). Helping Clients Find Their Wise Hearts. NICABM.

Lanius RA, Vermetten E, Pain C. (2010). Impact of Early Life Trauma on Health and Disease: The Hidden Epidemic.

Levine PA. (2005). Healing Trauma.

Levine PA. (6-1-11). In an Unspoken Voice: Somatic Experiencing. NICABM.com.

Levine PA. (10-15-14). Nature's Lessons in Healing Trauma. Retrieved 8-1-17: Youtube.com/watch?v=nmJDkzDMllc

Lewis T, Amini F, Lannon R. (2000). A General Theory of Love.

Loewy J, Stewart K, et. al. (2013). Effects of Music Therapy on Vital Signs, Feeding, and Sleep in Premature Infants. Pediatrics, April 2013.

MacLean, P. (1990). Triune Brain in Evolution.

Main, M, Hesse, E & Kaplan, N. (2005). Predictability of Attachment Behavior. In: Attachment from Infancy to Adulthood. Grossmann, Grossmann & Waters, p.245–304.

McCauley, KT. Disease Model of Addiction. DrKevinMcCauley.com.

Mindlin G, Durousseau D. (2012). Your Playlist Can Change Your Life.

Muktananda S. (1981). Mystery of the Mind.

Norwood R. (1985). Women Who Love Too Much.

Norwood R. (1997). Daily Meditations for Women Who Love Too Much.

Ogden P. (6-22-11). Sensorimotor Therapy. NICABM.com.

Ortner N. (2014). The Tapping Solution.

Porges S. (7-6-11). Polyvagal Theory for Trauma. StephenPorges.com /images/ stephen%20porges%20 interview%20nicabm.pdf. See also Attachment DisorderHealing.com/Porges-Polyvagal

Porges S. (April 2012). Polyvagal Theory. NICABM.com.

Redford J. (2015). Paper Tigers (film). KPRJfilm.co/paper-tigers

Ronstadt L. (1977). Poor Poor Pitiful Me. Album: Simple Dreams.

Rosenthal N. (2013). Gift of Adversity.

SAMHSA (was NIMH) (undated). How to Deal With Grief. Archive.samhsa. gov/MentalHealth/Anxiety_Grief.pdf

Schore AN. (1994). Affect Regulation and the Origin of the Self.

Schore AN. (6-15-11). Affect Regulation and Trauma. NICABM.com.

Schore AN. (2012). Interview, World Healing Electronic Network, minute 39. WhenWorldwide.org/films/dr-allan-n-schore-full-interview/

Schore AN. (9-28-14). Most Important Years of Life. Oslo and Akershus University College, Oslo, Norway. Youtube.com/watch?v=KW-S4cyEFCc

Siegel DJ. (1999). The Developing Mind.

Siegel DJ. (2011). How Mindfulness Can Change the Wiring of Our Brains. NICABM.com/mindfulness2011

Siegel DJ. (6-27-10). Domains of Integration. Retrieved 8-1-17: DrDanSiegel. com/uploads/DomainsofIntegration.mp3

Siegel DJ. (4-6-11). Developing Mind: Why Relationships Are so Critical. NICABM.com.

Siegel DJ, Perry B. et. al. (3-12-13). Trauma, Brain and Relationship. Youtube.com/watch?v=jYyEEMlMMb0

Siegel RD. (4-15-11). Neurobiology of Mindfulness. NICABM.com; The Chronic Back Pain Cycle. Backsense.org/bscycle_pg.htm

Stone T. (2008). Power of How. Paperback.

Stuart, Marty. (2005.) Way Down. Album: Souls' Chapel.

Taylor CL. (1991). Inner Child Workbook.

Taylor JB. (2008). My Stroke of Insight.

Taylor M, McGee S. (2000). The New Couple.

Thich Nhat Hanh (1991). Peace is Every Step.

Thich Nhat Hahn (1998). Heart of the Buddha's Teaching.

Thich Nhat Hanh (2001). Anger.

Third Day. (2008). Call My Name. Album: Revelation.

Tilak L. (1903). Arctic Home in the Vedas.

Townsend J. (7-27-09). Heartfelt Wisdom. CD; CTC.

Townsend J. (2010). Where Is God.

Townsend J. (2-13-10). "Where Is God" book debut, Irvine, CA.

Tronick E. (2007). Still-Face Experiment.

van der Kolk B. (2005). Developmental Trauma Disorder. Psych Annals 35:5, 401-408, May 2005.

van der Kolk B. (6-6-12). What Neuroscience Teaches About Trauma. NICABM.com.

van der Kolk B. (5-10-13). Childhood Trauma, Affect Regulation, and Borderline Personality. Ninth Yale NEA-BPD Conference. Youtube.com/watch?v=N2NTADxDuhA

Verrier N. (1993). The Primal Wound.

Verrier N. (2003). Coming Home to Self.

Weill A, Kabat-Zinn J. (2001). Meditation for Optimum Health. CD set.

Wexler DB. (2004). When Good Men Behave Badly.

Wikipedia (7-27-17). Attachment disorder.

About the Author

Kathy Brous, born on Long Island, New York, is an international economist turned technical writer and has written professionally on everything from monetary affairs to the design of satellite systems and power plants. She has penned and edited numerous complex technical documents for major aerospace companies.

She currently curates AttachmentDisorderHealing.com, a website on brain science, infant attachment, developmental trauma and child trauma, with the accent on "healing."

Kathy's experience includes nine years of research on the science of infant brain development, and seven years of deep psychotherapeutic healing of her own infant attachment trauma, including two years of neurofeedback. She is co-founder of the Orange County, California ACEs Task Force on Child Trauma, part of the ACEsConnection.com global network for public education on the Adverse Childhood Experiences (ACE) Study.

Kathy holds a BS in Mathematics from Simmons College in Boston. She is also a classically-trained singer in the *bel canto* tradition with 25 years of solo concert experience in five languages. She is the author of an introduction to a 2017 book of classical arias, *Korean Art Songs: An Anthology and Guide for Performance and Study*. Kathy resides in southern California, sings in local choirs and runs on the beach every chance she gets. Classical music and music of any kind are her passion, particularly German *Lieder* and country music two-step.

73940035R00164

Made in the USA
San Bernardino, CA
12 April 2018